Neither
White nor Black

Neither
White nor Black

Mormon Scholars
Confront the Race Issue
in a Universal Church

Lester E. Bush, Jr.
and
Armand L. Mauss

Editors

Midvale, Utah

And he inviteth them all
to come unto him, black and white,
bond and free, male and female;
and he remembereth the heathen;
and all are alike unto God.

2 Nephi 26:33

Table of Contents

Table of Contents

Foreword

Since its founding in 1966, *Dialogue: A Journal of Mormon Thought* has sought to publish the work of leading scholars whose research has examined or expressed Mormon culture, history, and theology. Over the years these articles have addressed important issues facing the Church and its members, and they have raised the level of discussion among Mormons and non-Mormons alike about problems of common concern. No series of articles illustrates this phenomenon better than those written by Lester Bush, Armand Mauss, and Newell Bringhurst about the origin, nature, and change of the policy that denied priesthood ordination to blacks.

During the turbulent 1960s and 1970s no issue so vexed the Mormon Church and its members as the categorical denial of the priesthood to black males. The subservient status of blacks in Mormon life and thought became a matter of national attention and internal stress. Leaders and members who were troubled by this paradox in a religion that had suffered its share of discrimination, and was otherwise committed to Christian ethics, scrambled for their scriptures and histories to explain what had become an acutely painful reality. There were those who found justification in Old Testament passages and in the Pearl of Great Price. Others, reading such Book of Mormon passages as II Nephi 26:33, found reason to believe—or hope—that the Church's position was not rooted in doctrine. Those who searched the historical record found as many questions as answers. The denial of priesthood to blacks was easily traced to the era of Brigham Young, but evidence for the proscription in Joseph Smith's time was hardly convincing.

In the ensuing years, some loyal members of the Church urged the leadership to reconsider the prevailing priesthood policy. At the same time, the Mormon community was the object of increasingly disdainful attacks from other sectors of the American community, as they too became more sensitive to the injustices of racial discrimination. A serious reassessment began. It was in this environment that Lester Bush, Armand Mauss, and Newell Bringhurst moved rationally to the center of the issue and sought, as scholars, to unravel the historical, theological, and sociological threads of the dilemma. Their articles, published in *Dialogue: A Journal of Mormon Thought* from 1967 to 1981, are of such enduring interest that the Editorial Boards of *Dialogue* and Signature Books now deem them worthy of reprinting in this special collection, complemented

Foreword

by introductory and concluding chapters that are published here for the first time. These new essays give perspective to the authors' earlier efforts to understand the origins and dimensions of the Church's former policy, and the processes by which change came.

Lester E. Bush, Jr., a native of Virginia, holds an M.D. degree from the University of Virginia and currently works in Washington, D.C. He served for six years as associate editor of *Dialogue*. Armand L. Mauss, Professor of Sociology at Washington State University, spent his early life in California and taught for several years in various community colleges there. He received his Ph.D. in Sociology at the University of California, Berkeley. Born in Salt Lake City, Utah, Newell G. Bringhurst received his Ph.D. at the University of California, Davis, and taught at several colleges and universities in Utah and California. Currently he teaches history and political science at the College of the Sequoias.

In June, 1978, when Spencer W. Kimball announced the revelation which accorded the opportunity for priesthood ordination to all worthy males, the Church of Jesus Christ of Latter-day Saints took its place among the major Christian religions. It also assumed new moral authority in a world still torn by racial and religious strife. But even as this volume goes to press the Reorganized Church of Jesus Christ of Latter Day Saints begins to implement its historic decision to ordain women— poignantly reminding us of another issue that will surely persist and require the attention of our best minds and most earnest spirits. The light shed by this volume on important earlier chapters in Mormon and American history may prove particularly instructive as we look to the future.

L. Jackson Newell, Editor
Dialogue: A Journal of Mormon Thought
April, 1984

Introduction: Conflict and Commitment in an Age of Civil Turmoil

Armand L. Mauss

Twins of the Times:
Dialogue and the Race Issue for Mormons

It is more than coincidence that the decade of the 1960s gave rise almost simultaneously to the Mormon confrontation with civil rights and to *Dialogue: A Journal of Mormon Thought*. It may also be symbolic and symptomatic that both should have begun outside of Utah. Not that Utah Mormons were unaccustomed to intellectual and social ferment or to the anguish of conflicts between church loyalties and other conscientious commitments. The history of Mormonism in Utah and well before has always had its share of hardy strugglers with conscience, from Oliver Cowdery and Sidney Rigdon to Edward Tullidge and B. H. Roberts to Lowell Bennion and Sterling McMurrin. Like many other Mormon intellectuals of equal or lesser notoriety (or none), these men at various times and places positioned themselves between the center and the periphery of official approbation—and sometimes beyond—depending upon their respective successes and failures in reconciling faith and reason. In general, however, Utah has largely been spared the civil turmoil over public policy that has from time to time engulfed campus, community, and conscience itself in the other areas of the United States.

Not so the Utah emigres who settled outside the Great Basin in increasing numbers from 1930 on. For them and their children, being Mormon has always meant having to answer for it regularly in the neighborhood, at school, at work, in politics, on the university campus, and ultimately to oneself. Such a predicament, however, was a blessing in disguise, as they were often reminded from the pulpit, for it presented many opportunities to share the faith. And rarely indeed were such encounters with the non-Mormon world actually acrimonious or hostile— rarely, that is, until the rise of the civil rights movement. For those becoming adults in the 1980s or later, it may be difficult to imagine the

1

American *zeitgeist* of the 1960s. Even those of us who lived through that period may have forgotten much about how it felt.

Up until about 1960, Mormons and other Americans living outside the South were able to enjoy the luxury of defining racial conflict as a Southern problem. That was the part of the country that had always had "trouble with the Negroes." The rest of the country naturally deplored slavery, lynchings, the KKK, and certain of the harsher aspects of black treatment by the white establishment in the South. Most were not inclined, however, to question Jim Crow laws, segregated schools and neighborhoods, or laws against interracial marriages. Indeed, most of these same features were commonplace *de facto*, if not *de jure*, in the Northern and Western states as well. It was with some ambivalence, then, that most of us read and heard about such federal assaults against school segregation as *Brown v. Board of Education* in 1954 and Little Rock in 1957; bus boycotts in Alabama in 1955 and 1956; and sit-ins at lunch counters and other businesses in various Southern states during the late 1950s and early 1960s. What the "Negroes" wanted sounded fair enough, on the one hand; but on the other hand, they seemed to be making an awful lot of trouble and perhaps should move "more gradually." In any case, it was not something *we* had to worry about, since, fortunately, we did not live in the South.

The folly of such complacency, Mormon and non-Mormon, is clear enough in retrospect. However, in those early days, American public opinion was remarkably conservative. In a carefully drawn national sample, for instance, only 38 per cent of white Americans favored school integration even as late as 1964, and that percentage did not increase much in subsequent years. In the same survey, only 41 per cent of white Americans nationwide were willing to grant blacks equal access to hotels and businesses; a bare majority (53 per cent) favored open housing; and a mere 27 per cent approved of the general desegregation of the races. At the same time, 68 per cent were convinced that civil rights advocates were "moving too fast," and 63 per cent felt that blacks had damaged their cause by their exertions on behalf of equal rights—and this was *before* any urban disorders in the North![1] Another major survey of white Protestants and Catholics, in the relatively liberal San Francisco area, found half of the sample agreeing that blacks did not adequately take care of their property, which was why their neighborhoods were "run down." Nearly half also believed that there would be no racial strife if "Communists and radicals" did not stir up trouble. One-fourth preferred segregated schools and churches and subscribed to the stereotype that "it's too bad Negroes are so immoral."[2] In the 1950s, a decade before these surveys, public opinion could only have been even more conservative.

Mormons, with a legacy of their own as victims of bigotry, might wish in retrospect that they had been more progressive in civil rights than the rest of the nation; but given the historical context, this would have been expecting too much. Whether because Haun's Mill, Carthage, and Johnston's Army were too remote in the collective Mormon memory, or because the assimilation of Mormons since those days had made them too much like other Americans, or because prosperity and respectability had vitiated the general prophetic impulse in the Mormon heritage, Mormon attitudes toward blacks remained very much like those of the rest of the nation.[3] The traditional denial by the Mormon Church of its lay priesthood to its few black members (the only ethnic group so excluded) was generally regarded by Mormons as their own business; and they preferred to avoid the subject whether within or outside the church. Mormons who questioned the exclusion policy, either as social criticism or out of a personal anguish of conscience, usually generated suspicion about their own loyalty to the Church, for it was nearly universally assumed that the policy had had its basis in revelation. Accordingly, few critical voices could be heard within the Church before the 1960s and not many more from the outside.[4] Even sociologist Thomas F. O'Dea, author of a distinguished 1957 work on Mormonism, did not think the Mormon policy toward blacks important enough to mention among the "strains and conflicts" to which he devoted his concluding chapter.[5]

The "Negro issue" within Mormonism took on increasing urgency only as the civil rights movement expanded outside the South after 1960. With a more sympathetic federal administration elected that year, civil rights pressure groups began to carry their protest northward and to enjoy a rapid growth in numbers and resources. Especially active were the National Association for the Advancement of Colored People (NAACP), the Congress of Racial Equality (CORE), and the Southern Christian Leadership Conference (SCLC), the latter having arisen out of the Alabama bus boycotts of the 1950s and led by Martin Luther King, Jr. Before long, however, these newly aroused organizations came to seem moderate in comparison to the startling doctrines, goals, and tactics of the mushrooming "black power" groups, sometimes called "black separatists" or "black nationalists," like the Student Non-Violent Coordinating Committee (SNCC), the Black Muslims, and the Black Panthers.[6] From across the entire ideological spectrum of the national civil rights movement came a swelling crescendo of lawsuits, boycotts, sit-ins, voter registration drives, and demonstrations of all kinds. Opponents of such activities frequently reacted with violence, in the North as well as in the South, and even routine interracial contacts became increasingly tense, sometimes erupting into major urban riots and disorders like the one in Watts (Los Angeles area) in August 1965. In this context, it was unrealistic to hope that a racially discriminatory policy within a major religious denomination could any longer be defined as strictly a parochial matter.

The Mormon collision with this burgeoning civil rights movement is recounted in some detail later in this volume so little need be said about it here, except to recall that it was a product of the 1960s, not earlier, and that it was the single most crucial issue in Mormon relationships with others during that entire decade. Mormons outside Utah may have had to face it first: it was clearly an issue in 1961-62, for example, when George Romney ran successfully for governor in Michigan. But Utah was not spared for long. NAACP plans to picket Temple Square during the October 1963 General Conference were apparently forestalled only by President Hugh B. Brown's unequivocal declaration in favor of civil rights at the beginning of the conference. However, picketing and other forms of public pressure on the Church in Utah later became common-place, climaxing with the campaign against Brigham Young University at the end of the decade. National media, which had paid no appreciable attention to the Mormon race issue before 1960, greatly increased the scope and frequency of their generally unfriendly coverage, and the press often badgered Church leaders for public statements.[7] Of course, the civil rights movement was not the only source of social ferment during the 1960s. Others included the controversial ameliorative programs embodied in the New Frontier and Great Society movements; the wholesale assault on traditional values, mores, and fashions epitomized by the "hippies" and their Age of Aquarius; and, perhaps most corrosive, the war in Viet Nam. Yet for Mormons, the race issue presented the most troubling and unavoidable conflict between conscience and commitment.

The *Dialogue* Response to the Race Issue

Dialogue, born in such a social and political environment, naturally addressed the matter of race and civil rights often in those early days. The first issue of the journal in the spring of 1966 carried a short but significant article by Robert Christmas describing a lecture series that had been sponsored by the LDS Institute at the University of Southern California in August 1965 on the Watts rioting earlier that month. The series featured speakers from various interest groups directly affected by the riot, including Mormons and non-Mormons, blacks and whites, all seeking to promote understanding about the causes and consequences of such disorders.[8] The next issue carried Karl Keller's memorable account of his own pilgrimage to the South one summer to help with a civil rights project there.[9] The 1967 issues of *Dialogue* carried a large number of letters to the editor on the race issue, starting with a lengthy one from former U.S. Interior Secretary Stewart Udall (Summer 1967), which sharply criticized Church policy. That letter provoked an outpouring of others in response, most of them in opposition to Udall and many of them very intense. That same issue of *Dialogue* also carried a brief article by sociologist Glenn Vernon reporting the findings of another social scientist on the admirable record of New Zealand Mormons in race relations, as though to remind us all that Mormons weren't doing as badly everywhere as in North America.[10] The final issue of that second year contained my "Mormonism and the Negro" (reprinted here as Chapter 2), the first *Dialogue* essay to consider explicitly (if briefly) the vagueness of the scriptural basis for Church policy and the separate question of that policy's impact on Mormon civil rights attitudes.[11]

In 1968, every issue contained at least a few letters to the editor on the topic, some in continued response to Udall, some in response to my essay, and some on other aspects like the perceived inadequacy of official Church reaction to the assassination of Martin Luther King. The winter issue carried an article by Dennis Lythgoe on the changing public image of Mormonism with an assessment of the price paid in bad publicity for the racial policy, and Royal Shipp's contribution to a "Roundtable on the Struggle for Justice and Order," in which he looked forward to a change in Church policy and called for a renewal of brotherhood in the meantime.[12]

In *Dialogue's* fourth year, 1969, the final issue coincided with and reprinted the first formal, public statement from the First Presidency on the priesthood policy in two decades. In the same issue was an extensive review essay by Lester Bush, which first raised the crucial question of the historical origins of the traditional position on blacks (see the commentary on Taggart's book, Chapter 3 of this volume),[13] a question that he would later treat more definitively. (See his historical overview in Chapter 4).

By 1970, the civil rights movement and most of the other exhausting issues of the period had begun to peak. The critics of the Mormon racial policy, having seen several universities break off athletic relations with Brigham Young University, seemed to relax the public pressure somewhat. *Dialogue* that year carried a cogent critique by Marvin Hill of an important lecture by Fawn Brodie on the transformation of Joseph Smith's racial ideas and a review by Lowell Bennion of a small book on the predicament of being a black Mormon.[14] As the final three chapters in this collection will demonstrate, other significant pieces on the race issue appeared in *Dialogue* after 1970, with an occasional letter to the editor as well. But never again was there such a concentration of articles and letters on that issue as during those first five formative years. It may not be an exaggeration to say that *Dialogue* itself was born in large part out of the travail of a generation of Mormons struggling to deliver itself of the burden of racial anachronisms.

That burden was, after all, only a particular manifestation of the classical dilemma of religious commitment vs. personal conscience experienced by anyone who has trouble reconciling the teachings and policies of his or her religion with the values and rationales acquired from secular sources. While such a dilemma may be more common among the well-educated or "intellectuals" in a religious community, it is by no means limited to them. It occurs wherever a person cares enough about his or her religious heritage to take it seriously in the face of challenges from the social and intellectual fashions around him. There are, of course, facile resolutions to the dilemma. Some turn their backs on their religion and dismiss it as irrelevant to the sophisticated mind and life; some flee to the bosom of blind faith and refuse to consider the relevance of ideas or issues not validated by official Church pronouncements. Those who have grappled with the Mormon race question (and many others) in the pages of *Dialogue* have chosen neither of these easy solutions. Instead, they have probed the substrata of Church doctrine and history, on the one hand, to delineate as fully as possible the origin and status of the traditional Mormon teachings on blacks; and, on the other hand, they have plumbed the depths of reason to ascertain the applicability and meaning of such teachings in the context of a universal gospel, trying all the while to avoid the shallows of sheer *apologia*. These efforts have helped illuminate the possible reconcilations between faith and reason. Not all questions have been answered, of course—at least not in the short run; but such truths as have been discovered have made thinking Mormons freer than before of uncritical dependence either upon ecclesiastical tradition or upon the collective social conscience of a secular and uncertain generation.

The chapters that follow, with the exception of Lester Bush's comprehensive concluding summary, have appeared as articles in *Dialogue*. They span nearly its entire history, now approaching two decades, and represent a major portion of the most important scholarly articles published on Mormon teachings and policies about blacks. While reedited here for stylistic consistency, they reflect the state of knowledge and the perspectives of the authors existing at the times when they were respectively first written. Together they constitute a history at two different levels simultaneously: (1) a history of the rise and fall of the Mormon policy of denying priesthood ordination to its black male members; and (2) a history of the efforts of Mormon scholars to grapple with that policy, to understand its origins, its meaning, its evolution, and its implications. In retrospect and when arranged, as here, in chronological order, these articles seem to pose, and then to answer, a logical sequence of questions, as indicated in the Contents. We invite the reader to join us now in reliving both of the histories mentioned above.

NOTES

1. Angus Campbell, *White Attitudes Toward Black People* (Ann Arbor, Mich.: The Institute for Social Research, 1971); esp. Ch. 7, "Stability and Change in Racial Attitudes, 1964-1970."

2. C. Y. Glock and Rodney Stark, *Christian Beliefs and Anti-Semitism* (New York: Harper and Row, 1966), p. 168.

3. See my "Mormonism and Secular Attitudes Toward Negroes," *Pacific Sociological Review* 9 (Fall 1966), pp. 91-99, for an explicit comparison of Mormon attitudes to those reported in Glock and Stark *Christian Beliefs*.

4. For the few outside criticisms of Mormon race policy before 1960, see Dennis L. Lythgoe, "The Changing Image of Mormonism," *Dialogue* 3 (Winter 1968): p. 50. The best-known, and perhaps only, insider to go public with criticism of the Church on this issue was Lowry Nelson, a sociologist with some history of service to the Church and also of internal criticism in the form of letters to Church leaders. See his "Mormons and the Negro" *The Nation* 174 (24 May 1952): p. 488. Two early authors critical of the Church's policy—at least in the scholarly sense and hence by implication in the polemical sense as well—were Fawn M. Brodie, *No Man Knows My History: The Life of Joseph Smith the Mormon Prophet*, 2nd ed., (New York: Alfred A. Knopf, 1971), and L. H. Kirkpatrick "The Negro and the L.D.S. Church," *Pen* (Winter, 1954): 12, 13, 29. Whether Brodie's book (originally published in 1945) should be considered here as "inside" or "outside" is hard to say, since she had not yet been formally excommunicated. Kirkpatrick, as far as I know, was not a Mormon. In any case, both of these early critics embraced the thesis that the exclusionary policy originated in Missouri, later to be more fully explored by others like Jan Shipps, Naomi Woodbury, Dennis Lythgoe, and Stephen G. Taggart in the 1960s.

5. Thomas F. O'Dea, *The Mormons*. University of Chicago Press, 1957, especially Chapter IX. Like everyone else, O'Dea had discovered the race issue by the time he wrote "Sources of Strain in Mormon History Reconsidered," in Marvin S. Hill and James B. Allen (eds.), *Mormonism and American Culture*. New York: Harper and Row, 1972.

6. Extensive treatments of some of these organizations and their activities will be found in Norval D. Glenn and Charles M. Bonjean (eds.), *Blacks in the United States*, San Francisco: Chandler Publishing Company, 1969; and in Lewis M. Killian, *The Impossible Revolution?: Black Power and the American Dream*, New York, Random House, 1968. A briefer treatment will be found in Chapter 14 of my *Social Problems as Social Movements*, Philadelphia: J. B. Lippincott Co., 1975.

7. See Lythgoe, "Changing Image."

8. Robert Christmas, "The Watts Riot." *Dialogue* 1 (Spring 1966): 162-63.

9. Karl Keller, "Every Soul Has Its South," *Dialogue* 1 (Summer 1966): 72-79.

10. Glenn M. Vernon, "Racial Integration and the Church, A Comparative Note," *Dialogue* 2 (Summer 1967): 148-49.

11. Armand L. Mauss, "Mormonism and the Negro: Faith, Folklore, and Civil Rights," *Dialogue* 2 (Winter 1967): 19-39.

12. Lythgoe, "Changing Image"; Royal Shipp, "Black Images and White Images: The Combustibility of Common Misconceptions," *Dialogue* 3 (Winter 1968): 77-91.

13. Lester E. Bush, Jr., "A Commentary on Stephen G. Taggart's *Mormonism's Negro Policy: Social and Historical Origins*," *Dialogue* 4 (Winter 1969): 86-103.

14. Marvin S. Hill, "The Manipulation of History," *Dialogue* 5 (Autumn 1970): 96-99. Lowell L. Bennion, "A Black Mormon Perspective." *Dialogue* 5 (Winter 1970): 93-94.

Mormonism and the Negro:
Faith, Folklore, and Civil Rights

Armand L. Mauss

The first Dialogue *essay to address in any depth what was then termed "the Negro doctrine" was this 1967 paper by Armand Mauss. Appearing near the peak of the public pressure against the Church, it briefly addressed the question of the limits of the Mormon canon on blacks and then presented the results of studies assessing the impact of Church teachings on the attitudes toward civil rights held by individual Mormons. Mauss's position that the noncanonical facets of Church teachings on blacks need not be considered Mormon "doctrine"—a common view among Church "liberals" at the time—anticipated the implicit message of official guidance issued by the First Presidency through a formal statement on the subject in 1969. This essay originally appeared in* Dialogue *2 (Winter 1967).*

It is probably a distressing turn of events for most Mormons to see the "Negro issue" replacing the "polygamy issue" as the one feature most likely to cross the popular mind whenever Mormonism is mentioned. Just when it was becoming almost respectable to be a Mormon, another skeleton is dragged out of our ecclesiastical closet for all the world to see. The world has begun to react with the equalitarian indignation appropriate to these times; particularly vocal have been the spokesmen of liberal religion, who, it would seem, have finally discovered discrimination in the churches during the last two decades.[1]

The recent attention directed to the Mormon Church over this issue is, however, only partly a consequence of the new American concern for racial equality; it is largely a consequence also of the greatly increased extensiveness of the Church's encounter with the secular urban world.[2] The Mormon Church is now a major American denomination, whose membership is comparable to that of such "old line" denominations as the Episcopal, Presbyterian, or Congregational. Furthermore, a majority of the Mormon membership now resides in urban areas mostly outside Utah and Idaho; and for the first time in our history, a prominent Mormon [George Romney] has been seriously and widely considered as a presidential candidate. In the midst of such social and demographic changes, Mormons can only expect *more* confrontations over their peculiar ways with sincere, enlightened, and sophisticated non-Mormons. That is why the "Negro issue" cannot be ignored or waited out or wished away. Pending a possible change in the official Church position (a change which we may never live to see), we must attempt to understand that position, insofar as it can be understood, rather than apologizing for it or trying to explain it away.

It is, of course, difficult for the thoughtful Mormon to understand the Church's policy of withholding the priesthood from Negroes, and many will probably frankly admit with me that the policy makes us quite uncomfortable; but my commitment to the religion is much too broadly based for me to become disaffected over what is, after all, a peripheral problem by comparison with the more fundamental tenets of the faith. Perhaps especially for academicians, one's intellectual life is a continuing struggle to resolve such puzzling gospel questions to some degree of satisfaction; so far, the "Negro issue" and a few others have defied resolution for me. However, in the process of pondering, while I have not as yet discovered what the scriptures really mean on this issue, I have come to some rather definite conclusions as to what they do *not* mean, a matter of even greater importance, perhaps, in the current social and political context.

If one finds the Church's policy on Negroes discomfiting, however, the "explanations" for it offered by well-meaning commentators (on all sides) are often even worse. On the one hand, we have those (conservatives?) who feel the need to "defend" the Church by "explaining" that the whole thing is somehow an unfortunate consequence of sins in the preexistence, or of something Cain did (or Ham, or both), apparently quite oblivious to the Second Article of Faith, which tells us that "men will be punished for their *own* sins...." On the other hand, we have those (liberals?) who are manifestly embarrassed that the Church has been caught with its civil rights down and who assure us that this Utah vestige of Jim Crow will give way ere long to enlightened counsel, or to picketing, or surely to George Romney's presidential campaign. In other words, the "defenders" are tying the issue to a heritage of American biblical folklore, while the "critics" are tying it to the current civil rights controversies. Neither position is warranted by the standard works, by official pronouncements of Church leaders, or by the logic of the Church policy itself.

This paper will expand upon these observations by arguing for three propositions: (1) the actual authoritative Church doctrine on the "Negro question" is extremely parsimonious, although it is not entirely without biblical precedent, and it is not too difficult to accept if it is linked cautiously with the doctrine of preexistence; (2) although there are, of course, scriptural references to the war in heaven, to the curse and mark on Cain, to the curse on Canaan, and to the blackness of Cain's descendants, there is *no* scriptural warrant for linking any of these to a denial of the priesthood; and (3) none of this has anything to do with the civil rights issue until it can be demonstrated (and not just inferred) that the Church's internal ecclesiastical policy carries over, in the form of civil bigotry, into the secular behavior of Latter-day Saints. As part of this last argument, I shall present recent empirical sociological evidence to the effect that there is no such carry-over.

Faith and Doctrine

The doctrine itself, as it is set forth in the Pearl of Great Price and in occasional pronouncements by the First Presidency, is quite simple— indeed, even cryptic: people of Hamitic (i.e. African) descent may be received into the Church and participate in all activities and ordinances, except those requiring that the participant hold the priesthood, for people of this lineage may not be given the priesthood.[3] In practice this has meant that although considerable Church activity and participation are still open to them, those members known to have any African Negro ancestry (no matter what their color) cannot hold the lay priesthood offices held by practically all other Mormon men, nor can they receive temple endow-ments or temple marriages. No reasons have been given in any scriptures, ancient or modern, for this proscription; the official stance of the Church leaders has been simply that the Lord has so decreed and that no change can take place in this policy until he decrees otherwise.[4]

If the Lord has been unwilling to provide us explanations for his judgment in this matter, the same cannot be said for Mormon theologians, whether of the scholarly or the lay variety. Understandably, a doctrine and practice seemingly so at odds with the generally equalitarian ethos of Mormonism could not go unexplained and unjustified. Although exceed-ingly little of an official or *ex cathedra* nature has been offered, many Church leaders and other doctrinal writers, in their private capacities, have provided explanations, ranging from the rather uncompromising "they-had-it-coming" versions of some of the brethren,[5] to the more humane, regretful, and hopeful position of President McKay.[6] Out of the academic world, too, have come explanations ranging from the scriptural-historical one of the very orthodox William E. Berrett to the critical American-historical versions of the less orthodox Sterling McMurrin or Lowry Nelson.[7] Meanwhile, Mormon Sunday School teachers, priest-hood quorum teachers, and seminary teachers, frequently supported by quotations from this or that unofficial Church book, have been innocent purveyors of a variety of fundamentalist folklore.

For the orthodox but thinking Mormon, the unfortunate fact is that we just don't know why the Lord has directed his Church to withhold the priesthood from those of Hamitic lineage; it is a policy that we simply accept on faith because of our general commitment to the rest of the restored gospel. If we want to turn to certain other gospel doctrines or scriptural precedents for possible "explanations" about this problem, we may do so, but we are on our own. For example, we might recall that under the Mosaic dispensation, there was also a connection between lineage and priesthood, and a far more restrictive one, for only the Levite lineage could provide the priests. Or we might observe that if, as Luke maintains, it was God who determined the times and places of our habitation, (Acts 17:26) then God knew he was "discriminating" against anyone born in a time (e.g., 900 A.D.) or a place (e.g., modern China) in which the priesthood (and indeed the gospel itself) would be just as unavailable to him as if he had Hamitic lineage. But these are not really explanations; they are only relevant precedents that perhaps might make us feel a little less uncomfortable.

The explanation which seems to have the greatest currency among Mormons derives from the rather unique Mormon doctrine of preexistence.[8] We have all heard it: before being born as mortals, all men [and women] lived as spirits with God in a conscious individual existence of unspecified duration, which represented a necessary phase in our eternal progression. In this preexistent life, God made many plans and decisions relating to the creation and destiny of the earth and its inhabitants. One of the decisions he made was that certain of his children should not be eligible to hold the priesthood during their mortal lives, and one of the ways (but only one) in which he seems to have implemented this decision was to use the Hamitic lineage for nonpriesthood holders. Notice that such a conceptualization *reverses* the cause-effect relationship which most Church critics presume, i.e., that Negroes aren't given the priesthood because they are Negro or because they are black. My interpretation of the "preexistence explanation," on the contrary, would hold that some are born through Hamitic lineage because they cannot hold the priesthood. Notice also that the distinguishing trait here is lineage, not color.[9]

One might tentatively accept this "preexistence explanation" without too much difficulty, as long as it stays in this simple and unembroidered form; for the doctrine does seem to have some official backing, if we are to judge by a letter from the First Presidency;[10] and furthermore, it seems to have a *prima facie* plausibility, given certain Mormon doctrinal premises. However, referring the problem back to the preexistence does not help too much, for we still don't know the reason for the divine proscription. A common folktale has it that those born through the "cursed" lineage somehow failed to measure up during the War in Heaven, which occurred in the preexistence between Jehovah and Lucifer. The notion that they were "neutral" in that war has gone out of vogue, only to be replaced by the equally dubious idea that they must have been among the "less valiant" in the war.[11] Any such notion involves the assumption (unacceptable to me) that a certain mortal condition which we perceive to be disadvantageous can be assumed to be the result of some failing in the preexistence. Such was not necessarily the case, according to Jesus, for the congenitally blind man whom he healed (John 9: 1-3), and we do not have the right, it seems to me, to assume that such is the case for any particular instance of unfortunate mortal circumstances. For one thing, the assumption is complicated by the question of relativity: e.g., one wonders on what possible grounds we can say that American Negroes must be paying for some failing in the preexistence, when their mortal circumstances are infinitely superior, one would think, to those of the contemporary inhabitants of China, who hold neither the priesthood nor much of anything else.

So far then, the following points have been made regarding Church doctrine on the subject: (1) neither the Lord nor the Church leaders have given us an adequate explanation for withholding the priesthood from the Negroes or from anyone else; we simply accept the policy on the basis of faith, a few partially relevant scriptures, and the position of the First Presidency; (2) apparent scriptural or historical precedents may help us feel a little less beleaguered on the issue, but they don't really explain anything; (3) the "preexistence explanation" may explain a little about *how* or *when*, and it suggests that Hamitic lineage is the result of ineligibility for the priesthood, not the cause; however, (4) this explanation tells us nothing about *why*, unless we mix in a dubious and speculative theory about the war in heaven.

Faith and Folklore

Having seen how sparse is the official and reliable doctrine on this subject, let us now turn to examine further some of the folklore which has rushed in to fill this doctrinal vacuum.[12] The story about insufficient valor during the war in heaven, mentioned above, is only one example. Two other folk tales have long been common among Mormons, both of which are also found among other Christians. Neither of them has any real basis in the standard works of the Church.

The first one is based upon the account in Genesis of Ham's disrespectful behavior toward his father, Noah, upon discovering the latter in a naked and unkempt condition. Among the rebukes which Ham received for his misbehavior was, "cursed be Canaan . . . ,"[13] to which many Mormons and other Christians of a fundamentalist variety have given the far-fetched interpretation that this curse was the origin of the postdiluvial Negro race and its troubles, including persecution, discrimination, and (for Mormons) the withholding of the priesthood. A tale which competes with this one for currency among Mormons and with which it is often linked, is the one about the curse on Cain. According to this one, when Cain killed Abel he was given a "curse" and a "mark" in consequence of his murder. The "mark" was black skin, and the "curse" was that he should always be persecuted and, by extension, not be given the priesthood. Mormons usually corroborate this interpretation of the biblical account with reference to our own Pearl of Great Price, where we are told that Ham's wife was a descendant of Cain, that Ham's lineage was "cursed ... as pertaining to the Priesthood," and that a "blackness came upon" the descendants of Cain.[14]

These interpretations placed upon the stories of Ham and of Cain are so widespread, and so authoritatively passed on in certain Church books and articles, that many of my more orthodox friends are surprised and annoyed at my characterization of them as folklore. To such I can only point out the difference between that which is scriptural and that which is not. I am aware that some distinguished Church writers over a period of more than a century have propounded the cursed-be-Canaan and mark-of-Cain "explanations,"[15] but these writers have written in their private capacities, and it is at least open to question whether they have been any more immune than the rest of us to the danger of mixing popular myths with sound doctrine. In any case, it is safe to say that their work is extra-scriptural and extra-doctrinal, and therefore not necessarily incumbent upon even the orthodox to accept. For the truth is that there is no real basis in the scriptures (Standard Works) for connecting any of these "curses" or "marks" with the denial of the priesthood to Negroes.[16]

Let us look carefully at what the scriptures really say on these matters: if we take either the Old Testament or the Pearl of Great Price account of Cain's punishment, we are told very little about the "curse" and nothing at all about the "mark" except the cryptic comment that it was to protect the bearer from being killed. Nor are we given any grounds to suppose that either the "curse" or the "mark" should apply to any of Cain's descendants. To tie any of this to the fact that Cain's or Ham's lineage was "cursed as pertaining to the priesthood" is to resort to pure conjecture. We simply don't know why Ham's lineage was chosen to carry the denial of the priesthood. Similarly, the datum given us that "a blackness came upon" some of the descendants of Cain has nothing necessarily to do with the "mark" put on Cain himself. We are nowhere in the scriptures told just what Cain's mark was, and the first mention of the "blackness" of Cain's descendants is in Enoch's time, six generations after Cain. (In fact, it is not really explicit that the "blackness" was even a literal blackness of the skin.)

The reference to the "curse" put on Ham by Noah is no more well-founded as an "explanation" than is the mark-of-Cain theory. There is absolutely no scriptural basis for assuming that anything Ham himself

14

did was involved in the denial of the priesthood to his descendants, except, of course, as the Pearl of Great Price indicates, he seems to have married into the non-priesthood-holding lineage (Abr. 1:20-27).

So far, then, I think I have demonstrated that three of the most widespread "explanations" in the Church for the denial of the priesthood to Negroes are unsupported in the scriptures of the Church and should therefore be regarded as speculation, or even folklore; these are (a) the war-in-heaven theory; (b) the curse-on-Ham theory; and (c) the mark-of-Cain theory. Whatever discomfiture we Mormons may feel at the lack of explanation for the Church's doctrine and practice relating to Negroes, we should once and for all disabuse ourselves and our Church friends of these folk tales. Not only do they lack theoretical viability, but they add an encumbrance of ridiculousness and superstition to a Church policy that is otherwise only enigmatic. Furthermore, and perhaps more seriously, these unscriptural tales may provide a pretext for those among us who are given to civil bigotry to rationalize it.

The Church Under Attack

At the national convention of the NAACP July, 1965, a strongly worded resolution condemning the Mormon "doctrine of non-white inferiority" was introduced by the Salt Lake and Ogden Chapters and passed by the entire convention. The resolution contained many misconceptions about the actual doctrines of the Church, most of which were understandable and forgivable errors, for they had only been taken from the folklore and the unofficial opinions of well-known Church writers, which I have criticized above (e.g., that the Church teaches of "spiritual inferiority," of "lesser valiance in the preexistence," etc.). One line of reasoning expressed in the resolution, however, was simply a case of gratuitous assumption and dubious logic, i.e., that the Mormon doctrine about the Negro "carries over into the civil life of Mormons... fosters prejudice and ... perpetuates the contention that Negroes deserve to be the subject of disadvantaged conditions during their lives on earth ...."[17] For this latter charge, no evidence was cited in the resolution, and I strongly suspect that none had been gathered, aside from vague subjective impressions of individual Negroes. Yet the validity and saliency of the entire resolution hangs upon this unsubstantiated assumption, for only if it can be shown that the Church's doctrine on the Negro "carries over into the civil life of Mormons" can the NAACP (or any other civil organization) legitimately concern itself with quaint Mormon doctrines and practices.

This tendency to assume that the internal Church policy on Negroes is somehow connected with the civil rights issue is found, unfortunately, among critics within the Church, as well as among outsiders. Stewart Udall, [former U.S. Secretary of the Interior], for example, makes this mistake in his recent letter to the editors of *Dialogue*, where he criticizes the Church policy explicitly in the context of a discussion of civil racial justice.[18] To say "we violate the rights and dignity of our Negro brothers" by withholding the priesthood from them makes no more sense than to say that we violate the rights and dignity of our women by withholding the priesthood from them. After all, one of the "imperious truths of the contemporary world" (which truths Udall wants us to "come to grips with") is that discrimination on the basis of sex is just as outdated as discrimination on the basis of race and is just as illegal, furthermore, in much of our recent civil rights legislation. So what? Even if Udall is right that the Church's Negro policy has "no real sanction in essential Mormon thought," he has apparently forgotten that the principle of continuous revelation through the prophets *is* essential in Mormon thought; and when the day comes that Church policies unfashionable to the times are changed by "we Mormons," or that our leaders feel they must "courageously [face] the moral judgment of the American people" for their inspired guidance, that will be the day that Mormonism will be just another dissipated denomination. That the Church must be open to change is a contention that probably no one will contest, and Mormonism is structurally and theologically better equipped for change than are most denominations, precisely because of the principle of continuous revelation. However, it is difficult to see how a committed Mormon could find any satisfaction or moral strength in watching his prophets make changes, either to satisfy Udall's "enlightened men everywhere," or to avoid running "counter to the great stream of modern religious and social thought." Nor will the Church be strengthened to face the modern age by Udall's cynical implication that what *really* brings about revelation (as in the abandonment of polygamy) is the realization by Church leaders that they are "unable to escape history."

However doubtful may be the validity of the efforts made by "inside" critics like Udall to tie the LDS "Negro problem" to the issue of civil racial justice, these efforts are met with great interest and satisfaction by non-Mormon critics and reformers, who are anxious to help bring Mormonism up to date in its doctrines and practices. One of these is the Reverend Lester Kinsolving, who is called an Episcopal "worker-priest," is religion correspondent for the *San Francisco Chronicle*, and produces a couple of religion programs for radio station KCBS in San Francisco. In his *Chronicle* column last June, the Reverend Kinsolving made an invidious comparison between Udall's recognition of a "fact of political life" and Governor Romney's "attempt to circumvent the [race] issue" in maintaining that he should be judged by his own civil rights record, rather than by what people think about his Church's doctrines.[19] Kinsolving seemed rather taken also with the apparent irony that while Governor Romney was criticizing Udall's comments in *Dialogue*, Mrs. Romney was resigning from a private women's club because of its policy of racial discrimination. To be consistent, Kinsolving suggested, the Romneys should also quit the Mormon Church, or at least "join fellow Mormons like Udall in protesting . . . racial discrimination within [their] church." In conclusion, the good Reverend offers us the charitable pastoral judgment that Governor Romney's "projected image of sincerity" will be open to question until he is willing to join in criticizing his church for its racial discrimination.[20]

Reverend Kinsolving had made similar observations during his KCBS Sunday evening program toward the end of May 1967. This program, the first in the series, was devoted entirely to a discussion of the "racial doctrines of the Church of Jesus Christ of Latter-day Saints." The usual format of the two-hour program calls for one or several guests appearing to discuss an issue for a half-hour or so, and then the Reverend and his guests entertain telephoned questions and comments from the radio audience. On this particular evening, however, the Reverend explained, he had been unable to get any Mormon representatives to appear on the program, in spite of many conscientious efforts to do so. In lieu of any guests in person, therefore, the Reverend, whose announced aim for the program is an "unencumbered search for truth," proceeded to "explain" the Mormon Church's position on Negroes by means of quotations from *Mormonism and the Negro* by John J. Stewart. Both in a phone call to the program and later in a letter to the Reverend, I strongly protested the use of such an unofficial source. My letter also attempted, without success, to disabuse the Reverend of his unsupported assumption that there is necessarily a tie between the Church's Negro policy and the secular issue of civil rights. As for Mrs. Romney, my letter pointed out, her behavior in remaining a Mormon, while quitting a discriminating club, was no more inconsistent than would be, say, the behavior of an Episcopalian (or Roman Catholic or Mormon) who might protest unfair employment practices against women while still affiliating with a church which does not let women hold the priesthood.

Reverend Kinsolving's reaction to my letter was to invite me to appear on his program 2 July 1967 when he would again deal with the "racial doctrines" of the LDS Church. Also invited, to provide an "alternative view," was the Reverend A. Cecil Williams, minister of worship at the Glide Memorial Methodist Church in San Francisco, and a Negro. The latter's contribution, in my opinion, was surprisingly limited and restrained, except for a very brief critical comment right at the end of the program, which time did not permit me even to try to answer. Almost all of the dialogue was between the Reverend Kinsolving and myself, with rather little time given to the few telephone calls that got through.[21]

I was given seven or eight minutes near the beginning of the program to read a brief prepared statement, but that was the only opportunity I had for an uninterrupted statement on any of the questions put to me. Some of the Reverend's questions were of an *ad hominem* nature (attacking me for "inconsistencies" or "inaccuracies" which he thought had appeared in some of my earlier papers on this subject), and still other matters that he raised seemed to me to be of doubtful relevance.

A matter of some substance which did arise and which, in fact, was recurrent throughout the program, was the controversy over what relevance the peculiar Mormon doctrine on the Negro has to the civil rights issue. The Reverend Kinsolving, and to a lesser extent the Reverend Williams, both took the position, expressed in the NAACP resolution... that one must naturally expect Mormons to translate their Church's policy into anti-Negro secular behavior. I, of course, denied that one can reasonably make such assumptions in the absence of systematic empirical evidence, and I cited my own research (discussed herein below) as evidence contrary to their assumption. Reverend Kinsolving had read the published results of my research, and he made no attempt to impeach either my findings or my methods; he simply continued to insist (apparently ignoring my evidence) that the internal Mormon policy on Negroes was a secular civil rights issue. Aside from "common sense," the only evidence the reverend offered was an article by Glen W. Davidson, which appeared about two years ago in *The Christian Century*.[22]

In this article, Davidson made a number of allegations about the unwholesome pressures which Mormon leaders have exerted to prevent fair employment, open housing, and other civil rights legislation from passing in Utah (and even in California). For all of these allegations, Davidson offers only hearsay as evidence nor does he give us any idea about his "sources" of information. One example of his "evidence" for the Church's influence on civil rights bills before the Utah legislature in 1965 was the statement that "rumor fanned speculation that the church was working behind the scenes to defeat the bills." Davidson is free also with his judgments about people's motives and innermost thoughts, charging that many Mormon converts are joining the Church mainly because it provides them with a "sanctimonious front" for their racism.

And the ordinary Mormon can only stand in awe of Davidson's intimate knowledge of what transpires at the meetings of the Twelve and in other high Church councils. We are informed, for example, that there is "heated debate... within the Council of the Twelve Apostles" over the Church's stand on the race question, with Joseph Fielding Smith leading the "conservative faction" and Hugh B. Brown leading the "liberal faction." However, by December of 1963, Davidson somehow discovers, "the leadership of the apostles' conservative faction... had passed from Joseph Fielding Smith to Ezra Taft Benson." The latter, of course, has a

"... warm friendship with Robert Welch, the 'revelator' of the John Birch Society ..." and thus Davidson ties the Mormon "Negro problem" to the right-wing conspiracy.

In his "unencumbered search for truth," the Reverend Kinsolving took several passages verbatim from Davidson's article and read them over the air as "evidence" of the kind of Mormon secular racism that derives from the "Negro doctrine" of the Church. I was then invited to answer the charges, which I started to do point by point, although I didn't get very far before being stopped by a series of interruptions. I tried two or three times to make the point that racism in Utah, even among Mormons, cannot be assumed to result from Mormon policies on the priesthood, any more than anti-feminism can be assumed to result from Episcopalian policies on the priesthood. For one thing, I insisted, racial attitudes in any population are shaped in large part by such secular social factors as education level and rural or urban origin, so that one cannot really know how much Utah racism is attributable to religion until rural Mormons are compared with rural others, poorly educated Mormons are compared with poorly educated others, etc. Apparently having difficulty with the subtleties of causal reasoning, the reverend then asked that if the Mormons were not responsible for Utah's backwardness in civil rights, was I suggesting that the blame should be laid to the Protestants in Utah, or, perhaps, to the Hindus? After all, I was reminded, Utah was the only state in the West by 1965 without any open housing legislation.[23] And so it went.

Whose Civil Rights?

The Kinsolving programs and articles, together with the growing volume of unfavorable publicity from critics inside and outside the Church, are all symptomatic of our failure to make clear to the world that our doctrines and policies on the Negro have no necessary bearing on secular issues like civil rights. For this gap in communication, there is probably blame on both sides. On the Mormon side, the leaders of the Church have shown a decided unwillingness to discuss the matter at all. The members at large, meanwhile, have tended to take one of three approaches to the problem, none of which has contributed much to public understanding: they have either (1) tried to avoid talking about it to non-Mormons, and then shuffled with embarrassment when "found out"; (2) tried to "explain" the Church position by resorting to unscriptural racial folklore; or (3) demanded that the prophet change the doctrine and policy. This last approach can only strengthen the popular tendency to think that the Church policy is somehow connected to the civil rights issue, and it is therefore likely, ironically, to foster even more public misunderstanding and hostility.

On the non-Mormon side of the communication gap, there has been a regrettable if understandable tendency to jump to conclusions about the meaning of the LDS "racial doctrines," without much effort to ascertain what the real meaning is. At its worst, this attitude is expressed in a reformist zeal reminiscent of that of our heresy-hating nineteenth century sectarian persecutors. After all, when a religious group is publicly condemned, picketed, and ridiculed because of an unfashionable doctrine that has no demonstrated social consequence, this is called religious bigotry. The fact that it may be carried on in the name of equality and brotherhood, or in such media of modern religious "liberalism" as *The Christian Century* and the Kinsolving show, does not alter the character of the calumny. Whatever happened to "civil rights" for religious minorities?

The contention that the LDS "Negro doctrine" has no necessary relevance to secular civil rights or racial justice is, of course, a crucial one for the case being here advanced. Although I would argue that the burden of proof lies with those who would contend to the contrary, I would here like to discuss some empirical evidence for my own contention. Let us note, first of all, that President Hugh B. Brown has gone to some length in recent general conferences of the Church to emphasize that "there is in this Church no doctrine, belief, or practice that is intended to deny the enjoyment of full civil rights by any person, regardless of race, color, or creed."[24] In other words, there is nothing in the *internal* ecclesiastical policy itself to warrant any kind of "carry over" into *external* civil life. In the same statement, President Brown warned that "all men are the children of the same God, and that it is a moral evil for any person or group of persons to deny any human being the right to gainful employment, to full education opportunity, and to every privilege of citizenship." This makes it clear to Church members that there must *not* be any carry over of the ecclesiastical practice into the civil world; not only does the Church's "Negro policy" not justify secular racial discrimination, but those who practice it are clearly failing to comply with the most fundamental and elementary injunctions of the gospel.

The Evidence Against Doctrine
Causing Prejudice

Just how well the Latter-day Saints succeed in complying with gospel standards in this regard is an open empirical question, and one which has been asked frequently about other denominations as well. Sociological studies on the relation between religious beliefs and race attitudes or practices are not numerous, and their findings are far from conclusive: apparently some religious beliefs "carry over" and some do not, and there are always many intervening variables. Glock and Stark, in their recent and penetrating study, *Christian Beliefs and Anti-Semitism*,[25] conclude that the relation between religious beliefs and race attitudes is clear where anti-Semitism is concerned, but not in the case of anti-*Negro* prejudice.[26] My own study, the only one I know of to deal with this question among Latter-day Saints, appears in the fall 1966 issue of the *Pacific Sociological Review.*[27] It is an analysis of survey data taken from three LDS wards (congregations) in the East Bay area of California, using an adaptation of the questionnaire upon which Glock and Stark based their recent study of Catholics and Protestants in the West Bay area. My access to the Glock-Stark data made it possible to compare item-by-item my Mormon responses with those of the Catholics and Protestants in the same general area. A number of questions can certainly be raised about the representativeness of my sample, and I would refer interested readers to the paper itself for my defense of the sample. Here I might simply point out that the sample represented every home in all three wards (with a net questionnaire return of 258), and that an extensive internal study of the samples was made, as well as a study of the differences between respondents and nonrespondents. All relevant sociological categories were well represented in the sample; and among the respondents there were no appreciable differences in attitude between the Utah-born and California-born, between those recently arrived from Utah (or Idaho) and those in California a long time, between those giving different reasons for leaving Utah, or between converts and life-long members. These considerations, combined with the demographic fact that the "typical" Mormon is now as likely to be found on the Pacific Coast as in Utah, make for more confidence in my sample than might be warranted at first glance.

Six indicators of anti-Negro secular attitudes received special attention in this study. Three of these were indicators of "prejudice": (1) a belief that Negroes have inferior intelligence; (2) a belief that Negroes are immoral; and (3) a belief that Negroes don't keep up property. Three others were taken as indicators of a tendency to practice "discrimination": (4) a stated preference for segregated schools; (5) a stated preference for segregated wards; and (6) a declaration of intention to sell the home and move if Negro families moved into the neighborhood.[28] (Whatever questions can be raised here about the difference between "admitted" and "actual" racism can also be raised, of course, about *any* study of this kind, including the one by Glock and Stark....)

The first level of analysis was a gross comparison between Mormons and other denominations in their responses to the above six items. (Table I in original paper).[29] This comparison showed that the Mormons, in spite of their peculiar doctrine on Negroes, were no more likely to give anti-Negro responses than were the Presbyterians, Episcopalians, Lutherans (whether American or Missouri Synod) or Baptists (whether American or

Southern), and furthermore that the Mormon responses were very nearly the same as the Protestant averages.

The rest of the analysis (the major portion) consisted of comparisons between (or among) *Mormon* categories: first of all, Mormons were compared according to their differential frequencies of church attendance, frequencies of scripture reading, and frequencies of private prayer (all considered indicators of devoutness). No consistent or systematic differences in the rate of anti-Negro secular attitudes appeared in any of these comparisons (Table II in original paper). Next, Mormons were compared according to their "orthodoxy" on certain key doctrines: the literal divinity of Jesus; the president of the Church as exclusive "prophet, seer, and revelator"; and the withholding of the priesthood from Negroes as the will of God. A dichotomized comparison between full believers and those expressing any degree of doubt in each of these doctrines revealed some modest percentage-point differences (i.e. the "orthodox" were somewhat more likely to express anti-Negro secular attitudes), but the differences were not statistically significant even at a ten percent probability level. Furthermore, the tendency among Mormons for anti-Negro attitudes to increase with degree of orthodoxy was found to be *at least* as true for Congregationalists, Methodists, and American Baptists also (Table III in original paper).

The third kind of intra-Mormon comparison involved social and ecological variables: education, occupation, age, sex, region of origin, community size of origin, and length of time in California (Tables IV and VI). Here, for the first time, many rather large differences occurred. The incidence of anti-Negro secular attitudes varied inversely with education, occupation, community size of origin, and youth. That is to say, the likelihood of expressed anti-Negro attitudes was considerably greater among the poorly educated, the manual occupations, those of rural or small town origin, and the old—those categories known by sociologists to be prone to prejudice in *any* denomination.

Finally, some multi-variate analysis was done, in which the "orthodox" or "believers" were compared with the "doubters" (cf. the three doctrines mentioned above) within categories of education and of community size; or, in the jargon of science, with education and with community size "held constant" (Tables V and VII). In these comparisons, the differences between the "believers" and the "doubters" (in the tendency to express anti-Negro secular attitudes) greatly diminished (and in many cases disappeared entirely) with increasing education and community size of origin. In fact, among those of urban origin, the "orthodox" or "believers" were consistently *less* likely to express anti-Negro attitudes than were the "doubters" of key Church doctrines. All of this evidence led me to conclude the paper as follows:

It would seem, from a study of the data here presented, that the null hypothesis must be allowed to stand for the *religious* variables; that is, no systematic differences in secular race attitudes were to be seen either between Mormons and others, *or* between orthodox and unorthodox Mormons. In most of their responses, Mormons resembled the rather "moderate" denominations (such as Presbyterian, Congregational, Episcopalian), rather than the "fundamentalists" or the sects. To be sure, Mormons *did differ among themselves* in the tendency to hold negative secular attitudes toward Negroes, but these differences were *not* so much between the orthodox and unorthodox, or the active and inactive, as they were between the educated and uneducated, the manual and the professional, the old and the young, or the rural and the urban (as in any denomination) . . . . This accords with other studies which have found socio-economic status an important determinant of attitudes toward minorities.[30]

Conclusion

My plea, then to the civil rights organizations and to all the critics of the Mormon Church is: get off our backs! The Mormon leadership has publicly condemned racism. There is no evidence of a carryover of the Mormon doctrine on the Negro into secular civil life; in fact, there is evidence to the contrary. No matter how much racism you think you see in Utah, you can't be sure it has anything to do with Mormonism. It might be related to the rural and small-town environment in much of the Mountain West (as in other parts of the country), or it might be the sickness of individual Mormon bigots, who would find some other way to rationalize their racism, even if the Mormon Church were without its peculiar "Negro doctrine."[31]

Will the Mormon Church ever change its stand on the Negro? There is no reason, in either Mormon doctrine or tradition, that it could not be changed. In fact, the unique doctrine of continuous revelation makes even drastic changes less difficult than in most denominations (recall the polygamy issue). Not only is there a precedent in the Manifesto of 1890 for a change of great magnitude, but the New Testament itself gives us a perhaps more appropriate precedent in the decision to admit gentiles into full fellowship without circumcision, an innovation which, like the present "Negro issue," was fraught with ethnic overtones and apparently strongly resisted in high places in the primitive church for some time. (Acts 10-11). Perhaps now, as then, the chief deterrent to a divine mandate for change is not to be found in any inadequacy among Negroes, but rather in the unreadiness of the Mormon whites, with our heritage of racial folklore; it

23

is perhaps we whites who have a long way to go before "the Negroes will be ready" for the priesthood.[32] One can speculate however, that if our missionary work ever gets going in black Africa (as apparently it almost did recently), it will only be a matter of time before at least Aaronic Priesthood leadership among Africans will be a necessity.[33]

Whenever change comes, however, it must come in the Mormon way; that is, the integrity of the principle of continuous revelation must be maintained. Without this and without the charisma of the "prophet, seer, and revelator," Mormonism would be without its most vital distinguishing attribute. Any perceived threat to the "due process" implied in the doctrine of continuous revelation will be resisted not only by the Church leadership but also by the overwhelming majority of the rank and file. Consequently, agitation over the "Negro issue" by non-Mormon groups, or even by Mormon liberals, is likely simply to increase the resistance to change. This consideration might not, in the eyes of the NAACP, provide sufficient grounds for ceasing the agitation if a question of civil rights were involved; *but it is not.* No one, I take it, would suggest that holding the priesthood in the Mormon Church is a right guaranteed under the Constitution of the United States. Membership in the Church is voluntary in the fullest civil sense: it is not a condition for holding a job, for owning property, for getting an education, for exercising the voting franchise, or for any other civil right. At the same time, there is nothing to restrain Mormons from engaging in civil rights campaigns and activities whenever conscience dictates, as indeed some have done.[34] So why denounce the Mormon Church for its "stand on civil rights"? To do so is not only inappropriate but is likely to have the opposite of the desired effect. Furthermore it is, in a sense, a form of religious persecution. Until it can be shown that the Mormon "Negro doctrine" has behavioral consequences in the civil world, it is just as much a form of bigotry and persecution to picket the Church Office Building as it would be, say, to picket an Orthodox Jewish synagogue because of pique at the traditional doctrine that Jews are God's chosen people!

In other words, except in cases of severely deviant or anti-social behavior, freedom of religious *belief* must not be breached, even in the name of "equality," no matter how galling a particular belief might be to non-believers, or how anachronistic it might seem to the current arbiters of modernity.

NOTES

1. I would regard the following articles as examples of the reactions of "liberal" religionists: Donald L. Foster (an Orem, Utah, Congregational minister), "Unique Gospel in Utah," *The Christian Century*, 14 July 1965, pp. 890 ff., in which the Mormon Church is chided for its denial of the priesthood to Negroes, and in general, for resisting ". . . such social change and ecumenical developments as have been firing the imaginations and engaging the energies of many other American churchmen"; also, Glen W. Davidson (Department of Philosophy and Religion, Colgate University), "Mormon Missionaries and the Race Question," *The Christian Century*, 29 Sept. 1965, pp. 1183 ff; and two *San Francisco Chronicle* articles by the Reverend Lester Kinsolving (formerly an Episcopal parish priest but now called a "worker-priest" and Religion Correspondent for the *Chronicle*): "The Mormons' Racial Doctrine," 4 June 1966, p. 35, and "Romney Ducks a Racial Issue," 24 June 1967, p. 26. Reverend Kinsolving has told me that he was an "agnostic" at the time he wrote the first of these articles.

As for my allegation that the concern shown by American churchmen about discrimination in the churches is only recent, no documentation should be needed for any informed student of American race relations. However, see for an example, Charles S. McCoy (professor of religion in higher education at Pacific School of Religion, Berkeley, California) "The Churches and Protest Movements for Racial Justice," in Robert Lee and Martin Marty, (eds.) *Religion and Social Conflict* (New York: Oxford University Press, 1964). My reference here is, of course, to white churchmen, as a group recognizing that there were, of course, a few pioneer voices crying in the wilderness much earlier about discrimination in the churches.

2. Discussed at some length in "Mormonism and Minorities," a Ph.D. dissertation in progress by the author in the Department of Sociology, University of California (Berkeley).

3. See Pearl of Great Price, Moses 7:8; Abr. 1:20-27; also the letter of the First Presidency of the Church dated 17 Aug. 1951, as reproduced on pp. 16-18 of the second part of a small book by John J. Stewart, *Mormonism and the Negro* (Orem, Utah: Bookmark Division, Community Press, 1960). The second part of this book, entitled "The Church and the Negroid People," with separate pagination, is authored by William E. Berrett.

4. The policy of the Prophet Joseph Smith himself regarding the ordination of American Negroes is difficult to establish from extant official records. On the one hand, we have the apparently authentic affidavits of Zebedee Coltrin and A. O. Smoot to the effect that the Prophet once said (in the 1830s) that Negroes should not be given the priesthood. (These documents are reproduced

in the Berrett section, pp. 9-11, of Stewart, *Mormonism and the Negro*). The contexts of these affidavits, however, make it somewhat ambiguous as to whether the Prophet meant to deny Negroes the priesthood on principle, or because they were for the most part, still slaves who would be unable to function with the priesthood. In any case, these documents are, at best, second-hand accounts rendered in 1879, forty years or more after the Prophet was supposed to have spoken on the question. On the other hand, it is apparently well established that at least one man of known Negro ancestry, Elijah Abel, was ordained both an Elder and a Seventy under the Prophet's jurisdiction.

Whatever ambiguity there may be in these records, it is clear from the Pearl of Great Price itself (Abr. 1:20-27) that the Prophet must have known, at least from 1842 on (when the Book of Abraham was first published), that Ham's lineage could not be given the priesthood. (Elijah Abel was first ordained in 1836.) The identification of African Negroes with Ham's lineage is apparently a matter of tradition, bolstered by some evidence from biblical scholars, and made explicit for Mormons in the letter from the First Presidency of the Church, reproduced in Stewart, *Mormonism and the Negro*. To an orthodox Mormon, such a formal and unanimous statement by the entire First Presidency, together with the passages in the book of Abraham, would seem to constitute sufficient grounds for regarding the denial of the priesthood to Negroes as the revealed will of God. On such grounds, it is difficult to agree with Samuel W. Taylor that this denial of the priesthood is based not upon doctrine, but only upon "policy." (See Taylor's letter to the Editor, *San Francisco Chronicle*, 11 July 1967, p. 32).

5. See, for example, Joseph Fielding Smith, *The Way to Perfection*, 2nd ed. (Salt Lake City: Genealogical Society, 1935), pp. 105-11; and Bruce R. McConkie, *Mormon Doctrine*, 2nd ed. (Salt Lake City: Bookcraft, 1966), pp. 526-28. These authors are drawing upon opinions apparently held by Joseph Smith and other early Church leaders who were writing (I would insist) in their private or nonprophetic capacities. See also Stewart's book, mentioned above in footnote 3, and John L. Lund, *The Church and the Negro* [Salt Lake City, Utah]: Paramount Publishers, 1967. The Lund and Stewart books, both of which are valuable as collections of historical documents and opinions on the subject, are nevertheless unfortunate contributions to the literature, in my opinion, because they help to perpetuate and popularize the folk notions discussed below.

6. See Llewellyn R. McKay, *Home Memories of David O. McKay* (Salt Lake City: Deseret Book Company), pp. 226-31.

7. See Berrett (in Stewart, *Mormonism and the Negro*). For the attitude of McMurrin on the subject I am relying on an article by Phil Keif appearing in the *Oakland Tribune* (California) for 5 April 1965; Lowry Nelson's position is

put forth in his article, "Mormons and the Negro" in *The Nation*, 174, (24 May, 1952); 488 ff.

8. In his presentation of the "preexistence explanation," Stewart (*Mormonism and the Negro*, pp. 20-36) is expressing what I have found to be the most common version. See also Joseph Fielding Smith, *Way to Perfection*, p. 43.

9. What is being set forth here, of course, is only the theory behind the actual (or presumptive) policy. The practical applications of the policy to specific cases of Hamitic lineage might be rather problematical. One wonders, for example, why the Lord permitted the ordination of Elijah Abel (and I have even heard it claimed that Church records would show Abel's sons and grandsons to have been ordained too, although I have never seen any such records or their facsimiles). One wonders also how we can be sure that all who are given the priesthood are free of even remote Hamitic lineage, especially in such ethnically mixed areas as Latin America and Fiji. I know first hand of at least one case (my boyhood friends) in which a family of completely Caucasian *appearance* was denied the priesthood for years because of genealogical evidence of remote Hamitic (i.e. Negro) ancestry. Even appeals to the General Authorities were to no avail, until the evidence itself was impeached and finally found to be dubious. Since then, members of the family have been ordained, but not, it should be noted, because of a relaxation in the policy itself. From time to time one hears rumors of incidents that do seem to constitute relaxations or "exceptions" to the policy, but first-hand information is extremely elusive. As far as I know, there is no official specification given as to how much, if any, Hamitic lineage is permissible for priesthood holders. Presumably, in such matters, we must rely on the pronouncements about lineage given in patriarchal blessings. In any case, I am concerned here only with trying to understand the theory and doctrine from which the policy derives. In cases of ordinations which seem to constitute "exceptions," or are otherwise questionable, it is not my responsibility to offer "explanations"; these must come, if they are to come, from the prophets themselves, who, we must presume, know what they are doing. Nothing is to be gained, it seems to me, by nit-picking about occasional exceptions to Church policies anyway, as long as these are rare; Mormon history has many such "exceptions" (e.g. the "rebaptisms" in Brigham Young's times), which the orthodox Mormon is usually willing to accept on faith, where no understandable explanation is available.

10. See Berrett, in Stewart, *Mormonism and the Negro* , pp. 16-18.

11. Ibid., 32-34; also Joseph Fielding Smith, *Way to Perfection* , p. 43.

12. The Fifes have shown us that Mormon ingenuity in folklore of all kinds is second to none, although much of it is ultimately of extra-Mormon origin, of course. See Austin and Alta Fife, *Saints of Sage and Saddle: Folklore Among the Mormons* (Bloomington: University of Indiana Press, 1956).

13. Gen. 9:18-29. Canaan was a son of Ham. His implication in the incident is not explained.

14. See Gen. 4:9-15 and Pearl of Great Price, Moses 5:16-40; 7:7-22; Abr. 1:20-27; also Joseph Fielding Smith, *Way to Perfection* , pp. 105-11.

15. Joseph Fielding Smith, *Way to Perfection* , pp. 105-11; see also Berrett, pp.13-15, in Stewart *Mormonism and the Negro*, provides a few examples from the writings of nineteenth-century Church leaders. In using the word "folklore" here, I do not mean to say that the scriptural references themselves can be regarded as folklore, but only the interpretation of them which ties denial of the priesthood to skin color, or to the curses and marks on Ham or Cain.

16. One of the more moot questions, especially on subjects of this kind, is the question of what is "official doctrine" and what is not. One would think that we should regard as official Church doctrine at least the standard works of the Church and those occasional pronouncements given by the First Presidency and/or the Twelve acting in formal and unanimous concert. Beyond that, there are many open questions, and the purport of my remarks in this paper, of course, is to deny that doctrines or opinions offered in books written by individual Church leaders, of however high callings, are binding upon the Latter-day Saints. In a lecture delivered on 7 July 1954, to Seminary and Institute teachers attending a BYU Summer Session, the late President J. Reuben Clark, Jr., dealt with this question and offered what I would regard as helpful counsel. He first referred his listeners to the Doctrine and Covenants 68:2-4, in which we are told that "scripture" is that which is spoken by those leaders who are "moved upon by the Holy Ghost," which implies, according to President Clark, that it is possible for leaders sometimes to speak *without* being so moved. Among the exact words of President Clark which bear particularly upon my contention are the following (all taken directly from this same lecture): "Only the President of the Church, the Presiding High Priest, is sustained as Prophet, Seer, and Revelator for the Church, and he alone has the right to receive revelations for the Church, either new or amendatory, or to give authoritative interpretations of scriptures that shall be binding on the Church....Yet we must not forget that the prophets are mortal men, with men's infirmities....Asked if a prophet was always a prophet, Brother Joseph quickly affirmed that a prophet is a prophet only when he is acting as such (from *History of the Church*, 5:265)....Even the President of the Church has not always spoken under the direction of the Holy Ghost, for a prophet is not always a prophet. I noted that the Apostles of the Primitive Church had their differences and that in our own Church, leaders have differed in their views from the first....When any man, except the President of the Church, undertakes to proclaim one unsettled doctrine, as among two or more doctrines in dispute, as the settled doctrine of the Church, we may know that he is not 'moved upon by the Holy Ghost,' unless he is acting under the direction and

by the authority of the President." As for the critical question of how to tell when a doctrine is pronounced by a prophet or leader who is "moved upon by the Holy Ghost," President Clark suggests only a subjective test; i.e., in the final analysis, we can tell when our leaders are so moved only when we ourselves are so moved, which has the effect, he points out, of shifting the burden from the speaker to the hearer.

17. A complete copy of the final resolution is in my files. It was more or less fully described in the news media (e.g. *San Francisco Examiner*, 2 July 1965, p. 6).

18. *Dialogue* 2 (Summer 1967): 5-6. All of my quotations of Udall in this section of the paper are excerpted from the same letter. Although I have taken most of them out of their specific contexts, I think I have not distorted the sense in which he used any of them.

19. Lester Kinsolving, "Romney Ducks a Racial Issue," *San Francisco Chronicle*, 24 June 1967, p. 26.

20. Ibid.

21. The description of my dialogue with the Reverend Kinsolving during the July 2 radio program is based upon my review of a tape recording of the program in my possession.

22. Glen W. Davidson, "Mormon Missionaries and the Race Question," *The Christian Century*, 29 Sept. 1965, pp. 1183-86.

23. This charge was, of course, inaccurate if only because of the case of California, whose voters, by a margin of 2 to 1, passed Proposition 14 in November 1964. This had the effect of wiping off the books all of the "fair housing" legislation ever passed in California (one wonders how the California Mormons were able to bring *that* about!). This situation prevailed throughout 1965 and 1966, until a recent Supreme Court decision striking down Proposition 14.

24. This unequivocal statement in the April, 1965, General Conference was quoted in the *San Francisco Chronicle*, 17 April 1965. Another statement by President Brown condemning racism, this time at the April 1966 General Conference, is quoted on the last page of *Dialogue* 1:2 (Summer, 1966).

25. Charles Y. Glock and Rodney Stark, *Christian Beliefs and Anti-Semitism* (New York: Harper and Row, 1966). The authors review some of the literature on the subject of religion and race attitudes. See also Gordon W. Allport, *The Nature of Prejudice* (New York: Doubleday Anchor Book, 1958): pp. 420-22, and John D. Photiadis and Arthur Johnson, "Orthodoxy, Church Participation, and Authoritarianism," *American Journal of Sociology*, Nov. 1963, pp. 244-48.

26. Glock and Stark, *Christian Beliefs*, ch. 10.

27. Armand L. Mauss, "Mormonism and Secular Attitudes toward Negroes," *Pacific Sociological Review* 9 (Fall 1966).

28. My distinction between "prejudice" and "discrimination" is after the well-known formulations appearing in Allport, *Nature of Prejudice*, pp. 14 ff. and Peter I. Rose, *They and We* (New York: Random House, 1964), ch. 4.

29. The tables in the original paper have been deliberately omitted to facilitate the reading. They are, I believe, adequately summarized here and can easily be obtained from the original article by interested persons. The *Pacific Sociological Review* is available in the library of virtually any four-year college or university west of the Rockies, and often in other regions as well.

30. Some of my Mormon critics have expressed disappointment in my findings to the effect that Mormons are not very different from others in the tendency to hold racist attitudes, pointing out that we can take small comfort indeed in the evidence that Mormons are no better than others in this regard. My reply to this understandable reaction is that *by comparison with* the charges of extraordinary Mormon racism, which are made by most of our critics, my findings are great comfort indeed! This would be no reason, however, for complacency; this much racist feeling in a Mormon population surely indicates the need for some religious education on the subject, which our seminaries and institutes could well provide.

31. Photiadis and Johnson, ("Orthodoxy, Church Participation," note 33) concluded that the secular variable of authoritarianism might be prior (or causal) to the *religious* variables of orthodoxy and participation.

32. Brigham Young (quoted in Berrett section of *Stewart, Mormonism and the Negro*, p. 14) was among those who held that no change could occur in the policy of denying Negroes the priesthood until all the rest of Adam's descendants had had a chance to receive it. President McKay (quoted in Llewellyn R. McKay, *Home Memories*, p. 231) seems to see no such required delay.

33. The now rather well known story about the Church's attempts to get missionary work started in Nigeria has been reported in various places in the news media. See, for example, the article in the "Religion" section of *Time* magazine for 18 June 1965, p. 56; the article by Wallace Turner, "Mormons Weigh Stand on Negro," *New York Times* (Western Edition) for 7 June 1963, p. 1; and Drew Pearson's column appearing in the *San Francisco Chronicle* of 5 July 1962, p. 39.

34. See, for example, the account by Karl Keller of his summer of civil rights activities in Tennessee, "Every Soul Has Its South," *Dialogue* 1 (Summer 1966): 72-79. Governor Romney of Michigan also was widely reported in the press to have participated in civil rights marches in his state.

A Commentary
on Stephen G. Taggart's
Mormonism's Negro Policy: Social
and Historical Origins

Lester Bush

*During the 1960s many authors attempted historical studies of the origins
of Mormon teachings on blacks. Most offered superficial analyses based
largely on assumptions, with little primary research. The most extensive
study came in 1969 in the form of an essay by Stephen Taggart which in
unpublished form received "Honorable Mention" in the first annual*
Dialogue *Prize for Social Literature. Drawing heavily on the recently
published Missouri-period research of Warren Jennings and the conceptual framework originally set forth by Fawn Brodie, Taggart proposed
more thoroughly than ever before the so-called "Missouri Thesis" of the
origins of Church teachings and practices related to blacks.*

*In response to oral presentations of this paper, Lester Bush submitted
to* Dialogue *the results of his own research which raised serious questions
about much of the traditional wisdom on Mormon teachings, including
many of the assumptions which underlay Taggart's analysis. Initially*
Dialogue *intended to carry both essays as a roundtable, with Taggart
being offered a chance to reply to the Bush critique. However, Taggart's
untimely death prevented this and his paper was withdrawn in favor of
publication in book form. The Bush essay, which in essence undermined
all previous historical explanations of the origins of church teachings, was
then published as follows, a review essay of Taggart's book version. This
essay originally appeared in* Dialogue *4 (Winter 1969).*

Stephen Taggart has attempted in *Mormonism's Negro Policy: Social
and Historical Origins* to show that the present Mormon Negro policy is
"a historical anachronism—an unfortunate and embarrassing survival of
a once expedient institutional practice" which emerged in response to
stress encountered in Missouri. With this demonstration that "the action
of social forces explains the present Mormon posture toward Negroes," it
becomes apparent that "the Church would need only declare its disposition

for a change to occur." Since other authors have previously "demonstrated" the socio-historical origin of this practice without noticeable effect on the Church,[1] one expects this to be an especially ironclad case—tightly reasoned, well documented, and presumably with some new references, perhaps even contemporary with the period.

The essay does indeed appear more comprehensive than previous treatments, and it cites some uncommon, though seemingly very relevant, references. One has the impression that a very good case is being made. If the Mormons in Missouri were so clearly swayed by their environment with regard to the Negro, why not the whole Church doctrine? Yet problems are evident which question the validity of Taggart's conclusions. After a generally accurate and well documented rehearsal of the Jackson County period of the Church, one finds an increasing incidence of speculative statements and secondary sources, and a sprinkling of factual errors. More disturbingly, one finds a number of relevant points omitted from Mormon history and doctrine and the general setting in which they arose.

We are informed, initially, that after the founding of the Church, Mormons with "abolitionist attitudes" went to Missouri, an area to which they became attached through "both economic and ideological forces." Facing, among other problems, hostile proslavery sentiment in the old settlers, the Mormons were willing to attempt "to reduce the conflict which threatened to drive them from the state by abandoning their initial abolitionist tendencies and adopting some form of proslavery posture."

Unquestionably the Mormons were viewed as a threat to slavery in Missouri. They were not slaveholders and had come from the home of the growing "antislavery impulse"; furthermore, their path—New York to Ohio to Missouri—paralleled in time and route the movement of abolitionist sentiment into the West.[2] Yet one is disappointed that essentially no effort has been made to document the claim that the early Mormons were, in fact, abolitionists.[3] The only evidence cited to defend this point is taken from an article in *The Evening and the Morning Star* which was an emphatic denial of any interference with the slaves.[4] Warren Jennings, to whom Taggart acknowledges a considerable debt for insight into the Jackson County period, deals with this question and concludes, "There is no concrete evidence that the Mormons ever incited, conspired, or tampered with the slaves."[5] Nonetheless, as is correctly observed, the Missourian perception of the Mormon position was important, and not the actual Mormon practice.

In 1833, Taggart proceeds, a crisis developed when "the Mormon press in Missouri" issued a cautionary note on immigration of free Negroes into Missouri. The article was misunderstood by the Missourians as an invitation to free Negro Mormons to come to Missouri. In response to the vigorous anti-Mormon activity which ensued, the Church within one month's time changed its stated position from having "no special rule" with regard to Negroes to a desire "to prevent them from being admitted as members of the Church."

This history is well substantiated. If one ignores the unnecessary speculative statements Taggart now inserts periodically,[6] the significant points are undeniable. The "Mormon press" (i.e., W. W. Phelps) responded most remarkably to the winds of environmental stress. One small point should be made; Elijah Abel was not the first Negro convert to the Church, as is suggested. At least one other, known variously as Black Pete and Black Tom, had joined in Kirtland, Ohio, within a year of the organization of the Church.[7] It is not clear that either Pete or Abel was known to Phelps, or that either had the necessary citizenship papers to go to Missouri. Pete's parents were slaves; and though Abel was born in Maryland, his family was later from Canada, raising the question of his having made use of the underground railroad.[8] In any event, there is no indication that Abel planned ("Abel ... may have intended ...") a trip to hostile Missouri. In fact, he originally went to Kirtland, not Nauvoo.

Taggart next relates that shortly after the expulsion of the Saints from Jackson County, Joseph Smith, upon obtaining a "clear impression of the explosiveness of the slavery issue" and "in the context of his recent firsthand experience in Missouri," reached the decision "to exclude Negroes from the priesthood"; however, he "advised only members who approached him on the subject, and who were concerned with the southern Church" (this in 1834). The following year reportedly brought "the first official declaration of policy regarding Negroes made by the Church," declaring "formally ... support of the legal institution of slavery ..."

With these claims come the first serious questions as to the adequacy of the research, as well as to the validity of the conclusions drawn. The remarkable "documentation" for the origin of the practice of denying the Negro the priesthood is the testimony of Zebedee Coltrin, and to a lesser extent the testimony of Abraham O. Smoot, given 31 May 1879.[9] These are the only references cited at any time in the article to support the claim that Joseph Smith taught denial of the priesthood to the Negro.[10] But the source needs further evaluation. Granting that "Coltrin's statement was recorded forty-five years after the fact" and that it therefore "would be unwise to accept its detail without question," Taggart still assumes "as generally correct the report" that Joseph Smith decided not to give the Negro the priesthood "in mid-1834."[11] This is indeed a commendable memory, especially in view of Taggart's stated belief that part of Coltrin's testimony is in error ("events show that tone in his testimony to be an artifact"). Of more serious concern is the absence of any attempt to evaluate the reliability of the sources. Nowhere is it mentioned that Coltrin's own account reflects prejudice to the subject;[12] nor that Coltrin, himself, two years after the reported conversation with Joseph Smith *ordained Elijah Abel* to the priesthood office of a Seventy[13] (to the Third Quorum, not the Second as Coltrin recalls in 1879);[14] nor is evidence given of Coltrin's later criticisms of Abel in a Seventies meeting.[15]

The testimony of Abraham O. Smoot is not emphasized because Smoot was unable to date the origin of the practice as early as 1834. Even so, it would have been worthwhile to point out that Smoot came from a line of slaveholders, and reportedly owned a slave himself while in Utah[16] (this slave described by him in later years as "one of the 'whitest Negroes' living");[17] or one might expect mention of Smoot's refusal, in 1844, under Southern pressuring to distribute Joseph Smith's presidential views which were critical of slavery.[18] More substantial documentation than the testimonies of Smoot and Coltrin seems indicated.

The first "official" Church position on slavery (there is no reference to Negroes in the 1835 statement referred to by Taggart) may not have come in 1835, but rather two years prior, immediately after the expulsion of the Saints from Missouri. And this would not have been in the form of a policy statement of support for slavery, but rather as a divine condemnation of it: "It is not right that any man should be in bondage one to another . . . ."[19] This statement, traditionally interpreted as meaning economic bondage by reference to a later revelation,[20] is never mentioned in early Mormon discourses on slavery. It is not entirely clear from the context that such a restriction is justified.

Careful reading of the policy statement passed in 1835 reflects that it was not so much an endorsement of legal slavery as it was a statement of support for legal institutions in general, which would include slavery where it was legal.[21] It should be noted that the statement was shortly thereafter amplified by Joseph Smith in a letter to the "elders abroad," in which he made it clear that the obligation to teach slaves the gospel had not been removed.[22] The elders were simply instructed to consult the masters first.[23] The Mormons had preached to Negroes from the earliest days of the Church. Black Pete was a member in February 1831; the *Journal History* speaks of preaching to Negroes in the summer of 1831; and Abel joined in 1832. The "Rules and Regulations to be Observed in the House of the Lord in Kirtland" drafted by Joseph Smith and others in 1836 provided for "black or white" (as well as "believer or unbeliever").[24] As late as 1840, the First Presidency issued a statement anticipating that "we may soon expect to seed flocking to this place [Nauvoo], people of every land and from every nation . . . [including] the degraded Hottentot . . . who shall with us worship the Lord of Hosts in His holy temple and offer up their orisons in His sanctuary."[25]

To return to Taggart's narrative, we are informed that because of a continuing "minority of verbal abolitionists within the Church," the "leadership" was forced "to develop a theological justification for its proslavery statements." This was "essential for the safety of the membership in Missouri, for the attainment of the land of Zion, and for the success of the Southern missionary effort . . . . The required argument had already been documented for him—complete with scriptural proof texts—by Southern churches . . ." and was utilized by Joseph Smith and others in the *Messenger and Advocate* (October 1836).

With these ideas, the article is briefly on firm ground again. The three discourses referred to embody virtually all the proslavery arguments then prevalent and represent the most extensive treatment of slavery found during the first decade of the Church.[26] Though the notion that Canaan, slavery, and the Negro were somehow related gained wide acceptance in the nineteenth century South, it was not new. This belief had been relatively common in seventeenth-century America as one of the justifications for enslaving Negroes, but had fallen into disuse until the biblical attacks of evangelical abolitionists (slave-holding became a "sin") in the nineteenth century forced its recall. Previously this connection had been found in sixteenth-century England at the time of the English "discovery" of Africans; and the concept can be traced to Hebraic literature of at least 200 to 600 A.D.[27] There is evidence that Joseph Smith believed this tradition, for he mentions parenthetically that Negroes were "descendants of Ham" as early as June 1831, well prior to any difficulty within the Church over the slavery issue.[28]

As Taggart notes, the statements in the *Messenger and Advocate* represented a personal (rather than "official") response to the growing frustration in the Church over the slavery issue. The suggestion, however, that this was primarily directed at Missouri difficulties, and in particular at abolitionists within the Church, lacks evidence. The Mormons long had been saddled with the charge of being abolitionists. Though the charge was repeatedly denied, it persisted and continued to plague them wherever slavery was "tolerated." Because of the growth of the Church in the South generally, the embarrassment of an abolitionist's visit to Kirtland was sufficient to trigger the extensive discourses found in the *Advocate*.[29]

During this same period (about 1836), Taggart proposes, a "theological justification" for the practice of denying the priesthood to the Negro was "evidently contemplated . . . . For some reason, however, [Joseph Smith] did not make his efforts public until 1842," when this justification "was published as part of *The Book of Abraham*." "Consequently, ordinations of Negroes continued . . . until as late as 1841."[30]

These are significant claims—if they have been justified. However, in looking for evidence to support the position, one is again disappointed to find a group of inferences and semi-relevant quotations. As with many of the other proposals, they may be correct, or they may not; unfortunately little light is shed on resolving the question. Several assumptions have been made. Basic is the unquestioned acceptance of the 1879 interview with Coltrin and Smoot. This allows Taggart to ignore his own observation that the book of Abraham "is vague and cannot by itself be said to justify denying the priesthood to Negroes," because "in the presence of an eight-year-old informal practice of denying the priesthood to Negroes" it becomes "sufficient" justification.

This ignores a lack of evidence that Joseph Smith ever used the book of Abraham to justify priesthood denial (nor apparently did any other Church leader, until the Utah period); neither is there any mention that Joseph Smith's "brief reversal" of opinion on slavery *preceded* the publication of the book of Abraham (which is difficult to reconcile with even the claim of its corroborating divine sanction of slavery by supporting Southern proslavery traditions).[31]

What of the claimed "contemplation" in 1835? The Egyptian alphabet and grammar now available has not yet been dated.[32] The specific references made by Joseph Smith in 1835 to the actual content of the grammar and alphabet (or to the book of Abraham) refer only to astronomy, not to the flood story.[33] In view of this, how can Taggart's conclusions be drawn? Simply: "The Egyptian alphabet and grammer... *appears* to have been the product of Joseph Smith's effort...[in] 1835.... It *appears* that the passage in *The Book of Abraham* concerning the curse of Canaan was written during the most intensive period of conflict[34]....Thus, *one year after his meeting* with Greene and Coltrin, Joseph Smith *evidently contemplated* the development of a theological justification for the practice of denying the priesthood to Negroes...." (q.e.d.) (my italics)

One must admit that in spite of the inadequacies of the above position, the parallels between Mormon scripture and the contemporary proslavery arguments are striking.[35] In the early 1840's the Mormon leadership could argue using only direct quotes from what were to become Church scriptures: "the seed of Cain were black" (Moses 7:22); "a blackness came upon all the children of Canaan" (Moses 7:8); "[the] king of Egypt was a descendant from the loins of Ham, and was a partaker of the blood of the Canaanites by birth" (Abr. 1:21); "and thus the blood of the Canaanites was preserved in the land" (Abr. 1:22); "and...from Ham, sprang the race which preserved the curse in the land" (Abr. 1:24); "[Pharaoh was] cursed...as pertaining to the priesthood" (Abr. 1:26); and Ham's son, Canaan, was cursed to be a "servant of servants" (Gen. 9:25). Those familiar with the "Inspired translation" of the Bible dating from 1831 could have added that Canaan had "a veil of darkness...cover him, that he shall be known among all men" (Gen. 9:50, JST).[36] Thus, Joseph Smith had armed the Church with evidence that clearly vindicated holding

Negroes as slaves, as well as denying them the priesthood. Or maybe it is not so clear. Why would he so extensively justify a position on slavery he had rejected?[37] Why does no Mormon publication utilize this "obvious" argument for slavery during Joseph Smith's lifetime?[38] Why does no one for many years tie these scriptures to the denial of the priesthood to the Negro?

These are perplexing questions. To assume without evidence that subsequent interpretations of scripture were necessarily those initially used is no more justified than the assumption that they were created for the purpose for which they later came to be used. A careful reading of the Mormon scriptures reveals a most confused picture—Cain's descendants, who "were black," are never again identified after Moses 7:22 (an antediluvian time) nor are Cain's brethren who were shut out with him (Gen. 5:26, JST). The antediluvian people of Canaan were apparently not black until they fought with the people of Shum (thus are questionably, if at all, connected with Cain) (Moses 7:8); and the JST renders Canaan as *Cainan*, and gives the impression that these were the prophet Enoch's own people (Gen. 7:6-10; for Enoch's background, Gen. 6:43-44). Nowhere is it stated that Ham married a descendant of the antediluvian people of Canaan. The closest suggestion of this is through reference to Pharaoh, a descendant of Ham and also a descendant of the "Canaanites" (Abr. 1:21), yet the other references in the book of Abraham to Canaanites refer to the descendants of Ham's son, Canaan, to whom the Pharaoh could have been related also. All that is said of Ham's wife is that her name was "Egypt, which in Chaldean signifies that which is forbidden" (Abr. 1:23);[39] yet we are told that Ham, shortly before the flood, was of such high standing that he "walked with God" (Moses 8:27). The Pharaoh and his lineage, the only persons identified as being denied the priesthood (Abr. 1:26-27), are minimally identified as descendants of Ham and Egypt. Only with the Pharaoh is any connection between the descendants of Ham through Egypt and those through Canaan even suggested, yet the Pharaoh was hardly a "servant of servants." Moreover, the Pharaoh is depicted a "white" in Facsimile 3 in the book of Abraham, in obvious contrast to a "black slave belonging to the prince." Finally, no reference is made to any son of Ham other than Canaan being cursed with servitude nor any lineage of Ham other than that of Pharaoh being denied the priesthood. The cause of the priesthood denial is not given (one wonders about idolatry), nor is there any continuous lineage of "black people" apparent in any of the scriptures. The "blackness" which overcomes individuals or groups periodically seems to represent the same divine displeasure found in Book of Mormon references to "blackness" overcoming the clearly non-Negro Lamanites.[40] Similarly, "curses" are adequately plentiful to make nonspecific allusions to "preserving" previous curses almost impossible to trace back to their origins with certainty.

The question of the historicity of the books of Abraham and Moses needs further analysis, especially as it pertains to the Negro and the priesthood.[41] The connection in English tradition, as noted earlier, of the Negro with Ham and Cain dates to at least the rediscovery of Africa by the English in the fifteenth and sixteenth centuries; the association with Ham is found in much older Hebraic writings.[42] Winthrop Jordan states that initially these beliefs were not associated with a justification for enslaving Negroes,[43] which reminds one of Joseph Smith condemning slavery at the very time he was claiming, in effect, validity for the tradition that Ham and Cain were associated with dark people. There is also a need for an adequate treatment of the biblical references used on the priesthood-slavery issue.[44]

Taggart has ended his historical survey with a disappointingly brief treatment of the period from the death of Joseph Smith until the end of the Brigham Young era—disappointing because it is in this period and later that most of the available contemporary source material is found. The first known documentation of the policy of priesthood denial comes in 1849.[45] By 1852, reports of this practice had become almost commonplace.[46] Notably these statements are without reference to Joseph Smith. One wonders just how early the documentation is for Joseph Smith having initiated the practice of denying the priesthood to Negroes. In spite of the many instances under Brigham Young in which this practice was reiterated, none of the quotations in general use refers to Joseph Smith as the originator[47] (although Brigham Young does say that Joseph taught that Negroes were not "neutral in Heaven").[48] One might infer from the 1879 interview that there was some question in the minds of John Taylor and Brigham Young, Jr., as to Joseph Smith's views on the subject.[49] And Lorenzo Snow, when president of the Church in 1900, is unsure whether Church teachings on the Negro originated with Brigham Young or Joseph Smith.[50] There are a few who attribute these teachings to Joseph Smith. Their written testimonies, as in the cases of Coltrin and Smoot, come many years after the fact, and coincidentally after decades of actual priesthood discrimination.[51] Among those who could have heard it from Joseph Smith, two were of note in Church leadership. George Q. Cannon reported in 1895 and again in 1900 that Joseph Smith originated the practice because of a connection of the Negro with Cain;[52] and Franklin D. Richards said essentially this in 1896.[53] However, by this time usage was being made of the Joseph Smith translation of the book of Abraham in support of the priesthood policy.[54] One wonders if it has been only in the twentieth century that the idea that this practice originated with Joseph Smith has become widely accepted.[55]

By contrast there is no question but that Joseph Smith thought the

Negro was descended from Ham; however, this belief when initially recorded was by no means in a revelatory context and would appear to have been little more than the contemporary view. As mentioned earlier, the original statement was expressed in 1831 and only parenthetically. At an early meeting, the gospel was preached to "all the families of the earth... several of the Lamanites or Indians—representatives of Shem; quite a respectable number of Negroes—descendants of Ham; and the balance was made up of citizens of the surrounding country (from Japeth)."[56] In 1836, as Taggart notes, Joseph Smith extended this belief to a justification of slavery; by 1842, while he still referred to the Negroes as descendants of Ham, he no longer felt this was a justification for slavery.

There is also contemporary evidence, at least in the 1840s, to show that Joseph believed the Negro to be descended from Cain. Here again the preserved statements are parenthetical, and one wonders if this idea, too, was not merely the reflection of a prevalent belief. The reference cited in documentations of the Prophet holding this opinion was from 1842, "The Indians have greater cause to complain of the treatment of the whites, than the negroes, or sons of Cain."[57] If Joseph Smith did hold this belief, might not his statements on Cain be a source to link him to the idea that the Negroes should be denied the priesthood.[58] This is an area which has been largely ignored, perhaps because it has not been particularly fruitful.[59]

As interesting as the sudden availability of sources on the priesthood policy shortly after the Utah period begins are the numerous justifications of slavery cited by the brethren in the West based solely on the curse on Canaan, and contrary to Joseph Smith's recent position.[60] One wonders how Joseph would have reacted to slave-owning apostles,[61] or to the formal legalization of slavery in Utah in 1852.[62] The belief that the Negroes were descended from Cain was soon very widespread in Utah, being commonly mentioned in early publications and was almost invariably the justification given for denial of the priesthood to Negroes.[63] And this remains the official belief to the present day.[64]

Taggart has concluded his essay with an "implication"— "Mormonism's practices regarding Negroes should be viewed as matters of policy rather than as points of doctrine," and therefore subject to nonrevelatory change. Though his historical analysis is subject to serious question, he renders the objections somewhat academic with his final quotation. Almost as an afterthought he supports his conclusion with an excerpt from a letter sent by Sterling McMurrin in August 1968 to Llewelyn McKay regarding a 1954 conversation with President David O. McKay: "[President McKay]... said with considerable feeling that 'there is not now, and there never has been, a doctrine in this Church that the negroes are under a divine curse.' He insisted that there is no doctrine of any kind pertaining to the Negro. 'We believe,' he said, 'that we have scriptural precedent for withholding the priesthood from the Negro. It is a practice, not a doctrine, and the practice will some day be changed. And that's all there is to it.'"[65] Taggart adds, in a note, that "Llewelyn R. McKay has informed the writer that when he received Dr. McMurrin's letter he read it to his father, David O. McKay, and he reports that President McKay told him that the letter accurately represents what he said to McMurrin in 1954." While the verification would have been more impressive had it come from President McKay,[66] this statement is obviously one for careful consideration. The fourteen-year time lapse[67] as well as McMurrin's acknowledged bias on this issue seem relevant, but the recent independent substantiation of the report largely neutralizes these objections.

One is struck by the contrast of the McMurrin quotation with other reports of the beliefs of President McKay. Though at least one well known letter may be partially reconcilable with this new quotation, most statements seem incompatible.[68] The First Presidency statement issued in August 1951, under President McKay, said: "The attitude of the Church with reference to Negroes remains as it has always stood. It is not a matter of the declaration of a policy but of a direct commandment from the Lord, on which is founded the doctrine of the Church from the days of its organization to the effect that Negroes . . . are not entitled to the Priesthood at the present time . . ."[69] Taggart cites no reference to President McKay other than the McMurrin quotation and thus avoids the problem of reconciling various statements. Though every prophet from Brigham Young to the present has concurred in denying the priesthood to the Negro, none publicly has made specific claim to a revelation of this matter—all (except perhaps Brigham Young) have deferred to preceding prophets. Nor does the First Presidency statement of 1951 cite a specific revelation, but rather quotes a Brigham Young discourse on the curse of Cain. Therefore, the McMurrin quotation does not contradict any explicitly claimed revelation. Moreover, the Church's position on the Negro historically has shown enough variability to suggest the possibility of a "policy" interpretation. Theologically, however, such a change in stated position by the Church would reflect a need for clarification of where, on the spectrum from "revelation" to "personal opinion," are found such concepts as "doctrine," "policy," and "First Presidency statement."

While it is clear that Taggart has not proved that "Mormonism's practices regarding Negroes" are solely "matters of policy," he nonetheless has added a number of significant documents to an already substantial list.[70] The evidence of these documents, and others, would seem to require a more extensive response by the Church. There remains no period source to support the contention that Joseph Smith was the author of the present Church Negro position. Joseph Smith did express the then-prevalent opinion that Negroes were descendants of Canaan and Cain; yet he did not relate this to the priesthood in any account now available. In contrast to others who believed the Cain-Canaan tradition, Joseph Smith came to teach that this did *not* justify Negro slavery and spoke clearly against that institution. In fact, a Negro known to him was ordained to the priesthood in Kirtland and held the priesthood in Nauvoo. And, under Joseph Smith's direction, the First Presidency anticipated soon having other black African converts joining them in worship in the Nauvoo temple.

With the move West under the leadership of Brigham Young, this history, as presently understood, changed dramatically. The curse on Cain is found central to many discourses and is seen to be the justification for priesthood denial to the Negro. The curse on Canaan is interpreted in a manner that not only justifies Negro slavery, but also places the institution beyond man's power to eliminate. Moreover, in contrast to Joseph Smith's high opinion of Negro potential,[71] Brigham Young expressed the view that Negroes were almost universally inferior to whites and had limited leadership potential.[72] Those succeeding Brigham Young have relied heavily on his discourses for documentation of early Mormon beliefs on the priesthood question (slavery was removed from discussion by the Civil War). Additionally, one begins to find common usage of the book of Abraham as "scriptural support" of modern beliefs, as well as the claim that the Church's view on the Negro has not changed since being set forth by Joseph Smith.

Because of the limited circulation or inaccessibility of some Church records, the history of this subject remains tentative and incomplete. There is an obvious need for more research into the views of the Negro held in the formative years on the Church. Equally obvious is that careful reading of Taggart's article, as well as this commentary, will reveal that little has been established in any absolute sense. Yet significant questions have been raised which subsequent study should attempt to clarify.

NOTES

1. Fawn Brodie's *No Man Knows My History* (New York:Knopf 1945) is probably widest known; most convincingly documented is Naomi F. Woodbury's "A Legacy of Intolerance: Nineteenth Century Pro-slavery propaganda and the Mormon Church Today," (M.A. thesis, University of California at Los Angeles, 1966). Other current works include Jerald Tanner's *The Negro in Mormon Theology* (Salt Lake City: Modern Microfilm Company, 1963); Jerald and Sandra Tanner's *Joseph Smith's Curse upon the Negro* (Salt Lake City: Modern Microfilm Company, 1965); and sections of general treatments of Mormonism, e.g., William J. Whalen, *The Latter-day Saints in the*

Modern World (New York: John Day Company, 1964), and Wallace Turner, *The Mormon Establishment* (Boston: Houghton Mifflin Company, 1966). See also Jan Shipp's, "Second Class Saints," *Colorado Quarterly* 11 (1962): 183 and Dennis Lythgoe, "Negro Slavery and Mormon Doctrine," *Western Humanities Review* 21 (1967): 327.

2. Many abolitionists were associated, additionally, with religious evangelism and the temperance movement.

3. For the most part. Taggart has made rather casual usage of the term "abolitionist," employing it interchangeably with passive opposition to slavery and failing to distinguish among the broad spectrum of views held by abolitionists (gradualists to immediatists); these distinctions become more important in the Nauvoo period. He also ignores the anti-Negro, antibolitionist sentiment in the Northeast, which shortly resulted in widespread disorder, including riots in Palmyra, New York, in 1834 and 1837. See John Hope Franklin, *From Slavery to Freedom: A History of Negro Americans*, 3d ed. (New York, 1969), p. 235.

4. *The Evening and the Morning Star* 2 (Jan. 1834): 122.

5. Warren A. Jennings, "Factors in the Destruction of the Mormon Press in Missouri, 1833," *Utah Historical Quarterly* 35 (1967): 67. This excellent work adds to many of Taggart's primary references for this period several other seemingly relevant testimonies concerning early Mormon views toward slavery.

6. E.g., "a few converts . . . who *probably* subscribed to the slave system . . . "; "the threat . . . *may have been* aggravated by a revelation . . ."; and, "to the extent that . . . , it would have been construed as an attempt . . ." (my italics).

7. He is spoken of as being a member of the Mormon Church in early February 1831 (*Ashtabula Journal*, 5 Feb. 1831, Stanley S. Ivins Collection, Utah State Historical Society, Notebook 2, p. 221). There are a number of later references to Pete, who was one of two Negro Mormons to claim to have received revelation.

8. Abel's mother reportedly was originally a slave in South Carolina. With slave parentage, neither could have obtained citizenship papers very easily.

9. Taggart's footnote cites a secondary source (William E. Berrett, *The Church and the Negroid People* [Orem, Utah, 1960]) which in turn refers to a *Journal History* entry of 31 May 1879. Actually, the *Journal History* contains no such entry near that date (if at all) and the correct source was actually John Nuttall's journal for that day. The quote, however, is accurately reported.

10. See *John Nuttall, Journal,* Vol. 1 (1876-1884) Typescript, pp. 290-93, the Library, Brigham Young University, Provo, Utah. A copy is also preserved in the Historical Dept. Archives of the Church of Jesus Christ of Latter-day Saints, Salt Lake City, Utah; hereafter cited as LDS Church Archives.

11. "Generally correct" comes to mean that after a forty-five-year time lapse, the dating is adequately precise to be used in specific reference to other events, e.g., Coltrin's visit took place "just after Joseph Smith returned to Kirtland"; "More than eighteen months after Joseph Smith was approached by Greene and Coltrin, Joseph Smith evidently...."; and, "during mid-1842...more than eight years after the practice was begun."

12. Coltrin speaks of a "warm" argument even prior to his talk with Joseph Smith, in which he advocated denying Negroes the priesthood; moreover, he reports that in administering to Abel, he had "such unpleasant feelings" that he vowed he "never would again Anoint another person who had Negro blood in him. [sic] unless I was commanded by the Prophet to do so" (Nuttall, *Journal*, 1:290, or Berrett, *The Church and the Negroid People*). In later years Coltrin is tied circumstantially to a practical joke carried out against an elderly Negro in Utah, see Kate B. Carter, *The Negro Pioneer* (Salt Lake City: Daughters of the Utah Pioneers, 1965), p. 24.

13. *Minutes of the Seventies Journal*, Hazen Aldrich, then a president of the Seventies; entry for 20 Dec. 1836. LDS Church Archives.

14. Ibid.; Aldrich, Coltrin, and J. Young were then presidents of the Third Quorum, and all were present.

15. Ibid., 1 June 1839. This reference suggests that Abel was out of favor with a number of the brethren in the quorum "because of some of his teachings." It is of interest that Abel was clearly in possession of his priesthood, a fact obviously known to Joseph Smith, who was at this meeting. Yet Smith is not recorded as having made any comment.

16. Carter, *The Negro Pioneer*, p. 24; also, C. Elliot Berlin, "Abraham Owen Smoot, Pioneer Mormon Leader" (M.A. thesis, Brigham Young University, 1955), for Smoot's family background.

17. In an 1897 letter by Smoot to Spencer Clawson, quoted in entirety in Carter, *The Negro Pioneer*, p. 25.

18. Berlin, "Abraham Owen Smoot," p. 33. This study was largely taken from Smoot's personal journal. Abraham Smoot is also the source in later years (under President Joseph F. Smith) of the account attributed to David Patten in 1835 in which Cain appears to Patten (in the South) as a large "very dark" person "covered with hair" and wearing "no clothing"; see Lycurgus Wilson, *Life of David Patten, the First Apostolic Martyr* (Salt Lake City: Deseret News Press, 1904), pp. 45-47.

19. D&C 101:79, given 16 Dec. 1833.

20. Ibid. 104:16-18, 83, 84, given 23 April 1834. Both revelations, as well as the statement issued in 1835 appeared in the 1835 edition of the Doctrine and Covenants.

21. Ibid. 134.

22. *Messenger and Advocate* 1 (Sept. 1835): 180, 2 (Nov. 1835): 210-11.

23. If permission was denied by the masters, "the responsibility be upon the head of the master of that house, and the consequence thereof..." (ibid.).

24. See Joseph Smith, Jr., *History of the Church of Jesus Christ of Latter-day Saints*, B. H. Roberts, ed. 7 vols. (Salt Lake City: Deseret News Press, 1902), 1:75.

25. Ibid., 4:213. The temple ordinances presently denied to Negroes were not announced until 1841 (sealing) and 1842 (endowments), and were not performed in the temple until 1846 and 1845, respectively.

26. A well-documented discussion of the similarity of antebellum proslavery arguments and Mormon teachings is found in Woodbury. *A Legacy of Intolerance*; a broader treatment without reference to the Mormons is J. Oliver Buswell's *Slavery, Segregation, and Scripture* (Grand Rapids, 1964); see also Caroline Shanks, "The Biblical Anti-slavery Argument of the Decade 1830-1840," *Journal of Negro History* 15 (1931): 132.

27. Winthrop D. Jordan, *White Over Black: American Attitudes Toward the Negro 1550-1812* (Baltimore, 1968), p. 36, and Part 1 in general.

28. Smith, *History of the Church*, 1:75. The earliest published version of the account (*Times and Seasons* 5 [1844]: 448) deletes this expression; however, it is present in the original handwritten entry of the Manuscript History of the Church, 19 June 1831, LDS Church Archives.

29. This, by Joseph Smith's own testimony. "I am prompted to this course, in consequence, in one respect, of many elders having gone into the Southern States, besides, there now being many in that country who have already embraced the fulness of the gospel...." (*Messenger and Advocate* 2:289); and, shortly thereafter, "[Y]ou can easily see it was put forth for no other reason than to correct the public mind generally without a reference of expectation of any excitement of the nature of the one now in your county [in Missouri]...." (*Messenger and Advocate* 2:354). There is no evidence that abolitionists within the Church played any substantial role at this time. The "many who profess to preach the gospel [who] complain against their brethren of the same faith, who reside in the south..." refers to the evangelical abolitionists in general.

30. Elijah Abel, to whom Taggart's source refers, was in reality ordained a Seventy in 1836. There have been numerous subsequent cases of men of Negro ancestry reportedly receiving the priesthood. The most commonly cited include a "colored" elder in Batavia, New York, ordained by "Wm. Smith" at an unknown date (*Journal History*, 2 June 1847); Samuel Chambers, a prominent Salt Lake Negro reportedly active in the Eighth Ward Deacon's Quorum in 1873-74 (noted in *Manuscripts History* card

reference); two unnamed Negro elders reported in South Carolina (*Journal History*, 18 Aug. 1900); Eduard Legroan, a "deacon" in Salt Lake City's Ninth Ward (reported in Carter, *The Negro Pioneer*, p. 51); and several of Elijah Abel's descendants, e.g., his son Enoch and grandson Elijah, both reportedly elders (Jerald and Sandra Tanner, *Joseph Smiths Curse upon the Negro*, pp. 8-12). Some of Abel's children, themselves with light complexions, married into "white" families, and the descendants of these marriages have largely "passed over" from Negro to white. The problem of what policy to follow in cases such as this, where a priesthood holder finds unexpected Negro ancestry, has not been resolved consistently by the Church. Though Brigham Young is said to have excluded anyone with as much as "one drop of the seed of Cain" in his blood, occasional exceptions are reported more recently, particularly if the individual was assigned a lineage other than Cain, Ham, or Canaan in his patriarchal blessing.

31. See the letters exchanged by John C. Bennett, C. V. Dyer (active in the abolition movement in Chicago), and Joseph Smith in January and March of 1842 (*Times and Seasons* 3:723-25). The Prophet continued to distinguish between his position (a friend of "equal rights and privileges to all men") and being an abolitionist (*Times and Seasons* 3:806-8), a distinction made very explicit in his presidential platform of 1844. Joseph Smith's stand when more fully expounded was very similar to the more gradual school of emancipationists of the 1830s, an approach largely superseded in the 1840s by advocates of immediate emancipation. As noted earlier, Taggart makes little reference to the historical setting in any other place than Missouri. He dispenses with the seven years in Ohio with the observation that there "the membership has been largely exempt from the slavery conflict," notwithstanding that Ohio had been the headquarters of most abolitionist activity in the West during the 1830's. Rather he prefers to emphasize the one year during which the Church headquarters had moved to Missouri (1838)—which "meant that the tone of normative Mormonism was now being set ... where the membership was directly exposed to the conflicts forcing the Church away from abolitionism ...." And he makes no reference to the growth of the abolitionist movement in Illinois in the 1840's. Relevant to his observation on the effect of being in Missouri was Brigham Young's statement, "If I could have been influenced by private injury to choose one side in preference to the other, I should certainly be against the pro-slavery side of the question, for it was pro-slavery men that pointed the bayonet at me and my brethren in Missouri . . ." *Journal of Discourses*, 10:110-11.

32. *Joseph Smith's Egyptian Alphabet and Grammar* (Salt Lake City, Modern Microfilm Co., 1966).

33. These comments were made on 1 Oct. and 16 Dec. 1835. Smith, *History of the Church*, 2:286, 2:334. At least nine other 1835 references to the papyri included by Roberts says nothing more than "Egyptian records" or "grammar"

about the content (July; 7 and 19 Oct.; 17, 19, 20, 24, 25, and 26 Nov).

34. The year 1835 saw a relative lull in the Missouri difficulties.

35. Most impressive, perhaps, is the letter by W. W. Phelps, referred to by Taggart in a footnote, in which Phelps proposes several months *before* the papyri was even in possession of the Church that Cain and his children were forever "cursed" with a black skin, that Ham married a Canaanite woman, preserving some of the "black seed" through the flood, and that Canaan, Ham's son, "inherited three curses: one from Cain for killing Abel; one from Ham for marrying a black wife, and one from Noah..." (*Messenger and Advocate* 1:82). Phelps has added to the traditional chronology that Ham's wife was a Canaanite, immediately reminiscent of the book of Abraham's "this king [the Pharaoh]...was a partaker of the blood of the Canaanites by birth" (Abr. 1:21). More likely the idea was drawn from the already extant book of Moses reference to an antediluvian people of Canaan who became black (Moses 7:8).

36. Joseph Smith, Jr., *The Holy Scripture* (Independence, Mo.: Herald House, 1944); hereafter cited as Joseph Smith Translation (JST).

37. Joseph Smith criticized slavery over at least the three years from 1842 to 1844. Contrary to the impression gained from Taggart's article ("brief reversal"), there are probably as many different published statements in condemnation of slavery by Joseph Smith late in his career as there were supportive statements earlier.

38. The earliest reference cited in previous treatments of this subject was an article by B. H. Roberts in 1885. Even at this late date the argument was still tentative, even speculative, in nature:
"Others there were, who may not have rebelled against God, and yet were so indifferent in their support of the righteous cause of our Redeemer, that they forfeited certain privileges and powers granted to those who were more valiant for God and correct principle. We have, I think, a demonstration of this in the seed of Ham. The first Pharaoh—patriarch-king of Egypt—was a grandson of Ham:...[Noah] *cursed him as pertaining to the Priesthood* ....
"Now, why is it that the seed of Ham was cursed as pertaining to the Priesthood? Why is it that his seed 'could not have right to the Priesthood?' Ham's wife was named 'Egyptus, which in the Chaldaic signifies that which is forbidden; and thus from Ham sprang that race which preserved the curse in the land.'... Was the wife of Ham, as her name signifies, of a race with which those who held the Priesthood were forbidden to intermarry? Was she a descendant of Cain, who was cursed for murdering his brother? And was it by Ham marrying her, and she being saved from the flood in the ark, that 'the race which preserved the curse in the land' was perpetuated? If so, then I believe that race is the one through which it is ordained those spirits that were not valiant in the great rebellion in heaven should come; who, through their

indifference or lack of integrity to righteousness, rendered themselves unworthy of the Priesthood and its powers, and hence it is withheld from them to this day" (*The Contributor* 6:296-97) (Roberts' italics).

The reference to "indifference" in pre-earthly life was not new. Orson Hyde expressed similar views in 1844 without reference to the priesthood ("lent an influence to the devil, thinking he had a little the best right to govern"); Joseph Smith Hyde, *Orson Hyde* (Salt Lake City, 1933), p. 56; cf. Orson Pratt in 1853 ("not valiant in the war"), *The Seer* 1:54-56. Hyde's remarks may be relevant to the otherwise unexplained statements of John Taylor that Cain's lineage was preserved through the flood that "the devil should have a representation here upon the earth..." (*Journal of Discourses* 22:304, 23:336).

39.   It is not totally evident that Egyptus is being portrayed as the literal wife of Ham, for in the patriarchal order individuals separated by several generations are often spoken of as daughters or sons of one another. In Abr. 1:25, an "Egyptus" is described as "the daughter of Ham."

40.   2 Nephi 5:21. The belief that a "black skin... has ever been the curse that has followed an apostate of the holy priesthood" is no longer considered grounds for priesthood denial based solely on darkness of skin color. The implications of this early belief for present practice need further study.

41.   Hugh Nibley has entered this field with his current *Improvement Era* series, "A New Look at the Pearl of Great Price" (Jan. 1968-present), but has only minimally discussed the priesthood question.

42.   Jordan, *White Over Black*, discusses the implications of these views for the institution of American slavery. His study was not designed primarily to trace these ideas to their origin. See also David B. Davis, *The problem of Slavery in Western Culture* (Ithaca, N.Y.: 1966).

43.   Jordan, *White Over Black*, pp. 18-19.

44.   Obviously relevant, for instance, are the numerous intermarriages reported between the house of Israel and the Canaanites, Egyptians, and Ethiopians.

45.   Journal History, 13 Feb. 1849. Lorenzo Snow had asked about the "chance of redemption for the Africans," and Brigham Young replied that "the Lord had cursed Cain's seed with blackness and prohibited them the Priesthood...."

46.   Lieutenant J. W. Gunnison mentions "blacks being ineligible to the priesthood" in his *The Mormons, or Latter-Day Saints, in the Valley of the Great Salt Lake, etc* (Philadephia: 1853), p. 143. This work, prefaced in July 1852, was written after a "year and one half among them." The practice of priesthood discrimination is also mentioned in a *Deseret News* article. "To the Saints," 3 Apr. 1852. Wilford Woodruff later reports that Brigham Young taught this idea in a speech to the legislature that year; however, Young's

January address states only that Negroes must always be servants to their superiors, without explicit reference to the priesthood; Matthias Cowley, *Wilford Woodruff* (Salt Lake City: Deseret News Press, 1909), p. 351; and "Governor's Message to the Legislative Assembly of Utah Territory, January 5, 1852," or *Deseret News* of January 10, 1852).

47. In addition to the references cited in notes 45-46, see *The Seer* 1 (1853): 54-56; *Journal of Discourses* 2 (1854): 142-43; *Journal of Discourses* 11 (1866): 272; and *Juvenile Instructor* 3 (1868): 173.

48. Journal History 25 Dec. 1869.

49. Taylor was investigating a report that Joseph Smith taught *not* to discriminate which was alleged to have originated with Coltrin.

50. This sentiment was expressed 11 Mar. 1900 and is recorded in a letter by George Gibbs to John Whitaker, 18 Jan. 1909, Whitaker Collection, University of Utah, and LDS Church Archives. President Snow, while discussing the curse of Cain, is reported as saying he did not know "whether the President [Brigham Young] had had this revealed to him or not...or whether President Young was giving his own personal views, or whether he had been told this by the Prophet Joseph." The observation was of particular significance as Lorenzo Snow had asked Brigham Young about the practice as early as 1849.

51. The "six" testimonies cited in Taggart's work, by reference to the 1879 meeting, are of course only two testimonies—those of Smoot and Coltrin.

52. Journal History, 22 Aug. 1895; and Gibbs to Whitaker.

53. Journal History, 5 Oct. 1896.

54. Although the earliest informal usage of the Cain-Egyptus-Ham-Pharaoh justification is probably lost, the generally available published sources utilizing this argument date from the post-Brigham Young period. As noted earlier, B. H. Roberts postulated this idea in 1885 (*The Contributor* 6:296-97); it was was repeated in 1891 in "Editorial Thoughts" in the *Juvenile Instructor* of which George Q. Cannon was editor (26:635-36); and appeared again in 1908 in *Liahona, the Elder's Journal* (5:1164). More recently this argument has found wide circulation.

55. Possibly through the influence of John Fielding Smith who attributed the practice to Joseph Smith (*Improvement Era* 27:564-65, 1924 and later). Recently this idea has been reiterated in a letter from the First Presidency to Dr. Lowry Nelson in 1947; quoted in John J. Stewart, *Mormonism and the Negro* [Orem, Utah: Community Press, 1960], pp. 46-47. Nonetheless, the majority of treatments of this subject by the Church leadership (and *all* documented discussions) still refer only as far back as Brigham Young. Thus, Joseph F. Smith in 1908 when asked about the Negro policy deferred to "the rulings of President Brigham Young, Taylor, and Woodruff" without

mention of Joseph Smith; and the First Presidency statements issued in 1949, and again in 1951, referred only to Brigham Young and Wilford Woodruff (see Berrett, *The Church and the Negroid People*, pp. 16-17), though the most recent (Dec. 1969) refers to "Joseph Smith and all succeeding presidents of the Church" as having taught that "Negroes . . . were not yet to receive the priesthood." (see appendix.)

56. As cited in note 28.

57. Manuscript History, 25 Jan. 1842; or Smith, *History of the Church,* 4:501. Recall that this idea was current in defense of slavery and had been used by W. W. Phelps eight years prior to this time.

58. This was the claim of those initially attributing the Negro doctrine to Joseph Smith, cited in notes 52 and 53.

59. E.g., in 1840 Joseph stated that Cain's priesthood had proved a cursing to him because of his "unrighteousness." There was no obvious tie to the Negro, but at least the priesthood is connected in some way to Cain. The same day this statement was made, the First Presidency issued the message anticipating the "Hottentot" soon worshipping with them in the Nauvoo Temple (Smith, *History of the Church* , 2:213; 4:298). If Joseph was not concerned with the curse of Canaan in his criticisms of slavery, might he not have viewed a curse on Cain as equally irrelevant to the present situation?

60. Not merely a justification of slavery, the belief became common that Negro slavery was divinely sanctioned, and that slaves could not be freed nationally in spite of the efforts of abolitionists or even a Civil War. For Brigham Young's views to this effect, see *Journal of Discourses*, 2 (1855): 184; *Millennial Star* 21:608-11, and *Journal of Discourses* 7:290-91, both 1859; and *Journal of Discourses* 10 (1863): 250. This belief had been expressed in a *Times and Seasons* article as early as 1845 (*Times and Seasons* 6:857). The progress of the Civil War initially posed no threat to this idea, as it was widely believed that the United States as then constituted would not recover from the war, that shortly masses of downtrodden would be fleeing from all over the world to Utah, and that the time when the Saints would return to Jackson County and assume control of the government was virtually at hand (see *Millennial Star* 23:60, 300, 396, 401; 24:158; *Journal of Discourses* 11:38; *Deseret News*, 10 July 1861; and *Deseret News*, 26 Mar. 1862, for sentiments to this effect). When war's end found the Saints still in Utah, little more was said: Orson Pratt did attempt an explanation in 1866 (*Millennial Star* 28:518).

61. Charles C. Rich, and possibly Heber C. Kimball; see Jack Beller, "Negro Slaves in Utah," *Utah Historical Quarterly* 2 (Oct. 1929): 122-26.

62. "An Act in relation to service," passed and approved, 4 Feb. 1852. This statute more nearly paralleled the practice of indentured slavery found in Illinois than it did Southern slave codes.

63. This idea was particularly common in the discourses of Brigham Young. Occasionally both the curses on Canaan and Cain would be discussed jointly (e.g., *Journal of Discourses* 7:290-91). Negroes receiving patriarchal blessings in Utah were assigned to the lineage of Cain, Ham, or Canaan as a rule. Elijah Abel, addressed as "Elder" and "orphan," was not assigned a lineage when given his blessing by Joseph Smith, Sr., in 1836.

64. Modified at present, as it was on occasion in early references, to the extent that the "blood" of Cain merely designates those to be denied the priesthood, for some reason not fully understood; being a descendant of Cain, per se, is not considered a sufficient justification (see the First Presidency statement of 1951, Berrett, *The Church and the Negroid People* pp. 16-17, and other sources).

65. Stephen G. Taggart, *Mormonism's Negro Policy: Social and Historical Origins* (Salt Lake City: University of Utah Press, 1970), p. 79. The comment came after McMurrin had "introduced the subject of the common belief among the Church membership that Negroes are under a divine curse. I told him that I regarded this doctrine as both false and morally abhorrent and that some weeks earlier, in a class in my own Ward, I had made it clear that I did not accept the doctrine and that I wanted to be known as a dissenter to the class instructor's statements about 'our beliefs' in this matter.

President McKay replied that he was 'glad' that I had taken this stand, as he also did not believe this teaching. He stated his position in this matter very forcefully and clearly said ... " (continued in text above).

66. Copies of the letter were sent to all the McKay sons, and there have been unofficial and conflicting reports about others verifying the sentiment also.

67. Though McMurrin made a "detailed record of the conversation ... within several hours of the time it occurred," these notes are reportedly lost. There was no one else present.

68. Although nearly everyone addressing the Mormon Negro policy quotes President McKay, virtually all references are taken from just two sources. One of these, a response to a reporter made at the dedication of the Oakland Temple in November 1964 states that the Negro will not be given the priesthood "in my lifetime, young man, nor yours" (quoted in John Lund, *The Church and the Negro*, 1967, p. 45; there are minor variations in other reports of this response). The other source is a letter dated 3 Nov. 1947, and written by President McKay (then counselor in the First Presidency) as his explanation of "why the Negroid race cannot hold the priesthood." Excerpts from this letter are commonly used to show President McKay's support for present church practices. The recent "policy statement" signed by Presidents Brown and Tanner included the three most cited passages:

> The seeming discrimination by the Church toward the Negro
> is not something which originated with man; but goes back

into the beginning with God . . .

Revelation assures us that this plan antedates man's mortal existence extending back to man's pre-existent state.

Sometime in God's eternal plan, the Negro will be given the right to hold the priesthood.

Curiously, in context these quotations lack some of their finality, and "this plan" spoken of in the second quote is found to be the general "plan of salvation" rather than a specific reference to the Negro-priesthood practice. The tone of the letter seems more searching and tentative than revelatory or doctrinaire. Finding no solution in "abstract reasoning" and knowing of "no scriptural basis for denying the Priesthood to Negroes other than one verse in the book of Abraham (1:26)," President McKay "believes" that "the real reason dates back to our pre-existent life." Citing the case of pharaoh as a precedent for priesthood denial (a denial that "may have been entirely in keeping with the eternal plan of salvation"). his ultimate answer to the problem is faith in a "God of justice." The letter, read in its entirety, seems more a defense of men individually not receiving the priesthood than an explanation of group discrimination based on race. See Llewelyn R. McKay's *Home Memories of President David O. McKay* (Salt Lake City: Deseret Book Co., 1956), pp. 226-31. No reference to Cain, Ham, or Canaan is made in either of the above quotations.

69. This statement, perhaps not drafted by President McKay, has been until now the only "official" Church statement cited in treatments of the Negro policy. Though generally dated 17 Aug. 1951. President Henry D. Moyle stated that it was actually made in 1949 and was subsequently reaffirmed under President McKay (Henry D. Moyle "What of the Negro?" address delivered in Geneva, Switzerland, 30 Oct. 1961). Similar views were expressed in the First Presidency letter of 1947 written to Dr. Lowry Nelson. In the future the December 15, 1969 statement will likely be referred to as most authoritative.

70. The McMurrin quotation, Lorenzo Snow statement of 1900, and Phelps letter of 1835 are each remarkable references which, to my knowledge, have not been cited in previously published studies.

71. E.g., "They came into the world slaves, mentally and physically. Change their situation with the whites, and they would be like them . . . .Find an educated negro, who rides in his carriage, and you will see a man who has risen by the powers of his own mind to his exalted state of respectability . . . ." *Millennial Star* 20:278

72. At one time Brigham Young described the Negro as "seemingly deprived of nearly all the blessings of the intelligence that is generally bestowed upon mankind" (*Journal of Discourses* 7:290-91), and in his governor's message of 5 Jan. 1852, he stated that "[we should not] elevate

them...to an equality with those whom Nature and Nature's God has indicated to be their masters." A view of Negro inferiority was also developed extensively in an unsigned series of articles in the *Juvenile Instructor* in 1867-68 entitled "Man and His Varieties." In this, it was said that the " Negro race" was "the lowest in intelligence and the most barbarous of all the children of men," and that they "appear to be the least capable of improvement of all people" (*Juvenile Instructor* 3:141). As recently as 1907, evidence of Negro racial inferiority was cited in a priesthood manual (B. H. Roberts' *Seventy's Course in Theology*, Year Book 1 (Salt Lake City: Deseret News Press, 1907), pp. 165-66. This is a seemingly relevant area which has not been adequately treated as yet. A related area in need of investigation is the possibility of an initial distinction being made between free Negroes and slaves, particularly in view of the claims of Coltrin and Smoot, who were in the south, and the two earliest Negro priesthood holders, who were in the North.

Mormonism's Negro Doctrine: An Historical Overview

Lester E. Bush, Jr.

Four years after undermining the facile assumptions of the "Missouri thesis," Lester Bush offered his own reconstruction of the history of church teachings on blacks. In his essay, by far the most comprehensive survey of the subject to date and winner of both the Dialogue *and* Mormon History Association *Best Article awards, Bush implicitly refuted virtually all the orthodox "church" explanations of the origins of Mormon teachings on blacks in much the same documentary manner he previously applied to the secular, "environmental" Missouri thesis.*

While outside criticism of Mormon racial policy had crested several years prior to the publication of this article, the doctrinal implications of Bush's research made this essay one of the most sensitive ever carried by Dialogue. *In an effort to insure a constructive discussion of the subject, several scholars—representing a variety of disciplines—were invited to respond in the same issue. Three of these short responses were printed.* Dialogue's *concern over the potential explosiveness of the issue was not unfounded. Ecclesiastical pressure from varying levels was applied to several individuals and two who had originally agreed to respond withdrew from participation.*

To the credit of the editors, the article itself was published as submitted except for two Uncle Remus quotations used as a preface. A preface preceding Section 1 had read: "'Tu'n me loose, fo' I kick de natchul stuffin' out'n you,' sez Brer Rabbit, sezee, but de Tar-Baby, she ain't saying nothin'. She des hilt on, en den Brer Rabbit lose de use er his feet in de same way. Brer Fox, he lay low." (From "The Wonderful Tar-Baby Story").

The concluding summary Section 6 was originally introduced by this quotation: "'En who stuck you up dar whar you is? Nobody in de roun' worl'. You des tuck en jam you' se'f on dat Tar-Baby widout waitin' for enny invite, 'sez Brer Fox, sezee, 'en dar you is...'" (From "How Mr. Rabbit Was Too Sharp For Mr. Fox"). This essay originally appeared in Dialogue 8 (Spring 1973).

Neither White nor Black

I

... So long as we have no special rule in the Church, as to people of color, let prudence guide, and while they, as well as we, are in the hands of a merciful God, we say: Shun every appearance of evil.

W.W. Phelps, 1833

There once was a time, albeit brief, when a "Negro problem" did not exist for the Church of Jesus Christ of Latter-day Saints. During those early months in New York and Ohio no mention was even made of Church attitudes towards blacks. The gospel was for "all nations, kindreds, tongues and peoples,"[1] and no exceptions were made. A Negro, "Black Pete," was among the first converts in Ohio, and his story was prominently reported in the local press.[2] W. W. Phelps opened a mission to Missouri in July 1831 and preached to "all the families of the earth," specifically mentioning Negroes among his first audience.[3] The following year another black, Elijah Abel, was baptized in Maryland.[4]

This initial period was ultimately brought to an end by the influx of Mormons into the Missouri mission in late 1831 and early 1832. Not long before the arrival of the Mormon vanguard, the "deformed and haggard visage" of abolitionism was manifest in Missouri; elsewhere Nat Turner graphically reinforced the southern phobia of slave insurrection.

At this time the Mormons were mostly emigrants from northern and eastern states, and were not slaveholders. In less than a year a rumor was afoot that they were "tampering" with the slaves. Not insensitive to this charge, the Mormons agreed to investigate and "bring to justice any person who might ... violate the law of the land by stirring up the blacks to an insurrection, or in any degree dissuade them from being perfectly obedient to their masters."[5] Their investigations proved negative as only one specific accusation was uncovered, and the elder accused had returned to the East; however the rumors continued unabated.[6]

One aspect of the slaveholders' paranoia not initially touched by the Mormon presence was the dictum that free Negroes promoted slave revolts. Ten years earlier Missouri had been delayed admission into the Union for barring free Negroes from the state. A modification in the state constitution was compelled which allowed entry to the few free blacks who were citizens of other states. Consequently free Negroes were rare in Missouri; Jackson County had none.

In the summer of 1833, the older settlers perceived a new threat to this status embodied in the Church's *Evening and Morning Star*. Because of special requirements in the Missouri law affecting the immigration of free Negroes into the state, Phelps had published the relevant material "to prevent any misunderstanding among the churches abroad, respecting free people of color, who may think of coming to the western boundaries of Missouri, as members of the Church."[7] The Missourians interpreted the article as an invitation to "free negroes and mulattoes from other states to become 'Mormons,' and remove and settle among us."[8] This interpretation was probably unfair to Phelps as he had stated twice that the subject was especially delicate, and one on which great care should be taken to "shun every appearance of evil." However, he also included a remarkably injudicious comment, "In connection with the wonderful events of this age, much is doing towards abolishing slavery, and colonizing the blacks, in Africa."[9]

The local citizenry immediately drafted a list of accusations against the Saints, prominently featuring the antislavery issue and Phelps' article. In response, Phelps issued an "Extra" explaining that he had been "misunderstood." The intention, he wrote, "was not only to stop free people of color from emigrating to this state but to prevent them from being admitted as members of the Church" and stated that, furthermore, "none will be admitted into the Church."[10] Since Phelps had stated in his first article that there was "no special rule in the Church, as to people of color," this new restriction was obviously an expedient adopted in Missouri. Incredibly, Phelps also reprinted his previous reflection on the "wonderful events . . . towards abolishing slavery."

The reversal of position on Negro membership had no discernible impact on the settlers; a redraft of their charges, with additional demands, was incorporated into several "propositions" which flatly rejected Phelps' explanation.[11] The subsequent events are well known—mob violence, the destruction of the *Star* press, and ultimately the expulsion of the Saints from Jackson County.

The Missouri accusations had gone "considerably the rounds in the public prints," so, on reestablishing of the *Star* in Ohio, an extensive rebuttal was published. No Mormon, it was asserted, had ever been implicated on a charge of tampering with the slaves. And, in a broader context, the *Star* added,

> All who are acquainted with the situation of slave States, know that the life of every white is in constant danger, and to insinuate any thing which could possibly be interpreted by a slave, that it was not just to hold human beings in bondage, would be jeopardizing the life of every white inhabitant in the country. For the moment an insurrection should break out, no respect would be paid to age, sex, or religion by an enraged, jealous, and ignorant black banditti. And the individual who would not immediately report any one who might be found influencing the minds of slaves with evil, would be beneath even the slave himself, and unworthy the privilege of a free Government.[12]

The Mormons had their own reasons for being alert to the possibility of slave insurrection (and their early publications reflect this preoccupation)—for back in late 1832 Joseph Smith had prophesied that a war was imminent pitting the South against the North, and that "after many days, slaves shall rise up against their masters."[13]

The Jackson County experience demonstrated the need for a clear statement of Church policy on slavery. In December 1833, immediately following the expulsion from Jackson County, Joseph Smith received a revelation that seems to bear directly on this question. In part it declared that "it is not right that any man should be in bondage to another."[14] Though the most recent Church pronouncement on the Negro (1969), [See Appendix] tied this revelation to Negro slavery, it does not appear to have been used in early discourses on either side of the slavery question.[15]

The statement which did come to serve as the "official" Church position on slavery was adopted in August 1835. This statement, worded so that it avoided comment on the morality of slavery *per se*, was part of a general endorsement of legal institutions. One section dealt with governments "allowing human beings to be held in servitude," and stated that under these circumstances the Church felt it to be "unlawful and unjust, and dangerous to the peace" for anyone "to interfere with bond-servants, neither preach the gospel to, nor baptize them contrary to the will and wish of their masters, nor to meddle with or influence them in the least to cause them to be dissatisfied with their situations in this life, thereby jeopardizing the lives of men."[16]

The restriction on proselyting was not felt to conflict with the universal calling of the Church. Any possible question on this point was eliminated the following month in a letter from Joseph Smith to the "elders abroad." In this the Prophet reaffirmed that the Church believed "in preaching the doctrine of repentance in all the world, both to old and young, rich and poor, bond and free." While the elders were instructed to teach slaves only with their master's consent, if this permission were denied "the responsibility be upon the head of the master of that house, and the consequences thereof, and the guilt of that house is no longer upon thy skirts."[17]

During the 1830s the national debate over slavery increased sharply. Abolitionists shifted from a plea for gradual release of the slaves to a demand for immediate emancipation. Biblical arguments became more prominent as slaveholding was attacked as a sin, or defended with scriptural precedents. Anti-slavery evangelists travelled circuits proselyting northern communities; and in the spring of 1836 an abolitionist visited Kirtland, Ohio, and established a small anti-slavery society. The Mormons, in spite of their repeated denials, continued to be charged with anti-slavery activity in Missouri. Now these accusations were spreading to fertile missionary areas elsewhere in the South. It was not the best time for an abolitionist to visit Church headquarters.

Lest anyone gain "the impression that all he said was concurred in," the next issue of the *Messenger and Advocate* was devoted largely to a rebuttal of abolitionism.[18] A lengthy article was contributed by Joseph Smith, and there were others from Warren Parrish and Oliver Cowdery. Together these essays constitute the most extensive discussion of slavery to appear during the first two decades of the Restoration, and they provide an invaluable insight into the thinking of Church leaders at that time.

At least five major objections to the abolitionist cause can be identi- fied in Joseph Smith's discussion:

—First, he believed the course of abolitionism was "calculated to ... set loose, upon the world a community of people who might per- adventure, overrun our country and violate the most sacred principles of human society,—chastity and virtue...."

—Second, any evil attending slavery should have been apparent to the "men of piety" of the South who had raised no objections to the institution.

—Third, the Prophet did "not believe that the people of the North have any more right to say that the South *shall not* hold slaves, than the South have to say the North *shall*..."; the signing of petitions in the North was nothing more than "an array of influence, and a declaration of hostilities against the people of the South...."

—Fourth, the sons of Canaan (or Ham) whom Joseph Smith identi- fied with the Negro were cursed with servitude by a "decree of Jehovah," and that curse was "not yet taken off the sons of Canaan, neither will be until it is affected by as great power as caused it to come ... and those who are determined to pursue a course which shows an opposition ... against the designs of the Lord, will learn ... that God can do his work without the aid of those who are not dictated by his counsel...."

—Fifth, there were several other biblical precedents for slavery (in the histories of Abraham, Leviticus, Ephesians, Timothy).

In concluding his article, the Prophet partially withdrew his previous stand on proselyting slaves, "It would be much better and more prudent, not to preach at all to the slaves, until after their masters are con- verted...."

Parrish and Cowdery pursued similar arguments. Parrish's main points were that the Constitution was divinely inspired and had sanc- tioned slavery and that the people should comply with the laws of the land. He also cited the curse on Ham and declared that it would continue in effect until the Lord removed it, at which time he would "announce to his servants the prophets that the time has arrived." Until such time all the "abolition societies that now are or ever will be, cannot cause one jot or tittle of the prophecy to fail." Parrish concluded with a comment on the danger to society if rebellion were fomented among the blacks.

Oliver Cowdery's article was more directly concerned with race. He touched on most of the points raised in the other two articles, but dwelt at much greater length on the problems of insurrection and the social implications of emancipation:

> ... Let the blacks of the south be free, and our community is overrun with paupers, and a reckless mass of human beings, uncultivated, untaught and unaccustomed to provide for themselves the necessaries of life—endangering the chastity of every female who might by chance be found in our streets— our prisons filled with convicts, and the hangman wearied with executing the functions of his office! This must unavoidably be the case, every rational man must admit, who has ever travelled in the slave states, or we must open our houses, unfold our arms, and bid these degraded and degrading sons of Canaan, a hearty welcome and a free admittance to all we possess! A society of this nature, to us, is so intolerably degrading, that the bare reflection causes our feeling to recoil, and our hearts to revolt....

He also saw little alternative to slavery:

> ... The idea of transportation is folly, the project of emansipation [sic] is destructive to our government, and the notion of amalgamation is devilish!... And insensible to feeling must be the heart, and low indeed must be the mind, that would consent for a moment, to see his fair daughter, his sister, or perhaps, his bosom companion, in the embrace of a NEGRO![19]

At last an unequivocal position on Negro slavery had been taken. Should the question of Mormon attitudes arise, an unambiguous statement was now available that should satisfy the most ardent slaveholder. Questions did arise and the articles were put to use with mixed results.[20]

A question immediately arises as to the basis for these statements originating with the Prophet and other prominent spokesmen of the Church. Many Mormons have supposed that at least part of the information was doctrinal or even revelatory. However, far from professing divine insight, the authors made it expressly clear that these were their *personal* views.[21] Moreover, a comparative study will demonstrate that the ideas presented reflect a cross section of the popular arguments of the day in support of slavery.

The growth of the abolitionist movement in the mid-1830s had led to the wide circulation of anti-slavery literature. The proponents of slavery also became more active and were equally prolific pamphleteers. Many and varied defenses of slavery were to appear over the next quarter century, and several themes were evident from the start. The natural inferiority and alleged sexual depravity of the blacks alluded to in all the *Messenger and Advocate* articles were rarely missing from any general defense of Negro slavery. States' rights and the Constitutional sanction of slavery provided the standard legal justifications; and *all* scriptural defenses of slavery cited Noah's curse on Canaan and applied it directly to Negroes. Other scriptural "precedents" were generally cited as well.

Though none of these arguments were truly unique to this period or even to the nineteenth century, their prominence in national debate was greatest during the years from 1830 to 1860. With very little effort one can duplicate the Mormon arguments to the most specific detail from these contemporary non-Mormon sources.[22] To claim these ideas originated independently within the Church would require considerable justification, none of which has ever been presented.

Because of its later prominence in Mormon history, one particular argument requires careful attention—the belief that Negroes were descended from Ham. Though particularly common in the first half of the nineteenth century this idea was actually very old. Recent studies have traced the association to at least 200 to 600 A.D. Jordan reports that early Jewish writings invoked Noah's curse to explain the black skin of the Africans. Among early Christian fathers, both Jerome and Augustine accepted the Ham genealogy for Negroes, and this belief is said to have become "universal" in early Christendom. More recently the association is evident in the earliest English descriptions of Africans in the fifteenth and sixteenth centuries. By the eighteenth century the connection had become common in the New World, where it was not infrequently cited in justification of black slavery.

However, there was always disagreement on the implications of Noah's curse. Those opposed to slavery contended that the Africans were related to Ham through Cush, rather than Canaan (or occasionally, through all four sons), and therefore a curse affecting Canaan could not be applied to the blacks as a group. Furthermore, it was argued, the curse *predicted* rather than *justified* enslavement. The fundamental association with Ham was not so frequently challenged. Even among nineteenth century anti-slavery elements, the Ham genealogy was widely accepted, and among the pro-slavery forces the association was virtually axiomatic.[23]

It is clear that Joseph Smith accepted this traditional genealogy. As early as 1831 he had noted parenthetically that Negroes were "descendants of Ham," and he again applied Noah's curse to Negro slavery in 1841.[24] There is no record of his "teaching" the Ham genealogy as Church doctrine. This would have been unnecessary, of course, as the association of Ham and the Negro was already common knowledge.

The first pointed reference to the Ham genealogy had actually come not with the articles in 1836 but rather a year earlier in a letter published in the *Messenger and Advocate*. W. W. Phelps proposed at that time that a lineage of blacks could be traced from Cain, through a black "Canaanite" wife of Ham, to Canaan.[25] The Cain genealogy had a somewhat less extensive tradition than the more straightforward Ham thesis, though it also was widely reported and can be traced back several centuries, generally in connection with the enslavement of Africans.[26] It had the "advantage" of including all of Ham's sons within a cursed lineage. The problem of transmitting Cain's lineage through the flood was generally handled as Phelps did, through the wife of Ham; there have been some bizarre variants of his explanation.[27] Joseph Smith may also have believed that Negroes were descended from Cain, though the evidence for this claim is not very convincing. Certainly there is presently no case at all for the idea that he "taught" this genealogy.[28]

It is significant, I believe, that in spite of the many discussions of blacks and slavery that had been published by 1836, *no* reference had been made to the priesthood. Yet, while there was not a written policy on blacks and the priesthood, a precedent had been established. Shortly before publication of the articles on abolitionism, a Negro was ordained to the Melchizedek priesthood. It has been suggested, considerably after the fact, that this was a mistake which was quickly rectified. Such a claim is totally unfounded and was actually refuted by Joseph F. Smith shortly after being put forth.[29] Elijah Abel was ordained an elder 3 March, 1836, and shortly thereafter received his patriarchal blessing from Joseph Smith, Sr.[30] In June he was listed among the recently licensed elders[31] and on 20 December, 1836, was ordained a seventy.[32] Three years later, in June 1839, he was still active in the Nauvoo Seventies Quorum,[33] and his seventy's certificate was renewed in 1841, and again after his arrival in Salt Lake City.[34] Moreover, Abel was known by Joseph Smith and reportedly lived for a time in the Prophet's home.[35]

The charge that Abel was dropped from the priesthood originated with Zebedee Coltrin. It is unfortunate that his memory proved unreliable on this point, as he should have been in a position to provide valuable information—for it was he who ordained Abel to the office of seventy two years after purportedly being told that Negroes were not to receive the priesthood.[36] The circumstances of Coltrin's account may be of some relevance. He claimed to have questioned the right of Negroes to hold the priesthood after a visit to the South. Abraham Smoot, the only other person to claim first-hand counsel from Joseph Smith on this subject also had asked about the situation in the South: "What should be done with the Negroes in the South as I was preaching to them? [The Prophet] said I could baptize them by the consent of their masters, but not to confer the priesthood upon them." Additionally, a second-hand account related by Smoot in which Smith allegedly gave the same advice was also directed at Negroes "in the Southern States."[37] Most, if not all, of the Negroes involved in these accounts were slaves. It may be, notwithstanding the lack of contemporary documentation, that a policy was in effect denying the priesthood to slaves or isolated free southern Negroes. In any case, a *de facto* restriction is demonstrable in the South, and empirical justification for the policy is not difficult to imagine.

After 1836 the Mormons largely ignored the subject of slavery for nearly six years. During this time they periodically reaffirmed that they were not abolitionists, but the charge was no longer common in Missouri nor elsewhere in the South.[38] In spite of the small number of Negro converts, the gospel was still proclaimed as universal. The first Mormon hymnal, printed in 1835, included a hymn exhorting the members to proclaim the message "throughout Europe, and Asia's dark regions, To China's far shores, and to Afric's black legions."[39] Another hymnal, in 1840, contained a new hymn by Parley P. Pratt, encouraging the Twelve to carry the gospel throughout the world,

> ... India's and Afric's sultry plains
> Must hear the tidings as they roll
> Where darkness, death, and sorrow reign
> And tyranny has held controll'd ... [40]

No discrimination was evident in the 1836 rules governing the temple in Kirtland, which provided for "old or young, rich or poor, male or female, bond or free, black or white, believer or unbeliever...."[41] Nor was a discriminatory policy projected for the Nauvoo Temple when the First Presidency anticipated in 1840 that "we may soon expect to see flocking to this place, people from every land and from every nation, the polished European, the degraded Hottentot, and the shivering Laplander. Persons of all languages, and of every tongue, and of every color; who shall with us worship the Lord of Hosts in his holy temple, and offer up their orisons in his sanctuary."[42]

Early in 1842 Charles V. Dyer, a prominent Chicago physician, wrote to the mayor of Nauvoo, John C. Bennett, in an effort to gain Mormon support for the antislavery cause. Three abolitionists had recently been imprisoned in Missouri, and Dyer expressed indignation at the treatment received by abolitionists *and* Mormons in that state: "Have we not a right to sympathyze with each other?" Bennett, at the height of a brief but exalted career with the Mormons, replied that he had considered the question of slavery "years ago" and was uncompromisingly for "UNIVERSAL LIBERTY, *to every soul of man—civil, religious,* and *political.*" This exchange came to the attention of Joseph Smith, who wrote Bennett a short letter in apparent agreement: the subject of American slavery and the treatment of the three abolitionists made his "blood boil within me to reflect upon the injustices, cruelty, and oppression, of the rulers of the people—when will these things cease to be, and the Constitution and the Laws bear rule?"

Perhaps more unexpected than the contents of these letters was their subsequent publication by Joseph Smith in the March *Times and Seasons,* with an introduction that endorsed "UNIVERSAL LIBERTY' and characterized Bennett and Dyer as men of "brave and philanthropic hearts."[43] The antislavery sentiment in the letters was unmistakable, and their publication marked a virtual reversal of the published Mormon stance on slavery.

When and why this change occurred is not clear. Except for the relative silence of the preceding years there was no suggestion of an impending change. The circumstances were obviously much different in 1842 than they had been in 1836. The slavery issue was no longer threatening to the Mormons. Though the Church had previously received rough treatment at the hands of pro-slavery elements, it had no real prospect of returning to a slaveholding state. Illinois was theoretically a free state and had only a small residual of "indentured" slaves. While abolitionist organizations and activities had declined markedly after 1837, antislavery sentiment was more widespread both nationally and in Illinois. This was in part through association with the issues of freedom of speech, press, and petition—all of which were important to the Mormons. Personalities had also changed in the Mormon hierarchy.[44] However, for all the conducive circumstances, we have no contemporary explanation for the dramatic change in attitude.

Some authors have attempted to minimize the importance of Joseph Smith's antislavery views, and to suggest that his opposition to slavery was superficial or politically motivated. He did, after all, continue to deny that he was an abolitionist, rather preferring to characterize himself as a "friend of equal rights and privileges to all men."[45] A careful review of published sources, however, fails to reveal any evidence of duplicity. Rather one finds consistent opposition to slavery from early 1842 until the Prophet's death in mid-1844. Even in private conversation, the Prophet advised that slaves owned by Mormons be brought "into a free country and set . . . free—Educate them and give them equal Rights."[46] He recorded a similar sentiment in his history: "Had I anything to do with the negro, I would . . . put them on a national equalization."[47] Many similar expressions are to be found in 1843 and 1844, though his greatest attention to slavery was evident during his 1844 presidential campaign. Joseph Smith's "Views on the Government and Policy of the U.S.," prepared in February as a campaign platform, included a plan for the elimination of slavery within six years through federal compensation of slaveholders.[48] He later added that this might be accomplished a few states at a time or with a provision that slave children be freed after a "fixed period."[49]

The sincerity of the Prophet's anti-slavery statements was challenged for several reasons. Though he repeatedly expressed a desire to "abolish slavery," Joseph Smith condemned the abolitionists as self-seeking and destined for "ruin, infamy and shame." Actually the Prophet's paradoxical antipathy to both slavery and abolitionism was not atypical of churchmen of his day. In the preceding few years the majority of both the Protestant and Catholic clergy had opposed the abolitionist movement; and at the same time, many also condemned slavery.[50] They particularly feared the divisive effect that the movement was having within their denominations. Those abolitionists who had advocated a compensated emancipation in the previous decade were now gone, and the current uncompromising polemics were clearly aggravating badly strained intersectional relations. The possibility of a Civil War was especially real to the Prophet; reiterating his warning of ten years before, he prophesied in 1843 that "much bloodshed" would "probably arise over the slave question."[51]

It also has been claimed that the Prophet planned to allow Mormon slaveholders to retain their chattel property. The growth of the Church in the South had led to the conversion of several slaveholders, at least three of whom moved to Nauvoo prior to the Prophet's death. Two of the three claimed to have freed their slaves before coming north but also reported that eight "ex-slaves" had chosen to remain with their masters.[52] Theoretically a permanent move to Illinois should have brought freedom regardless. It appears that they were indeed freed, for in April 1844, the Prophet stated with some pride that in Nauvoo there was not a slave "to raise his rusting fetters and chains, and exclaim, O liberty where are thy charms?"[53] Oddly, some of these blacks and a number of others who later lived briefly in Nauvoo again appear to be slaves several years later in Utah.[54]

It occurred to several prominent Mormons working at the time in the Wisconsin pineries of the Church that there ought to be some special provision for slaveholders in the Church. This idea was presented in two letters from a "Select Committee" to the First Presidency and Quorum of the Twelve proposing that the Gospel be carried to the "South-Western States, as also Texas, Mexico, Brazil, &c" ("from Green Bay to the Mexican Gulf"), and that Texas be established as a "place of gathering for all the South." Were this done, the Committee believed, thousands of rich planters "would embrace the Gospel, and, if they had a place to plant their slaves, give all the proceeds of their yearly labour, if rightly taught, for building up the kingdom . . . ." Moreover, the Committee was "well informed of the Cherokee and the Choctaw nations who live between the State of Arkansas and the Colorado of the Texans, owning plantations and thousands of slaves, and that they are also very desirous to have an interview with the Elders of this Church, upon the principles of the Book of Mormon."[55]

Bishop George Miller, who delivered the letters, reported that the Prophet's response was favorable ("I perceive that the Spirit of God is in the pineries"), and that some preliminary steps were taken towards obtaining land in Texas.[56] Andrew Jenson later claimed that Joseph Smith himself made the suggestion that a place be established in the Southwest for slaveholding members of the Church.[57] As this was in March, 1844, in the midst of the Prophet's denunciations of slavery, a suggestion of duplicity is not unreasonable. The source of Jenson's statement was the Journal History copy of these letters. However, while the Prophet included them in his history, there is no indication of endorsement, and he never related them to the slavery issue. Unquestionably he favored the expansion of Mormon activities into the West, for within two weeks of receipt of the above letters he submitted a memorial to Congress asking that he be authorized to organize a company of 100,000 men to police the West, specifically naming Oregon and Texas.[58]

The rather lengthy treatment of slavery included in the Prophet's "Views" presented a remarkable contrast to his extensive discussion of 1836. For instance, the "Views" contained no reference to the social depravity of blacks. The "men of piety" of the South became "hospitable and noble" people who will help eliminate slavery "whenever they are assured of an equivalent for their property." States' rights were much less evident as both the Declaration of Independence and the Constitution were interpreted broadly to provide liberty for all "without reference to color or condition: *ad infinitem.*"[59] There was no hint of divine endorsement of slavery through a biblical curse; rather, the Prophet lamented a situation in which "two or three millions of people are held as slaves for life, because the spirit in them is covered with a darker skin than ours." The only scripture invoked was in support of the idea that a "noble" nation should work to "ameliorate the condition of all: black or white, bond or free; for the best of books says,'God hath made of one blood all nations of men, for to dwell on all the face of the earth.'" Moreover, the "Views" were promulgated much more actively than the earlier pro-slavery essays. Mormon missionaries were pressed into service to carry the Prophet's campaign and program throughout the country, and for a short while the Mormon Church could accurately be described as outspokenly against slavery.

In favoring "equal rights" for Negroes, Joseph Smith did not wish to remove all legal restrictions on that race. Nor should the impression be conveyed that he was completely free of nineteenth-century prejudices. The aversion to miscegenation apparent in the articles in 1836 was later incorporated into the laws of Nauvoo;[60] and in the same breath that the Prophet advocated "national equalization" for Negroes, he expressed a desire that they be confined "by strict law to their own species." Not unexpectedly, a wide range of racial attitudes was manifest within the Church during this time. These ranged from the relatively progressive Willard Richards remark about a respected exslave, "A black skin may cover as white a heart as any other skin, and the black hand may be as neat and clean as the white one, and all the trouble arises from want of familiarity with the two";[61] to the anonymous Mormon simile published in the *Elders' Journal* (Joseph Smith, editor) regarding an especially ungrateful and "mean" man: "One thing we have learned, that there are negroes who [wear] white skins, as well as those who wear black ones."[62] More subtle, but nonetheless revealing, was a remark on the extensive actions taken by European nations to end the slave trade, "But what would those nations think, if they were told the fact that in America— Republican America, the boasted cradle of liberty and land of freedom—

that those dealers in human flesh and blood, negro dealers and drivers, are allowed with impunity to steal white men."[63] There are very few statements on race directly attributable to Joseph Smith. While negative value judgments are occasionally suggested by his remarks, the most extensive comment reveals that he did not share the majority opinion of his day on the innate racial inferiority of Negroes.[64] The little that is recorded about his direct dealings with blacks is also more reflective of compassion than prejudice.[65]

In fourteen years Joseph Smith led the Church from seeming neutrality on the slavery issue through a period of antiabolitionist, proslavery sentiment to a final position strongly opposed to slavery. In the process he demonstrated that he shared the common belief that Negroes were descendants of Ham, but ultimately his views reflected a rejection of the notion that this connection justified Negro slavery. There is no contemporary evidence that the Prophet limited priesthood eligibility because of race or biblical lineage; on the contrary, the only definite information presently available reveals that he allowed a black to be ordained an elder, and later a seventy, in the Melchizedek priesthood. The possibility has been raised, through later testimony, that within the slave society of the South, blacks were not given the priesthood.

After the Prophet's death, most of his philosophy and teachings were effectively canonized. There was one significant subject on which this does not appear to have been the case—the status of the Negro. A measure of the influence of Joseph Smith's personal presence in shaping early Mormon attitudes on this subject can be obtained by contrasting the Church position prior to his death with the developments which followed.

II

... any man having one drop of the seed of [Cain] ... in him cannot hold the priesthood and if no other Prophet ever spake it before I will say it now in the name of Jesus Christ I know it is true and others know it ...
Brigham Young, 1852

The uncertainty which followed the martyrdom of Joseph Smith was not fully resolved for many months, and most of the efforts of the Church during this time were directed at self-preservation. Among the early changes to emerge, one of the most dramatic involved Mormon attitudes towards blacks and slavery. Joseph Smith's anti-slavery sentiment persisted for a short time, though this was partially due to delayed publications in the *Times and Seasons*. Several talks and letters advocating the Prophet's presidency and program for the abolition of slavery were published during the summer months.[66] The talks actually delivered during that summer were more concerned with the dwindling freedom within the Mormons' own community. Brigham Young did recommend that the Saints remain aloof from the upcoming election until "a man is found, who, if elected, will carry out the enlarged principles, universal freedom, and equal rights and protection" advocated by Joseph Smith.[67]

By the following spring, however, a shift had again become evident in the Church position on slavery. A "Short Chapter" appeared in the *Times and Seasons* which reverted almost literally to the arguments of 1836:

> History and common observation show [Noah's curse to] have been fulfilled to the letter. The descendants of Ham, besides a black skin which has ever been a curse that has followed an apostate of the holy priesthood, as well as a black heart, have been servants to both Shem and Japeth, and the abolitionists are trying to make void the curse of God, but it will require more power than man possesses to counteract the decrees of eternal wisdom....[68]

Why did this opinion reemerge? The short interval since Joseph Smith's death and the acknowledged basis for the article ("history and common observation") suggests that the change may not have been one of opinion so much as one of personalities. One other development may also have been a factor. Several Protestant denominations had been divided by the slavery question; in particular, the division of the Methodist, Baptist, and Presbyterian churches was covered at great length in the Mormon press. Though the articles were reprints from non-Mormon sources, comments were frequently appended, as the following example illustrates:

> The inference we draw from such church jars among the sectarian world, is, that the glory which professing clergymen think to obtain for themselves by division on slavery, temperance, or any other matter of no consequence to pure religion, is "nothing but vanity and vexation of spirit."
>
> Christ and his apostles taught men repentance, and baptism for remission of sins; faithfulness and integrity to masters and servants; bond and free, black and white...
>
> Like the fable of the dog and the meat, the christian community are preparing to lose what little religion they may have possessed, by jumping after the dark shade of abolitionism.—So passes falling greatness.[69]

The Mormon exodus to the Salt Lake Valley did not free the Saints from the slavery controversy, for much of the national debate was focused on the West. Southern congressmen were pressing for an extension of slavery into the new territories, while Northerners wanted the institution confined to the South. In this difficult situation the Saints organized the State of Deseret, and applied for national recognition. The Mormon lobbyists were aware of their delicate position and attempted to maintain complete neutrality on the slavery question. The Constitution of Deseret was intentionally without reference to slavery, and Brigham Young made it clear that he desired "to leave that subject to the operations of time, circumstances and common law. You might safely say that as a people we are averse to slavery, but we wish not to meddle with this subject but leave things to take their natural course...."[70] Congressional compromise eventually created the Territory of Utah in 1850, with no restriction on slavery. This was possible, according to lobbyist John Bernhisel, because northerners believed slavery was excluded from Utah "by the physical geography of the country and the laws of God."[71] However, Bernhisel wrote, "If they had believed that there were even half a dozen slaves in Utah, or that slavery would ever be tolerated in it, they would not have granted us a Territorial organization."[72]

Shortly thereafter the Mormons belatedly defined their position on slavery. Though no law authorized or prohibited slavery in Utah, there were slaves in the territory, and all appeared to be "perfectly contented and satisfied." They were fully at liberty to leave their masters if they chose. Slave-owning converts were being instructed to bring their slaves west if the slaves were willing to come, but were otherwise advised to "sell them, or let them go free, as your conscience may direct you."[73] In fact the first group of Mormons to enter the Salt Lake valley was accompanied by three Negro "servants." By 1850 nearly 100 blacks had arrived, approximately two-thirds of whom were slaves. Bernhisel had performed his task well.[74]

The official acceptance of slavery in the Mormon community extended fully to slave owners as well. Bishops, high councilmen, and even an apostle were ordained from their small number. However, by chance or design, a number of the slaveholders were sent to San Bernardino in 1851 to establish a Mormon colony, and in the process their slaves became free.[75]

The "laissez-faire" approach to slavery in Utah was short-lived, and came to an end early in 1852. As the Mormons quickly learned, Mexicans had carried out slaving expeditions into the region for decades, buying Indians from local tribes who staged raids for "captives of war." Periodically children were offered for sale to the Mormons. The enslavement of Indians, a "chosen people" in Mormon theology, posed a much more serious problem than had Negro slavery. Governor Brigham Young took action to stop the raiding parties, and in January 1852, requested legislation on the slavery question.[76]

In his request Brigham Young made a definite distinction between Indian and Negro. After condemning the Indian slave trade, he observed, "Human flesh to be dealt in as property, is not consistent or compatible with the true principles of government. My own feelings are, that no property can or should be recognized as existing in slaves, wither Indian or African." However, in view of the "present low and degraded situation of the Indian race" and their current practices of "gambling, selling, and otherwise disposing of their children," the Governor would condone a "new feature in the traffic of human beings"— "essentially purchasing them into freedom, instead of slavery." This was not simply buying the children and setting them free, but also caring for them and elevating them to "an equal footing with the more favored portions of the human race." There were, of course, certain economic considerations, and "if in return for favors and expenses which may have been incurred on their account, service should be considered due, it would become necessary that some law should provide the suitable regulations under which all such indebtedness should be defrayed."

Negro slavery was different:

> It has long since ceased to become a query with me, who were the most amenable to the laws of righteousness; those who through the instrumentality of human power brought into servitude human beings, who naturally were their own equals, or those who, acting upon the principle of nature's law, brought into this position or situation, those who were naturally designed for that purpose, and whose capacities are more befitting that, than any other station in society. Thus, while servitude may and should exist, and that too upon those who are naturally designed to occupy the position of 'servant of servants' yet we should not fall into the other extreme, and make them as beasts of the field, regarding not the humanity which attaches to the colored race; nor yet elevate them, as some seem disposed, to an equality with those whom Nature and Nature's God has indicated to be their masters, their superiors . . . .[77]

The suitable regulations were shortly forthcoming, and within a few weeks Young signed into law acts legalizing both Negro and Indian slavery.[78] Though Negro slaves could no longer choose to leave their masters, some elements of consent were included. Slaves brought into the Territory had to come "of their own free will and choice"; and they could not be sold or taken from the Territory against their will.[79] Though a fixed period of servitude was not prescribed for Negroes, the law provided "that no contract shall bind the heirs of the servant . . . for a longer period than will satisfy the debt due his [master] . . . " Several unique provisions were included which terminated the owner's contract in the event that the master had sexual intercourse with a servant "of the African race," neglected to feed, clothe, shelter, or otherwise abused the servant, or attempted to take him from the Territory against his will. Some schooling was also required for slaves between the ages of six and twenty.

By contrast the more liberal act on Indian servitude required persons with Indian servants to demonstrate that they were "properly qualified to raise or retain said Indian," and limited the indenture to a maximum of twenty years. Masters were also required to clothe their "apprentices . . . in a comfortable and becoming manner, according to his, said master's, condition in life." Yearly schooling was mandatory between the ages of seven and sixteen, and the total education requirement was significantly greater than for Negroes.

No other territory legalized both Indian and Negro servitude. New Mexico eventually legalized slavery in 1859, but census figures the following year listed slaves only in Utah among the western territories. Actually the Negro population throughout the West was negligible, and several territorial legislatures even banned Negro immigration. A recent study has argued convincingly that antislavery sentiment in frontier territories was in part reflective of racial prejudice, and was designed to exclude Negroes from the region.[80] Brigham Young interpreted Utah's anomalous proslavery legislation as accomplishing this same end. In a message commending the legislature late in 1852, he observed, "The law of the last session so far proves a salutary measure, as it has nearly freed the territory of the colored population; also enabling the people to control all who see proper to remain, and cast their lot among us."[81]

Other more obvious factors contributed to the legalization of Negro slavery in Utah. Without the influx of southern converts with their slaves, no legislation would have been required. Perhaps the most fundamental factor was the declaration by Brigham Young and other Mormon leaders that the Lord had willed that Negroes be servants to their "superiors." During his tenure as head of the Church, Young showed none of the variability on this subject manifest under Joseph Smith. He fully accepted the traditional genealogy of the Africans through Canaan and Ham to Cain, and repeatedly taught that this connection gave divine sanction to the servile condition of the Negroes. Nonetheless, he did not claim new information on the subject. As early as "our first settlement in Missouri . . . . we knew that the children of Ham were to be 'servant of servants,' and no power under heaven could hinder it, so long as the Lord should permit them to welter under the curse, and those were known to be our religious views concerning them."[82]

Though Brigham Young clearly rejected Joseph Smith's manifest belief that the curse on Ham did not justify Negro slavery, possibly an even greater difference of opinion is reflected in the importance Young ascribed to the alleged connection with Cain. "The seed of Ham, which is the seed of Cain descending through Ham, will, according to the curse put upon him, serve his brethren, and be a 'servant of servants' to his fellow creatures, until God removes the curse; and no power can hinder it";[83] or, "The Lord put a mark upon [Cain], which is the flat nose and the black skin. Trace mankind down to after the flood, and then another curse is pronounced upon the same race—that they should be the 'servant of servants'; and they will, until that curse is removed; and the Abolitionists cannot help it, nor in the least alter that decree."[84]

Brigham Young derived a second far-reaching implication from the genealogy of the Negro. Asked what "chance of redemption there was for the Africans," Young answered that "the curse remained upon them because Cain cut off the lives of Abel....The Lord had cursed Cain's seed with blackness and prohibited them the Priesthood." The Journal History account of this conversation, dated 13 February, 1849, is the earliest record of a Church decision to deny the priesthood to Negroes.[85] At the time practical implications of the decision were limited. Though reliable information is very scanty, there appear to have been very few Negro Mormons in 1849. Only seven of the twenty thus far identified were men, and three of these were slaves; two of the four freemen had already been given the priesthood.[86]

Though Brigham Young reaffirmed his stand on priesthood denial to the Negro on many occasions, by far the most striking of the known statements of his position was included in an address to the territorial legislature, 16 January, 1852, recorded in Wilford Woodruff's journal of that date. In this gubernatorial address, Young appears to both confirm himself as the instigator of the priesthood policy, and to bear testimony to its inspired origin: "Any man having one drop of the seed of [Cain]... in him cannot hold the priesthood and if no other Prophet ever spake it before I will say it now in the name of Jesus Christ I know it is true and others know it." This clearly is one of the most important statements in the entire history of this subject.

Placed in a fuller context, these remarks are part of one of several discussions of slavery and Negro capability by Governor Young in conjunction with the enactment of Utah's slavery codes in February and March, 1852. Other significant points in the address include Young's statement, "The Negro cannot hold one part of Government" (this immediately followed the above quotation); he would "not consent for the seed of [Cain] to vote for me or my Brethren"; "the Canaanite cannot have wisdom to do things as white man has"; miscegenation required blood atonement (offspring included) for salvation; and the curse would some day be removed from the "seed of Cain."

While it will be seen that the Church eventually abandoned a number of Young's contentions, and though one hesitates to attribute theological significance to a legislative address, were this account to be unequivocally authenticated it would present a substantial challenge to the faithful Mormon who does not accept an inspired origin for Church priesthood policy. That such statements exist and have not appeared in previous discussions of this problem, either within the Church or without, is an unfortunate commentary on the superficiality with which this subject traditionally has been approached.

Though it is now popular among Mormons to argue that the basis for the priesthood denial to Negroes is unknown, no uncertainty was evident in the discourses of Brigham Young. From the initial remark in 1849 throughout his presidency, every known discussion of this subject by Young (or any other leading Mormon) invoked the connection with Cain as the justification for denying the priesthood to blacks. "Any man having one drop of the seed of Cain in him cannot receive the priesthood." (1852);[87] "When all the other children of Adam have had the privilege of receiving the Priesthood....it will be time enough to remove the curse from Cain and his posterity" (1854);[88] "Until the last ones of the residue of Adam's children are brought up to that favourable position, the children of Cain cannot receive the first ordinances of the Priesthood" (1859);[89] "When all the rest of the children have received their blessings in the Holy Priesthood, then that curse will be removed from the seed of Cain" (1886).[90]

A more specific rationale is suggested by the foregoing extracts. Cain, in murdering Abel, had "deprived his brother of the privilege of pursuing his journey through life, and of extending his kingdom by multiplying upon the earth." Cain had reportedly hoped thereby to gain an advantage over Abel—the number of one's posterity somehow being important in the overall scheme of things. Brigham Young further explained that those who were to have been Abel's descendants had already been assigned to his lineage, and if they were ever to come "into the world in the regular way, they would have to come through him." In order that Cain's posterity not gain an advantage the Lord denied them the priesthood until such time as "the class of spirits presided over by Abel should have the privilege of coming into the world." Those spirits formerly under Cain's leadership were reportedly aware of the implications of this decision, yet "still looked up to him, and rather than forsake him they were willing to bear his burdens and share the penalty imposed upon him."[91]

Unfortunately Brigham Young gave no indication as to when Abel's "strain" would receive their entitlement; certainly it was not foreseen in the near future: "When all the other children of Adam have the privilege of receiving the Priesthood, and of coming into the kingdom of God, and of being redeemed from the four quarters of the earth, and have received their resurrection from the dead, then it will be time enough to remove the curse from Cain and his posterity."[92]

   While none in the Church saw fit to question the connection of the Negroes to Cain or Ham, it did occur to several that if men were not responsible for Adam's transgressions, the restriction on the Negro could not consistently be attributed solely to his genealogy. As early as 1844 Orson Hyde had explained the status of the "accursed lineage of Canaan" in terms of the preexistence:

> At the time the devil was cast out of heaven, there were some spirits that did not know who had authority, whether God or the devil. They consequently did not take a very active part on either side, but rather thought the devil had been abused, and considered he had rather the best claim to government. These spirits were not considered worthy of an honorable body on this earth . . . . Now, it would seem cruel to force pure celestial spirits into the world through the lineage of Canaan that had been cursed. This would be ill appropriate, putting the precious and vile together. But those spirits in heaven that lent an influence to the devil, thinking he had a little the best right to govern, but did not take a very active part any way, were required to come into the world and take bodies in the accursed lineage of Canaan; and hence the Negro or African race.[93]

Several years later Orson Pratt also attempted to explain why "if all the spirits were equally faithful in their first estate," they "are placed in such dissimilar circumstances in their second estate," and concluded, "Among the two-thirds who remained [after the Devil was cast out], it is highly probable, that, there were many who were not valient [sic] in the war, but whose sins were of such a nature that they could be forgiven . . . ."[94] Hyde and Pratt were primarily concerned with an explanation of the debased status of the Negro race in these early speculations, and not specifically with the priesthood.

   The preexistence "hypothesis" gained wide acceptance among the Mormons, and was even included in non-Mormon accounts of Church teachings.[95] Brigham Young, however, did not feel it necessary to appeal beyond the curse on Cain to the preexistence. When asked "if the spirits of negroes were neutral in Heaven," he answered, "No, they were not, there were no neutral [spirits] in Heaven at the time of the rebellion, all took sides . . . . All spirits are pure that came from the presence of God. The posterity of Cain are black because he committed murder. He killed Abel and God set a mark upon his posterity. But the spirits are pure that enter their tabernacles . . . ."[96]

   A second fundamental assumption supported Mormon beliefs. This was their unqualified acceptance of the innate inferiority of the Negro—the undeniable evidence of the curse on that race. In significant contrast to Joseph Smith's optimistic evaluation of Negro potential, the Church under Brigham Young characterized the blacks as "uncouth, uncomely, disagreeable in their habits, wild, and seemingly deprived of nearly all the blessings of the intelligence that is bestowed upon mankind";[97] as potentially "blood-thirsty," "pitiless" and a "stranger to mercy when fully aroused," and "now seemingly tame and almost imbecile."[98] In the fullest treatment of race to appear in a Church publication in the nineteenth century, the Negro was characterized as "the lowest in intelligence and the most barbarous of all the children of men. The race whose intellect is the least developed, whose advancement has been the slowest, who appear to be the least capable of improvement of all people. The hand of the Lord appears to be heavy upon them, dwarfing them by the side of their fellow men in every thing good and great."[99]

Moreover, they were black, and for Mormons "blackness" was no mere literary figure. Two Church scriptures had recounted blackness befalling people in divine disfavor, and this was understood to extend beyond the metaphorical to a real physical change.[100] Nor was this phenomenon just an historical curiosity, for apostates from the latter-day Church were seen to darken noticeably, while more dramatic changes could still be viewed in the African and Indian races.[101] What clearer sign that they were cursed?

Notwithstanding the repeated denunciations of racism by the modern Church, the evidence for "racist" attitudes among nineteenth-century Mormon leaders is indisputable. Despite the implications of these attitudes for modern Mormonism, their significance in the nineteenth century was negligible. "Mormon" descriptions of Negro abilities and potential can as readily be obtained from the publications of their learned contemporaries. Such a book, not atypical of this era, could be found in Brigham Young's library—*Negro-Mania: Being an Examination of the Falsely Assumed Equality of the Various Races of Men*....[102] Though blatantly racist by any modern standard, this work cited men of acknowledged intellect from a variety of fields—Johann Friedrich Blumenbach, Baron Cuvier, Champollion, Samuel G. Morton, Rosellini, George Gliddon, Samuel Stanhope Smith, Thomas Jefferson, to name but a few. Brigham Young could find ample support for his racial views in this collection alone, and it was by no means exhaustive. Many others could have been included. The American scientific community though divided on the question of slavery was virtually unanimous in ascribing racial inferiority to the Negroes. So also did Louis Agassiz, Count de Gobineau, statesmen of the North as well as the South, abolitionists (excepting Garrison and a few others), slaveholders, ministers, and university presidents. In short, the "laws of nature" were interpreted in essentially the same way by most nineteenth century Americans, Mormons included. [103] Possibly Brigham Young never read his copy of *Negro-Mania*; even today the book reveals little evidence of usage. It is nonetheless important to realize that those few enlightened individuals who anticipated the mid-twentieth century understanding of race were not generally termed "enlightened" for their racial insight a century ago.

This is not meant to minimize the prejudices of the period nor of the leaders of the Church during that time. The regrettably uniform racial attitudes of white America from colonial to modern times have been no source of pride to anyone who has studied the subject. Nor can one mistake the implicit racial judgments conveyed in many Church statements. Consider, for example, the implications of the following simile from Brigham Young: "Here are the Elders of Israel who have got the Priesthood, who have to preach the Gospel....They will stoop to dance like nigers. I don't mean this as debasing the nigers by any means." [104]

During the 1850s the Mormons were finally able to observe the national slavery controversy with some detachment, no longer as part or pawn of the struggle. Yet even as the prophesied war became more and more probable, there were remarkably few expressions of concern for the welfare of the Union. Jedediah M. Grant said, "They are threatening war in Kansas on the slavery question, and the General Government has already been called upon to send troops there. Well, all I have to say on that matter is, 'Success to both parties.'" [105] The long-harassed Mormons had come to view the anticipated conflict not only as the fulfillment of prophecy, but also as divine retribution upon the heads of those who had persecuted the people of the Lord. [106]

One thing was certain, no act of man was going to free the slaves. Late in 1859 Brigham Young again reiterated that those who have been cursed to be "servant of servants" would continue to be, "until that curse is removed; and the Abolitionists cannot help it, nor in the least alter the decree." [107] Two years of war and Lincoln's Emancipation Proclamation failed to change his opinion:

> ... Will the present struggle free the slave? No; but they are now wasting away the black race by thousands ...
>
> Treat the slaves kindly and let them live, for Ham must be the servant of servants until the curse is removed. Can you destroy the decrees of the Almighty? You cannot. Yet our Christian brethren think they are going to overthrow the sentence of the Almighty upon the seed of Ham. They cannot do that, though they may kill them by thousands and tens of thousands. [108]

President Young's confidence may have stemmed from more than his interpretation of the curse on Ham. Mormon discourses during the Civil War convey the impression that the Saints did not anticipate the United States surviving the war. Rather the conflict was to spread until it had "poured out upon all nations." Moreover, the expectation was high that the Saints would shortly return to Jackson County and begin work on the New Jerusalem. In such a context the entire slavery debate was somewhat academic.[109]

Though war's end found the Mormons still in Utah and the slaves apparently freed, the belief persisted for some time that the peace was to be short-lived, and that the Saints "would most certainly return and build a temple [in Jackson County] before all the generation who were living in 1832, have passed away."[110] Brigham Young, in a slight shift of emphasis, acknowledged in 1866 that slavery may have been abolished: "One of the twin relics—slavery—they say, is abolished. I do not, however wish to speak about this; but if slavery and oppression and iron-handed cruelty are not more felt by the blacks today than before, I am glad of it. My heart is pained for that unfortunate race of men."[111] However, while the war had unexpectedly ended legalized slavery, President Young left no doubt of its impact on the Negro priesthood policy. In the same speech, he affirmed once again, "They will go down to death. And when all the rest of the children have received their blessings in the Holy Priesthood, then that curse will be removed from the seed of Cain, and they will come up and possess the priesthood."

As it became apparent that the war was indeed over, and Congress acted to extend Constitutional rights to all, irrespective of race, the subject of Canaan's curse of servitude disappeared from Mormon discourses. Racial restrictions were eliminated from the constitution of Utah[112]; and for the last decade of Brigham Young's presidency, the Negro was less frequently discussed in Mormon discourses. Though in retrospect the Church leadership had misread the implications of the biblical curse, no explanation was put forth for the error. There were more pressing problems at hand, for as one of the "twin relics of barbarism" was eliminated, national attention was turned to the other—polygamy.

Through three decades of discourses, Brigham Young never attributed the policy of priesthood denial to Joseph Smith, nor did he cite the Prophet's translation of the book of Abraham in support of this doctrine. Neither, of course, had he invoked Joseph Smith on the slavery issue. Nor had any other Church leader cited the Prophet in defense of slavery or priesthood denial. It is perhaps not surprising then that shortly after the departure of President Young's authoritative voice, questions arose as to what Joseph Smith had taught concerning the Negro.

III

With reference to the [Negro] question President [Joseph F.] Smith remarked he did not know that we could do anything more in such cases than refer to the rulings of Presidents Young, Taylor, Woodruff and other Presidencies on this question...
Council Minutes, 1908

When John Taylor assumed the leadership of the Church in 1877 there was no real question as to the basic Mormon policy towards Negroes. Brigham Young had made it quite clear that blacks, as descendants of Cain, were not entitled to the priesthood. It shortly became apparent, however, that all the related questions had not been resolved. In fact, decisions made during the next four decades were nearly as critical for modern Church policy on the blacks as those made by Brigham Young.

By virtue of his role as first prophet of the Restoration, Joseph Smith has always been especially revered, and it is a rare Church doctrine that has not been traced, however tenuously, to the Prophet to demonstrate his endorsement. It was therefore no mere curiosity when just two years after Brigham Young's death, a story was circulated that Joseph Smith had taught that blacks could receive the priesthood. As these instructions were allegedly given to Zebedee Coltrin, John Taylor went for a firsthand account.

When presented with the story Coltrin replied that on the contrary Joseph Smith had told him in 1834 that "the Spirit of the Lord saith the Negro had no right nor cannot hold the Priesthood." Though Coltrin acknowledged washing and anointing a Negro, Elijah Abel, in a ceremony in the Kirtland Temple after receiving these instructions, he stated that in so doing he "never had such unpleasant feelings in my life—and I said I never would again Annoint another person who had Negro blood in him. [sic] unless I was commanded by the Prophet to do so." Coltrin did not mention ordaining Abel a seventy (at the direction of Joseph Smith?), but he did state that he was a president of the seventies when the Prophet directed that Abel be dropped because of his "lineage." Abraham Smoot, at whose home the 1879 interview took place, added that he had received similar instructions in 1838.[113]

President Taylor reported the account to the Quorum the following week, and Joseph F. Smith disagreed. Abel had not been dropped from the seventies, for Smith had seen his certifications as a seventy issued in 1841 and again in Salt Lake City. Furthermore, Abel had denied that Coltrin "washed and annointed" him but rather stated that Coltrin was the man who originally ordained him a seventy. Moreover, "Brother Abel also states that the Prophet Joseph told him he was entitled to the priesthood." Abel's patriarchal blessing was read, verifying among other things that he was an elder in 1836.[114]

The question under discussion was not whether the Negro should be given the priesthood, but rather what had been the policy under Joseph Smith. Significantly, John Taylor, an apostle under the Prophet for over five years, added no corroboration to the claims of Coltrin or Smoot. Rather, he observed that mistakes had been made in the early days of the Church which had been allowed to stand and concluded that "probably it was so in Brother Abel's case; that he, having been ordained before the word of the Lord was fully understood, it was allowed to remain."[115]

Abel's case was further complicated by a corollary to the Negro policy. Brigham Young had not viewed the curse on Cain's lineage as limited solely to social and biological factors, and ineligibility to the priesthood; he further believed that blacks should not participate in Mormonism's most important ordinances—the temple ceremonies. To devout Negro Mormons this restriction was even more serious than the policy of priesthood denial, for in Mormon theology these ordinances were necessary for ultimate exaltation in the life hereafter.[116] This was not an unexpected restriction for the men, as only Mormon men holding the Melchizedek priesthood were eligible for the ordinances. However, Brigham Young had to appeal directly to the curse on Cain to extend the restriction to black women, for women normally needed only be in "good standing" to gain access to the temple.[117] Elijah Abel, the anomalous black who had been ordained to the priesthood, was also excluded by President Young because of the curse.[118]

Abel was convinced of his right to the priesthood and felt that he should be eligible for the temple ordinances. Consequently, on the death of Brigham Young, he appealed his case to John Taylor. Not only had the Prophet knowingly allowed him to hold the priesthood, Abel argued, but his patriarchal blessing also promised him that he would be "the welding link between the black and white races, and that he should hold the initiative authority by which his race should be redeemed."[119] His patriarchal blessing had come close to this sentiment, "Thou shalt be made equal to thy brethren, and thy soul be white in eternity and thy robes glittering; thou shalt save thy thousands, do much good, and receive all the power that thou needest to accomplish thy mission...."[120] Nonetheless, John Taylor upheld Brigham Young's ruling. Undaunted, Abel repeatedly renewed his application, until Taylor referred the case to the Quorum of the Twelve, who sustained the President's decision.[121] In 1883 John Taylor finally called the 73-year-old Abel on a mission from the Third Quorum, to which he had been ordained some 46 years prior. After a year on his mission, Abel became ill and returned to Utah, where he died, 25 December, 1884.[122] With Abel's death the Church lost the only tangible evidence of priesthood-Negro policy under Joseph Smith.

Even after his death, Abel continued to be a recurring problem for the Church leadership, particularly when they reconsidered Joseph Smith's alleged teachings on the subject. Ten years later Wilford Woodruff was faced with repeated applications for temple ordinances from another black Mormon, Jane James. He eventually took the matter to the Quorum, and asked "the brethren if they had any ideas favorable to her race." Once again Joseph F. Smith pointed out that Elijah Abel had been ordained a seventy "under the direction of the Prophet Smith."[123] However, on this occasion a new voice was heard. George Q. Cannon countered with the pronouncement that Joseph Smith had "taught" this doctrine: "That the seed of Cain could not receive the priesthood nor act in any offices of the priesthood until the seed of Abel should come forward and take precedence over Cain's offspring; and that any white man who mingled his seed with that of Cain should be killed, and thus prevent any of the seed of Cain coming in possession of the priesthood."[124]

This is startling information. Even Wilford Woodruff, apostle under the Prophet for five years, had said nothing about Joseph Smith's views. Actually, it was not first-hand information, for when Cannon repeated these sentiments in 1900, it had become, "he understood that the Prophet had said . . . ."[125] Nor did the latter version include the reference to miscegenation; in the interim Cannon had attributed this idea to John Taylor ("he understood Prest. Taylor to say that if the law of the Lord were administered upon him he would be killed and his offspring").[126] A more likely origin for these "quotations" was Brigham Young, who expressed similar sentiments on many occasions without reference to Joseph Smith.[127]

Another problem was considered that year. Two Negroes were discovered who had been given the priesthood, and local leaders wanted to know what should be done. Once again George Q. Cannon spoke up: "President Young held to the doctrine that no man tainted with negro blood was eligible to the priesthood; that President Taylor held to the same doctrine, claiming to have been taught it by the Prophet Joseph Smith." President Snow expressed the thought that the subject needed further consideration, to which Cannon replied "that as he regarded it the subject was really beyond the pale of discussion, unless he, President Snow, had light to throw upon it beyond what had already been imparted."[128]

Perhaps more than any other during this time, George Q. Cannon's confident pronouncements influenced Church decisions on the Negro. At his instigation, a "white" woman *formerly* married to a Negro was denied the sealing rites to her second husband because it would be "unfair" to admit the mother but not her daughters by the previous marriage and because "Prest. Cannon thought, too, that to let down the bars in the least on this question would only tend to complications."[129] Similarly, Cannon on another occasion was instrumental in a decision that denied the priesthood to a white man who had married a black woman.[130]

Notwithstanding George Q. Cannon's assertions, the Council was never presented with a direct quotation from Joseph Smith nor is there any record of Presidents Taylor or Wilford Woodruff (both apostles under Joseph Smith) citing the Prophet as author of the priesthood policy. There are, however, records of several meetings where the Prophet was discussed in relation to the priesthood-Negro matter, and in which they did *not* attribute the doctrine to Joseph Smith. Lorenzo Snow, who asked Brigham Young about the "Africans" in 1849, and who received at some point a lengthy explanation of the subject from Young, also avoided attributing the doctrine to Joseph Smith.[131]

Joseph F. Smith, on becoming president of the Church in 1901, faced problems similar to those of his predecessors. In discussing eligibility for the priesthood in 1902, Smith reviewed the rulings of Brigham Young and John Taylor, and once again remarked that Elijah Abel had been "ordained a seventy and received his patriarchal blessing in the days of the Prophet Joseph."[132] In 1908 the Council heard President Smith recount the story for at least the fourth time—but this time the story was different. Though Abel had been ordained a seventy, "this ordination was declared null and void by the Prophet himself."[133] With this statement the "problem" of Elijah Abel was finally put to rest. Why Joseph F. Smith should come forth with this information after testifying to the contrary for nearly thirty years remains a mystery. Perhaps he was influenced by others who by then had invoked Joseph Smith on behalf of the priesthood policy for nearly twenty years[134] and who were now citing the book of Abraham as a major justification for the policy. Perhaps his memory lapsed, for he erred in other parts of the account as well: he contradicted his earlier (correct) report that Abel was ordained by Zebedee Coltrin, and he further said that Presidents "Young, Taylor, and Woodruff" had all denied Abel the temple ordinances, even though Woodruff did not become president until five years after Abel's death. Beyond the historical inconsistencies, President Smith also described a situation he defined that same year as a doctrinal impossibility. In answering "whether a man's ordination to the priesthood can be made null and void, and he still be permitted to retain his membership in the Church," President Smith wrote that "once having received the priesthood it cannot be taken . . . except by transgression so serious that they must forfeit their standing in the Church."[135]

With Abel out of the way, the Prophet Joseph Smith increasingly became the precedent-maker for priesthood denial. In 1912 George Q. Cannon's second-hand account of the Prophet's views was cited in a First

Presidency letter on Church policy[136]; and slightly over a decade later Apostle Joseph Fielding Smith could write, simply but definitively, "It is true that the negro race is barred from holding the Priesthood, and this has always been the case. The Prophet Joseph Smith taught this doctrine, and it was made known to him....[137]

A second emerging theme can be traced almost in parallel with the beliefs concerning Joseph Smith. Writing in the *Contributor* in 1885, B. H. Roberts had speculated on the background of the priesthood restriction on blacks, and drew heavily on the recently canonized Pearl of Great Price:

> Others there were, who may not have rebelled against God [in the war in heaven], and yet were so indifferent in their support of the righteous cause of our Redeemer, that they forfeited certain privileges and powers granted to those who were more valiant for God and correct principle. We have, I think, a demonstration of this in the seed of Ham. The first Pharaoh-patriarch-king of Egypt—was a grandson of Ham:..." [Noah] *cursed him as pertaining to the Priesthood...*"
>
> Now, why is it that the seed of Ham was cursed as pertaining to the Priesthood? Why is it that his seed "could not have right to the Priesthood?" Ham's wife was named "Egyptus, which in the Chaldaic signifies Egypt, which signifies that which is forbidden;...and thus from Ham sprang that race which preserved the curse in the land."... Was the wife of Ham, as her name signifies, of a race which those who held the Priesthood were forbidden to intermarry? Was she a descendant of Cain, who was cursed for murdering his brother? And was it by Ham marrying her, and she being saved from the flood in the ark, that "the race which preserved the curse in the land" was perpetuated? If so, then I believe that race is the one through which it is ordained those spirits that were not valiant in the great rebellion in heaven should come; who through their indifference or lack of integrity to righteousness, rendered themselves unworthy of the Priesthood and its powers, and hence it is withheld from them to this day."[138]

Several years later George Q. Cannon repeated the essentials of this explanation (excluding the references to the preexistence) in the *Juvenile Instructor*,[139] and by 1900 Cannon was citing the Pearl of Great Price in First Presidency discussions.[140] This explanation appeared again in the *Millennial Star* in 1903[141] and in *Liahona, the Elders' Journal* in 1908.[142] Additional allusions were also evident in First Presidency and Council discussions,[143] and by 1912 this relatively new argument had become a foundation of Church policy. Responding to the inquiry, "Is it a fact that a Negro cannot receive the priesthood, and if so, what is the reason?" The First Presidency wrote, "You are referred to the Pearl of Great Price, Book of Abraham, Chapter 1, verses 26 and 27, going to show that the seed of Ham was cursed as pertaining to the priesthood; and that by reason of this curse they have no right to it."[144]

When fully developed the Pearl of Great Price argument went as follows: Cain became black after murdering his brother Abel; among his descendants were a people of Canaan who warred on their neighbors, and were also identified as black.[145] Ham, Noah's son, married Egyptus, a descendant of this Cain-Canaan lineage; Cain's descendants had been denied the priesthood, and thus Ham's descendants were also denied the priesthood. This was confirmed in the case of Pharaoh, a descendant of Ham and Egyptus, and of the Canaanites, and who was denied the priesthood; the modern Negro was of this Cain-Ham-lineage, and therefore was not eligible for the priesthood.[146]

Actually a careful reading of the Pearl of Great Price reveals that the books of Moses and Abraham fall far short of so explicit an account. Negroes, for instance, are never mentioned. Though Cain's descendants are identified as black at one point before the Flood, they are never again identified. The people of Canaan are not originally black and are thus unlikely candidates for Cain's "seed." There is no explicit statement that Ham's wife was "Egyptus"; rather the account reads that there was a woman "who was the daughter of Ham, and the daughter of Egyptus." In patriarchal accounts this would not necessarily imply a literal daughter, as individuals are not infrequently referred to as sons or daughters of their grandparents or even more remote ancestors. Within Abraham's own account an "Egyptus" is later referred to as the "daughter of Ham," and the Pharaoh who has been identified as "Egyptus' eldest son" is elsewhere seemingly the son of Noah. Moreover, the book of Moses records that Ham was a man of God prior to the Flood, and that the daughters of the sons of Noah were "fair." The effort to relate Pharaoh to the antediluvian people of Canaan is especially strained, for in characterizing Pharaoh as a descendant of Egyptus and the "Canaanites" there is no suggestion that this latter group was any other than the people of Canaan descended from Ham's son, Canaan (who also had been cursed).[147]

How then was the Pearl of Great Price put to such ready use in defense of the policy of priesthood denial to Negroes? Very simply, the basic belief that a lineage could be traced from Cain through the wife of Ham to the modern Negro had long been accepted by the Church, independently of the Pearl of Great Price. It was a very easy matter to read this belief into that scripture, for if one *assumes* that there was a unique continuous lineage extending from Cain and Ham to the present and that this is the lineage of the contemporary Negro, then it must have been accomplished essentially as B. H. Roberts proposed.

A better question is, why wasn't the Pearl of Great Price invoked earlier on this matter?[148] Most probably there was no need. The notion that the Negroes were descended from Cain and Ham was initially common-enough knowledge that no "proof" or corroboration of this connection had been necessary. This belief remained in evidence throughout the nineteenth century, and as late as 1908 a Mormon author could write: "That the negroes are descended from Ham is generally admitted, not only by latterday Saint writers but by historians and students of the scriptures. That they are also descended from Cain is also a widely accepted theory, though the sacred history does not record how this lineage bridged the flood."[149]

In reality these ideas were not nearly so widespread at this time as they had been a half century before. Fewer and fewer scientists were subscribing to a literal Flood, and the evidence they presented was convincing an increasing number of laymen that there had not been a general destruction as recently as Genesis suggested. Evolutionary theories even challenged Adam's position as progenitor of the human family. This dwindling "external support" probably accounts in part for the increased attention to the Pearl of Great Price evident during this time, for the traditional beliefs regarding both Cain and the Flood were essential to the Church's Negro doctrine.

The shift of the rationale ("doctrinal basis") for the Negro policy on to firmer or at least more tangible ground developed not only at a time when traditional beliefs concerning Cain and Ham were fading from the contemporary scene, but also as fundamental assumptions concerning the Negro's social and intellectual status were being challenged. Even within the Church this change can easily be identified. As early as 1879 Apostle Franklin D. Richards departed significantly from antebellum Mormon philosophy in a discussion of slavery and the Civil War, "without any argument as to whether slavery should be justified or condemned...[The Negro's] ancestor said they should be servant of servants among their brethren, making their servitude the fulfilment of prophecy, whether according to the will of God or not."[150] Twenty years later the Church's *Deseret News* was not only questioning the old notions of racial inferiority but had become somewhat of a champion of Negro political rights.[151] An ironic extreme was achieved in 1914 when a Mormon writer for the *Millennial Star* concluded, "Even the mildest form of slavery can never be tolerated by the one true church....The slavery of Catholic Rome must be looked upon as one great proof of apostasy."[152] There were reservations, and even in the midst of its "liberal" period, the *Deseret News* still felt the need for "some wise restrictions in society, that each race may occupy the position for which it was designed and is adapted."[153] Similarly, a seventy's course in theology could quote extensively from "perhaps the most convincing book in justification of the South in denying to the negro race social equality with the white race."[154] However, the very need for "evidence" reveals a significant change from the assumptions of an earlier time.

Notwithstanding the initial failure to cite Joseph Smith on Church Negro policy, there had never been any question among the leadership as to the lineage of the blacks nor of the implications of this genealogy. John Taylor had been editor of the *Times and Seasons* in 1845 when the "Short Chapter" marked the return of the Church to the "hard line" on the curse of Ham.[155] He accepted the traditional genealogy for the blacks[156] and as president of the Church denied them access to the temple because of their lineage. Also while president, he made the unique observation that this lineage had been preserved through the Flood "because it was necessary that the devil should have a representation upon the earth as well as God...."[157]

Wilford Woodruff, an apostle to Joseph Smith, Brigham Young, and John Taylor before becoming president, believed fully in the Cain genealogy. At one point he went so far as to cite the "mark of darkness" still visible on the "millions of the descendants of Cain" as evidence for the Bible.[158] As with his two predecessors, Woodruff denied blacks the temple ordinances as one of the "disadvantages ... of the descendants of Cain."[159] Nonetheless he authorized the compromise allowing Jane James into the temple for an unusual sealing ordinance.

Less information is available on Lorenzo Snow. His concern for the subject is reflected in his early inquiry into the "chance of redemption" for the Africans.[160] As a senior apostle he proposed that a man ruled ineligible for the priesthood for marrying a black be allowed "to get a divorce ... and marry a white woman, and he would be entitled then to the priesthood."[101] While President of the Church he upheld the decisions of his three predecessors, citing as they had the curse on Cain.[162]

Greater attention was focused on the Negro doctrine while Joseph F. Smith was president than at any time since the presidency of Brigham Young. Though several changes are evident in Mormon teachings during his administration, President Smith relied very heavily on the rulings of his predecessors in determining the fundamentals of Church policy ("he did not know that we could do anything more in such cases than refer to the rulings of Presidents Young, Taylor, Woodruff and other Presidencies ... ").[163]

The most important of the new developments was the incorporation of Joseph Smith and the Pearl of Great Price into the immediate background of the Negro policy. There were also several important decisions.

In 1902 the First Presidency received an inquiry concerning the priest-hood restriction to a man who had one Negro great-grandparent. The basic question was what defined a "Negro" or "descendant of Cain." There were precedents for a decision, and Joseph F. Smith recounted that Brigham Young applied the restriction to those with any "Negro blood in their veins." Even so, Apostle John Henry Smith "remarked that it seemed to him that persons in whose veins the white blood predominated should not be barred from the temple." It is not clear exactly what Apostle Smith had in mind, but if he meant cases in which there were more Caucasian grandparents, for instance, than Negro, he would have been much more liberal in his definitions than the vast majority of his con-temporaries.[164] It had long been the peculiar notion of American whites that a person whose appearance suggested any Negro ancestry was to be considered a Negro, notwithstanding the fact that perhaps fifteen of his sixteen great-great-grandparents were Caucasians. This was particularly so if it were known that there was a black ancestor. Theoretically, the presence of a "cursed lineage" should have been discernible to a Church patriarch. However, a previous Council had already been faced with a problem which arose when a patriarch assigned a man of "some Negro blood" to the lineage of Ephraim.[165] Joseph F. Smith's answer to the proposal by Apostle John Henry Smith was unusually revealing:

> President Smith...referred to the doctrine taught by Presi-dent Brigham Young which he (the speaker) said he believed in himself, to the effect that the children of Gentile parents, in whose veins may exist a single drop of the blood of Ephraim, might extract all the blood of Ephraim from his parents' veins, and be actually a full-blooded Ephraimite. He also referred to the case of a man named Billingsby, whose ances-tors away back married an Indian woman, and whose descend-ants in every branch of his family were pure whites, with one exception, and that exception was one pure blooded Indian in every branch of the family. The speaker said he mentioned this case because it was in line with President Young's doctrine on the subject; and the same had been found to be the case by stockmen engaged in the improvement of breeds. Assuming, therefore, this doctrine to be sound, while the children of a man in whose veins may exist a single drop of negro blood, might be entirely white, yet one of his descendants might turn out to be a pronounced negro. And the question in President Smith's mind was, when shall we get light enough to deter-mine each case on its merits? He gave it as his opinion that in all cases where the blood of Cain showed itself, however

slight, the line should be drawn there; but where children of tainted people were found to be pure Ephraimites, they might be admitted to the temple. This was only an opinion, however; the subject would no doubt be considered later.[168]

By 1907 the First Presidency and Quorum had reconsidered, and ruled that "no one known to have in his veins negro blood, (it matters not how remote a degree) can either have the priesthood in any degree or the blessings of the temple of God; no matter how otherwise worthy he may be."[167] The doctrinal concept related by Joseph F. Smith is virtually identical to the now outdated theory of "genetic throwback." Though once a widely accepted phenomena, modern geneticists doubt that such cases ever existed.[168]

Another important decision made during this period involved missionary work. Under the Prophet Joseph Smith the Church repeatedly claimed that its mission was to everyone, and in the year of the Prophet's death over 500 missionaries were set apart to carry forth the gospel. The trials faced by the Saints after 1844 were such that it was nearly fifty years until that level was again attained. Nonetheless, under Brigham Young the Church's universal call was a common theme, and this was particularly the case in the days prior to the Civil War.[169]

Notwithstanding Joseph Smith's early instructions and the concern under Brigham Young that the gospel at least symbolically be carried to all nations a new understanding was evident after 1900. A former South African Mission president reported an unusual problem. "An old native missionary" had been converted to Mormonism and was anxious to begin missionary work among the natives, as was the recently converted son of a Zulu chief. Should the gospel be preached to native tribes? The Quorum in response cited rulings of the First Presidency that "our elders should not take the initiative in proselyting among the negro people."[170] The rationale was set forth in response to an inquiry from another South African mission president who wrote in 1910 to ask if "a promiscuously bred white and Negro" could be "baptized for his dead," adding that "he did not wish it to be inferred that he and his fellow missionaries were directing their work among the blacks, as they were not, he having instructed the elders to labor among the white race."[171] In reply the First Presidency noted the policy of discrimination and stated, "this is as it should be, and we trust that this understanding will be clearly had by all of our missionaries laboring in South Africa, and who may be called there hereafter. In the Book of Moses (Pearl of Great Price) Chapter 7, verse 12, we learn that Enoch in his day called upon all the people to repent save the people of Canaan, and it is for us to do likewise."[172] Once instituted this policy remained in effect for over fifty years.

What of Negroes being baptized for the dead? President Smith could see "no reason why a negro should not be permitted to have access to the baptismal font in the temple to be baptized for his dead, inasmuch as negroes are entitled to become members of the Church by baptism." Consequently, the First Presidency informed the mission president that while it was not the current practice, they did not "hesitate to say that Negroes may be baptized and confirmed" for the dead.[173] With this the temple was once again opened to Negro Mormons.

One additional area of doctrinal import was considered during this period. In spite of Brigham Young's statement to the contrary, the notion that the curse on Negroes was somehow related to their relative neutrality in the War in Heaven had gained popularity. It was evident in B. H. Roberts's *Contributor* article in 1885, and by 1912 the idea was being advanced by many elders as Church doctrine. In response to an inquiry as to the authority for this belief, the First Presidency wrote, "there is no revelation, ancient or modern, neither is there any authoritative statement by any of the authorities of the Church . . . [in support of the idea] that the negroes are those who were neutral in heaven at the time of the great conflict or war, which resulted in the casting out of Lucifer and those who were led by him."[174] An explanation based solely on an ancestral connection still must have been unsatisfying, for the Presidency later wrote, "Our preexistence, if its history were fully unfolded, would no doubt make the subject much plainer to our understanding than it is shown at present."[175]

Though most studies of the Church's Negro policy ignore the decades from 1880 to 1920, it is apparent that few periods have been as important for modern Church teachings. During this time the Church adjusted to the effective loss of two external rationales for the priesthood policy—the general acceptance of the Negro's biblical lineage and his inherent inferiority. In their place were introduced the much more substantial evidences of the Pearl of Great Price, and the increasing weight (or inertia) of Church rulings that could now be traced through six presidents to the very earliest days of the Restoration. In addition the policy had been elaborated and refined to such a point that no real modifications were felt necessary for nearly fifty years.

IV

The attitude of the Church with reference to Negroes remains as it has always stood.

The First Presidency, 1949

No major changes in Church Negro policy were evident during the second quarter of the twentieth century. Both Heber J. Grant, and his successor, George Albert Smith, continued to base the priesthood restriction ultimately on the curse on Cain; and both cited the Pearl of Great Price as concrete evidence of the divine origin of this practice.[176] There were a few new developments of theoretical significance.

Joseph Fielding Smith's *The Way to Perfection* was published in 1931, and it contained by far the most extensive treatment of the Negro policy to date and remains even today the only comparable work by a General Authority. Through the influence of this book and other publications, Apostle Smith became very closely identified with the Negro policy, perhaps more so than any other figure of the twentieth century. In his writings, he effectively summarized Church policies under his father, Joseph F. Smith, and at the same time provided a theoretical foundation for these policies based on his understanding of history and the Pearl of Great Price. In many ways his works constitute the fullest development of Mormon thought on the Negro, and they were considered by many to be the definitive background study.[177] Where the progress of science and popular sentiment had left the Church almost totally without support for its assumed genealogy of the black ("There is no definite information on this question in the Bible, and profane history is not able to solve it."), Apostle Smith put forward "some definite instruction in regard to this matter" from the "Pearl of Great Price and the teachings of Joseph Smith and the early elders of the Church who were associated with him." In so doing he moved confidently through the negligible evidence concerning the Prophet's views, and concluded, "But we all know it was due to his teachings that the negro today is barred from the Priesthood."[178]

His most significant contribution to the Negro doctrine may well have involved the "preexistence hypothesis." Apostle Smith was aware that both Brigham Young and Joseph F. Smith had denounced the idea that Negroes were "neutral" in the war in heaven and that Young had particularly objected to the implication that the spirits of Negroes were tainted before entering their earthly bodies. On the other hand, Smith also knew that other prominent Mormons had felt it necessary to appeal beyond this life to some previous failing for ultimate justification of the present condition of the blacks.[179] *The Way to Perfection* seemingly reconciled these two positions. Treading a fine line, Apostle Smith distinguished between the neutrality condemned by Brigham Young and another condition comprised of those "who did not stand valiantly," who "were almost persuaded, were indifferent, and who sympathized with Lucifer, but did not follow him." The "sin" of this latter group "was not one that merited the extreme punishment which was inflicted on the devil and his angels. They were not denied the privilege of receiving the second estate but were permitted to come to the earth-life with some restrictions placed upon them. That the negro race, for instance, have been placed under restrictions because of their attitude in the world of spirits, few will doubt."[180] With regard to Brigham Young's comment that "all spirits are pure that came from the presence of God," Smith wrote, "They come innocent before God so far as mortal existence is concerned."[181]

As with those previously proposing this general explanation, Apostle Smith viewed the priesthood restriction as evidence for his thesis, rather than the reverse: "It cannot be looked upon as just that they should be deprived of the power of the Priesthood without it being a punishment for some act, or acts, performed before they were born."[182] After 1931 the "preexistence hypothesis" was presented with increasing frequency and confidence until 1949 when it formed a major portion of the first public statement of Church policy towards blacks to be issued by the First Presidency.[183]

The decision to deny the priesthood to anyone with Negro ancestry ("no matter how remote"), had resolved the theoretical problem of priesthood eligibility[184] but did not help with the practical problem of identifying the "blood of Cain" in those not already known to have Negro ancestry. The need for a solution to this problem was emphasized by the periodic discovery that a priesthood holder had a black ancestor. One such case came to the attention of the Quorum in 1936. Two Hawaiian members of the priesthood who had performed "some baptisms and other ordinances," were discovered to be "one-eighth negro" and the question arose, what should be done? A remarkably pragmatic decision was reached. The case was entrusted to senior apostle George Albert Smith who was shortly to visit the area, with instructions that if he found that their ordinances involved "a considerable number of people . . . that ratification of their acts be authorized . . .; [but] should [he] discover that there are only one or two affected, and that the matter can be readily taken care of, it may be advisable to have re-baptism performed."[185] A decade later similar cases were reported from New Zealand, and it was "the sentiment of the Brethren" on this occasion that "if it is admitted or otherwise established" that the individuals in question had "Negro blood in his veins," "he should be instructed not to attempt to use the Priesthood in any other ordinations."[186]

The growth of the international Church was clearly bringing new problems. Brazil was particularly difficult. Later that year J. Reuben Clark, First Counselor to George Albert Smith, reported that the Church was entering "into a situation in doing missionary work . . . where it is very difficult if not impossible to tell who has negro blood and who has not. He said that if we are baptizing Brazilians, we are almost certainly baptizing people of negro blood, and that if the Priesthood is conferred upon them, which no doubt it is, we are facing a very serious problem."[187] No solution was proposed, though the Quorum once again decided on a thorough review. Elsewhere the problem was not so complicated. South African "whites" had simply been required to "establish the purity of their lineage by tracing their family lines out of Africa through genealogical research" before being ordained to the priesthood.[188] Polynesians, though frequently darker than Negroes, were not generally considered to be of the lineage of Cain.[189] Within the United States, cases in which there was no acknowledged Negro ancestry were ultimately determined on the basis of appearance. Responding to an inquiry about a physical test for "colored blood," the First Presidency wrote that they assumed "there has been none yet discovered. People in the South have this problem to meet all the time in a practical way, and we assume that as a practical matter the people there would be able to determine whether or not the sister in question has colored blood. Normally the dark skin and kinky hair would indicate but one thing."[190]

In spite of the progressive editorials of a few decades before, Utah joined the nation in segregating blacks in hotels, restaurants, movie theaters, bowling alleys, etc., and in otherwise restricting their professional advancement in many fields.[191] Following the Second World War the general movement to guarantee more civil rights to blacks was also manifest in Utah. Though Church and civic leaders spoke in favor of "equal rights" during this time, this was in the context of the "separate equality" of *Plessy* v. *Ferguson* [192]; and between 1945 and 1951 the Utah legislature killed public accommodation and fair employment bills on at least four occasions.[193] As elsewhere, the ultimate argument advanced against a change in policy was that it would lead to miscegenation. While there was no published instruction from the First Presidency on this matter, their response to a personal inquiry is illuminating. A member had written from California to inquire whether "we as Latter-day Saints [are] required to associate with the Negroes or talk the Gospel to them . . . ." Their answer, in part:

> . . . No special effort has ever been made to proselyte among the Negro race, and social intercourse between the Whites and the Negroes should certainly not be encouraged because of leading to intermarriage, which the Lord has forbidden.
>
> This move which has now received some popular approval of trying to break down social barriers between the Whites and the Blacks is one that should not be encouraged because inevitably it means the mixing of the races if carried to its logical conclusion.[194]

An aversion to miscegenation has been the single most consistent facet of Mormon attitudes towards the Negro. Though the attitudes towards the priesthood, slavery, or equal rights have fluctuated significantly, denunciations of interracial marriage can be identified in discourses in virtually every decade from the Restoration to the present day. Though these sentiments can never be said to have dominated Mormon thought, they did become a major theme in the years following the Second World War and are to be found in both published and private remarks, generally in connection with the civil rights discussion.[195] The Church viewed miscegenation from the unique perspective of the priesthood policy but was, of course, by no means unique in its conclusions; in fact, the leadership generally invoked "biological and social" principles in support of their conclusions on the subject.[196]

Within the Church segregation was not a major concern. Occasionally the few Negro members did pose a problem; and, not unexpectedly, these difficulties were resolved after the manner of their contemporaries. Responding to a situation in Washington, D.C., in which some Relief Society sisters had objected to being seated with "two colored sisters who are apparently faithful members of the Church," the First Presidency advised: "It seems to us that it ought to be possible to work this situation out without causing any feelings on the part of anybody. If the white sisters feel that they may not sit with them or near them, we feel sure that if the colored sisters were discretely approached, they would be happy to sit at one side in the rear or somewhere where they would not wound the sensibilities of the complaining sisters."[197]

It is, of course, no more justified to apply the social values of 1970 to this period than it was to impose them on the nineteenth century, and the point to be made is not that the Church had "racist" ideas as recently as 1950. No one who has lived through the past two decades can doubt but that the racial mood of America has been transformed, as it has been on a grander scale in the past two centuries; these changes greatly complicate the assessment of the ethics of earlier times. On the other hand, from our present perspective it is impossible to mistake the role of values and concepts which have since been rejected in the formulation of many aspects of previous Church policy. The extent to which such influences may have determined present policy is clearly an area for very careful assessment.

This was not the view twenty-five years ago. In spite of the numerous reviews of Church policy towards the Negro that had taken place since 1879, the First Presidency could write as recently as 1947, "From the days of the Prophet Joseph until now, it has been the doctrine of the Church, *never questioned* by any of the Church leaders, that the Negroes are not entitled to the full blessings of the Gospel"[198] (*emphasis* mine). The reevaluations have always started with the assumption that the doctrine was sound.

In 1949 the Church issued its first general statement of position on the Negro, and thereby provided an "official" indication of current thinking at the end of this phase of the history. Four basic points can be identified in the statement. First, there was no question as to the legitimacy of the doctrine, as it was asserted that the practice of priesthood denial dated "from the days of [the] organization" of the Church and was based on a "direct commandment of the Lord." Second, though no rationale for the practice was given, there was a short quotation from Brigham Young on the "operation of the principle" which stated that a "skin of blackness" was the consequence of "rejecting the power of the holy priesthood, and the law of God" and that "the seed of Cain" would not receive the priesthood until the "rest of the children have received their blessings in the holy priesthood." Third, Wilford Woodruff was quoted as stating that eventually the Negro would "possess all the blessings which we now have." (Woodruff had actually been quoting Brigham Young.) The largest portion of the statement was devoted to a fourth point which presented the "doctrine of the Church" that "the conduct of spirits in the premortal existence has some determining effect upon the conditions and circumstances under which these spirits take on mortality." As the priesthood restriction was such a handicap, there was "no injustice whatsoever involved in this deprivation as to holding the priesthood by the Negroes."[199]

One cannot help but wonder why, in view of the hundreds of millions of men who have been denied the priesthood either because it had not been restored or because of their inaccessibility to the gospel, a relatively insignificant additional handful should be singled out for the same restriction based on the elaborate rationales that have accompanied the Negro policy. Though Church leaders have frequently spoken of the millions who have been denied the priesthood because of the curse on Cain, Negroes were really no less likely to receive the priesthood prior to the Restoration than anyone else, nor are they presently any less likely to receive the priesthood than the majority of mankind.[200] Ironically, the few men who have been denied the priesthood *only* because they were Negroes are the rare blacks who have accepted the gospel; yet acceptance of the gospel is frequently cited as a sign of "good standing" in the preexistence when the individual is not a Negro.

The "fourth period" in the history of the blacks in Mormonism has not been especially eventful. Changes were again evident in the stated rationale for priesthood restriction; and though the curse on Cain and Pearl of Great Price arguments were still considered relevant, they were superseded to a significant degree by the new emphasis on the role of Negroes in the preexistence. Basic Church policy, however, remained essentially unchanged; and while the Church confronted new social and anthropological problems, these problems were generally dealt with in the context of previously established policy.

V

Negroes [are] not yet to receive the priesthood, for reasons which we believe are known to God, but which He has not made fully known to man.

The First Presidency, 1969

The most widely publicized development of the past two decades has been the transformation of the segregationist sentiments of the Forties and early Fifties into an official endorsement of a civil rights movement associated with the elimination of a segregated society. As a result (or in spite) of the persistent and publicized pressure of the Utah NAACP, Hugh B. Brown read the following statement in 1963, on behalf of the Church:

> During recent months, both in Salt Lake City and across the nation, considerable interest has been expressed on the matter of civil rights. We would like it to be known that there is in this Church no doctrine, belief, or practice, that is intended to deny the enjoyment of full civil rights by any person regardless of race, color, or creed.
>
> We say again, as we have said many times before, that we believe that all men are the children of the same God, and that it is a moral evil for any person or group of persons to deny any human being the right to gainful employment, to full education opportunity, and to every privilege of citizenship, just as it is a moral evil to deny him the right to worship according to the dictates of his own conscience.
>
> ... We call upon all men, everywhere, both within and outside the Church, to commit themselves to the establishment of full civil equality for all of God's children.[201]

Though dissenting voices were heard from within the Church hierarchy, it has become evident that this was not a temporary change of position. In December, 1969, the First Presidency issued a statement which said in part that "we believe the Negro, as well as those of other races, should have full Constitutional privileges as a member of society, and we hope that members of the Church everywhere will do their part as citizens to see that these rights are held inviolate."[202]

Less well publicized but of greater doctrinal significance was the decision to open the first mission to blacks. In a virtual reversal of the policy laid down a half century before, David O. McKay announced in 1963 that missionaries were shortly to be sent to Nigeria, Africa, "in response to requests ... to learn more about Church doctrine."[203] This was not a decision made without lengthy deliberation. Requests for missionaries for Nigeria had been received for over 17 years, and an in-depth assessment had been under way for several years prior to the 1963 announcement.[204] Sadly, the Nigeria government became more fully aware of the scope of Mormon teachings on the blacks and denied the Church resident visas.[205] This decision was appealed, and the Church negotiated for over two years in an effort to establish the mission as planned. These efforts were finally terminated shortly before the outbreak of the Nigerian civil war. The initial plan envisioned the creation of a large number of independent Sunday schools to be visited periodically by the missionaries to teach and administer the sacrament and other ordinances. Estimates for the number of "Nigerian Mormons" who would have been involved ranged from 10,000 to 25,000, nearly all of whom were Biafrans.[206]

Receiving no publicity, though possibly of greater significance than the foregoing developments, were subtle indications of a new flexibility in the basic Negro doctrine itself. With the concurrence of President McKay, a young man of known Negro ancestry was ordained to the priesthood after receiving a patriarchal blessing which did not assign him to a "cursed" lineage.[207] In another case, President McKay authorized two children with Negro ancestry to be sealed in the temple to the white couple who had adopted them.[208] Additionally, the last vestige of discrimination based solely on skin color was eliminated, as priesthood restrictions were removed from all dark races in the South Pacific.[209] Finally, it became evident that still another policy had been supplanted as the rare members of the priesthood who married blacks were not debarred from their offices.

President David O. McKay, the man who presided over these developments, was widely acclaimed at his death as a man of unusual compassion who had truly loved all his fellowmen.[210] With regard to the priesthood policy, it was frequently said that he had been greatly saddened that he never felt able to remove the racial restriction. Curiously a somewhat different claim had been made by Sterling McMurrin in 1968. He reported that President McKay told him in 1954 that the Church had "no doctrine of any kind pertaining to the Negro," and that the priesthood restriction was "a practice, not a doctrine, and the practice will some day be changed."[211] Though there was never an official statement of McKay's views as president of the Church, many have doubted that he expressed the latter sentiment exactly in the form McMurrin presented it.[212] Just a few years prior to his alleged comments to McMurrin, McKay had endorsed the First Presidency statement of 1949 to the effect that the priesthood restriction was "not a matter of the declaration of a policy but of a direct commandment from the Lord, on which is founded the doctrine of the Church... to the effect that Negroes... are not entitled to the Priesthood at the present time."[213]

Some of the confusion over President McKay's opinion may be attributable to word choice. A clearcut distinction between "practice," "policy," "doctrine," and "belief" has not always been maintained in the history of this subject. Normally a "doctrine" is a fundamental belief, tenet, or teaching, generally considered within the Church to be inspired or revealed. A "policy" is a specific program or "practice" implemented within the framework of the doctrine. Some policies or practices are so loosely tied to their doctrinal base that they may be changed administratively; other policies or practices are so closely tied to a doctrine as to require a revision of the doctrine before they can be changed. The First Presidency statement in 1949 was emphasizing that there was more to giving the Negroes the priesthood than an administrative decision to change the practice or policy. The McMurrin quotation cited above may reflect a rejection by President McKay of the previous "doctrinal" bases for the priesthood restriction, without at the same time questioning the appropriateness of the practice.

If one reads "no known doctrinal basis" in place of McMurrin's reported "no doctrine," then the sentiment is very similar to the view previously expressed by McKay in 1947.[214] Responding to the question of "why the Negroid race cannot hold the priesthood," he had written that he could find no answer in "abstract reasoning," that he knew of "no scriptural basis . . . other than one verse in the book of Abraham (1:26)," and that "I believe . . . that the real reason dates back to our preexistent life." There is no hint of a "Negro doctrine" here, but McKay had made it even clearer when he explained that the "answer to your question (and it is the only one that has ever given me satisfaction) has its foundation in faith . . . in a God of Justice . . . [and] in the existence of an eternal plan of salvation." In so many words, he had expressed his dissatisfaction with an explanation limited to a curse on Cain or quotations from the Book of Abraham. Yet he did not reject a Church policy extending back well over a hundred years, and which was believed to have originated with the first prophet of the Restoration. Rather he chose to place his trust in God's justice, and (as he later elaborates) his belief that earthly limitations are somehow related to the preexistence.

In dissociating the priesthood restriction from its historical associations, McKay anticipated the current belief that there is no known explanation for the priesthood policy. President McKay was too ill to sign his endorsement to the First Presidency statement of 1969; however, it is surely no mere coincidence that after eighteen years under his leadership the Church would state that the Negro was not yet to receive the priesthood "for reasons which we believe are known to God, but which He has not made fully known to man."[215] Unlike the First

Presidency statement of twenty years before, there was now no reference to a "doctrine," but rather the practical observation that "Joseph Smith and all succeeding presidents of the Church have taught . . . ."

As relieved as the educated Mormon may be at not having to stand squarely behind the curse on Cain or a non sequitur from the Pearl of Great Price, nor ultimately to defend a specific role for blacks in the preexistence (e.g., "indifferent," "not valiant"), there is little comfort to be taken in the realization that the entire history of this subject has been effectively declared irrelevant. For if the priesthood restriction now stands independently of the rationales that justified its original existence, the demonstration that these rationales may have been in error becomes an academic exercise.

There have been no official statements on the Negro since President McKay's death. Though Joseph Fielding Smith had previously left little doubt as to his views on the subject, he did not reiterate them as president of the Church. He did continue the progressive policies of his predecessor and authorized still another innovation—the formation of the black Genesis Group.[216]

During the few months that Harold B. Lee has led the Church, he has been quoted in the national press as explaining the priesthood restriction in terms of the preexistence.[217] In spite of the precedent established while President McKay led the Church for scrutinizing such remarks from all angles, it does not seem indicated to speculate on future possibilities based on this type of "evidence."

A few final remarks should be made regarding a relatively new variant on the preexistence theme. For over a century those who dealt with the preexistence hypothesis derived the idea that Negroes had performed inadequately in the preexistence from either the assumed inferiority of the race or the policy of priesthood denial. Recently, however, one finds that a critical transposition has been made which transforms the earlier belief that Negroes were substandard performers in the preexistence *because* they had been denied the priesthood into the claim that Negroes are denied the priesthood *because* of their status in the preexistence. Thus, one who questions the priesthood policy must now, by extension, involve himself in the speculative maze of premortal life. This development has probably been encouraged by an error in context found in the last First Presidency statement, which reads:

> Our living prophet, President David O. Mckay, has said,
> "The seeming discrimination by the Church toward the Negro is not something which originated with man; but goes back into the beginning with God . . .
> "Revelation assures us that this plan antedates man's

mortal existence extending back to man's preexistent state."... [218]

Beyond the fact that McKay was a Counselor when he made these observations, two false impressions are conveyed. The initial quotation was not a "pronouncement" but rather was the conclusion of his reasoning that if the Lord originated the priesthood restriction, and if the Lord is a "God of Justice," then there must be an explanation that "goes back into the beginning with God." The paragraph which preceded the second quotation is also relevant:

> Now if we have faith in the justice of God, we are forced to the conclusion that this denial was not a deprivation of merited right. It may have been entirely in keeping with the eternal plan of salvation for all of the children of God.
>
> Revelation assures us that this plan...[219]

President McKay had not said that a revelation assured us that the Negro was denied the priesthood as part of the plan of salvation. *We* have assured ourselves that this is the case.

VI

Mormon attitudes towards blacks have thus followed an unexpectedly complex evolutionary pattern. When first apparent, these beliefs were sustained by the widely accepted connection of the Negro with Ham and Cain, the acknowledged intellectual and social inferiority of the Negro, his black skin, and the strength of Brigham Young's testimony and/or opinion. With the unanticipated termination of the curse of slavery on Canaan, the death of Brigham Young, increased evidence of Negro capability, and the decline of general support for the traditional genealogy of the blacks, justification of Church policy shifted to the Pearl of Great Price and an interpretation derived from earlier beliefs, and the belief that the policy could be traced through all the presidents of the Church to the Prophet Joseph Smith. By the middle of the twentieth century, little evidence remained for the old concepts of racial inferiority; skin color had also lost its relevance, and the Pearl of Great Price alone was no longer considered a sufficient explanation. Supplementing and eventually surpassing these concepts was the idea that the blacks had somehow performed inadequately in the preexistence. Most recently all of these explanations have been superseded by the belief that, after all, there is no specific explanation for the priesthood policy. Significantly this progression has not weakened the belief that the policy is justified, for there remains the not inconsiderable evidence of over a century of decisions which have consistently denied the priesthood to blacks.

No one, I believe, who has talked with leaders of the contemporary

Church can doubt that there is genuine concern over the "Negro doctrine." Nor can there be any question that they are completely committed to the belief that the policy of priesthood denial is divinely instituted and subject only to revelatory change. The not infrequent assumption of critics of Church policy that the demonstration of a convincing historical explanation for modern Church teachings would result in the abandonment of the Negro doctrine is both naive and reflective of a major misunderstanding of the claims of an inspired religion. Yet among the parameters of revelation, careful study has been identified as a conducive, if not necessary, preliminary step (D & C 9:7-8). A thorough study of the history of the Negro doctrine still has not been made. In particular, three fundamental questions have yet to be resolved:

First, do we really have any evidence that Joseph Smith initiated a policy of priesthood denial to Negroes?

Second, to what extent did nineteenth-century perspectives on race influence Brigham Young's teachings on the Negro and, through him, the teachings of the modern Church?

Third, is there any historical basis from ancient texts for interpreting the Pearl of Great Price as directly relevant to the black-priesthood question, or are these interpretations dependent upon more recent (e.g., nineteenth-century) assumptions?

For the faithful Mormon a fourth question, less amenable to research, also poses itself: Have our modern prophets received an unequivocal verification of the divine origin of the priesthood policy, regardless of its history?

The lack of a tangible answer to the fourth question emphasizes even more the need for greater insight into the first three. We have the tools and would seem to have the historical resource material available to provide valid answers to these questions. Perhaps it's time we began.

NOTES

I

1. The injunction was found in many places in the then-recently published Book of Mormon (e.g., 1 Ne. 19:17; 22:28; 2 Ne. 30:8; Mosiah 27:25; Alma 29:8; 3 Ne. 28:29; similarly, 1 Ne. 17:35; 2 Ne. 26:26-28, 33; Mosiah 23:7; Alma 26:37), and was reaffirmed in a revelation to Joseph Smith, 9 Feb. 1831, published the following July: "And I give unto you a commandment that ye shall teach them unto all men; for they shall be

taught unto all nations, kindreds, tongues and peoples"; *Evening and Morning Star*, July 1832; presently Doctrine & Covenants 42:58.

2. *Ashtabula Journal*, 5 Feb. 1831, and *Albany Journal*, 16 Feb. 1831. These papers attribute the account to the *Painesville Gazette*, and *Geauga Gazette*, respectively.

3. *Manuscript History of the Church of Jesus Christ of Latter-day Saints*, entry undated. Last preceding dated entry was from June 1831, though an intervening reprint from July suggests that the account originated in the latter month.

4. Andrew Jenson, *Latter-day Saint Biographical Encyclopedia* (Salt Lake City: A. Jenson History Co., 1901-1936), 3:577.

5. "Outrage in Jackson County, Missouri," *Evening and Morning Star* 2 (Jan. 1834): 122.

6. A discussion of this problem is to be found in Warren A. Jennings, "Factors in the Destruction of the Mormon Press in Missouri, 1833," *Utah Historical Quarterly* , 35 (1967), 59-76.

7. "Free People of Color," *Evening and Morning Star* 2 (July 1833): 109.

8. "The Manifesto of the Mob," as recorded in *John Whitmer's History*, p. 9; also found in Joseph Smith, Jr., *History of the Church of Jesus Christ of Latter-day Saints*, B.H. Roberts, ed., 7 vols. (Salt Lake City: 1902-12), 1:378.

9. *Evening and Morning Star* 2 (July 1833): 111.

10. *Evening and Morning Star* "Extra" reprinted in *Times & Seasons* 6:818; also *History of the Church* 1:378.

11. "Contemporaneous with the appearance of this article, was the expectation among the brethren here, that a considerable number of this degraded caste were only awaiting this information before they should set out on their journey." *Times & Seasons*, 6:832-3, which cites the *Western Monitor* of 2 Aug. 1833, though Jennings, "Factors," dates the *Monitor* article 9 Aug. 1833.

12. "Outrage in Jackson County, Missouri," *Evening and Morning Star* 2 (Jan. 1834): 122.

13. D&C 87, received 25 Dec. 1832, as quoted in the 1851 edition of the Pearl of Great Price. Though not published until 1851, Orson Pratt reported in 1870 that this prophecy was in circulation in 1833, and that when "a youth of nineteen...I carried forth the written revelation, foretelling this contest, some twenty-eight years before the war commenced." *Journal of Discourses* 13:135; 18:224; also 14:2 where Wilford Woodruff also reported early familiarity with the prophecy.

14. The present D&C 101:77-79, revealed 16 Dec. 1833 and included in the 1835 edition of the Doctrine and Covenants.

15. "In revelations received by the first prophet of the Church in this dispensation, Joseph Smith (1805-44), the Lord made it clear that it is 'not right that any man should be in bondage one to another.' These words were spoken prior to the Civil War. From these and other revelations have sprung the Church's deep and historic concern with man's free agency and our commitment to the sacred principles of the Constitution.

"It follows, therefore, that we believe the Negro, as well as those of other races, should have his full Constitutional privileges as a member of society...." First Presidency Statement, 15 Dec. 1969, *Church News*, 10 Jan. 1970.

16. D&C 134:12, "adopted by unanimous vote at a general assembly" in Kirtland. Though some claim that this was the work of Oliver Cowdery, the statement was supposed to have been drafted by a committee composed of Joseph Smith, Cowdery, Sidney Rigdon, and Frederick G. Williams. The statement was included in the 1835 edition of the Doctrine and Covenants as section 102.

17. Published in *Messenger and Advocate* (September and November, 1835), 1:180-81; 2:210-2ll.

18. *Messenger and Advocate* 2 (April 1836), 289-301.

19. *Messenger and Advocate* 2:299-301.

20. In July, 1836, Wilford Woodruff and Abraham Smoot, on being charged as "abolitionists" in Tennessee, "read the seventh number of the *Messenger and Advocate* to them, which silenced the false accusations" (L. C. Berrett, "History of the Southern States Mission," Master's thesis 1960, Brigham Young University, p. 117); similar charges were made the same month in Missouri, and the First Presidency advised, "Without occupying time here, we refer you to the April (1836) No. of the 'Latter Day Saint's Messenger and Advocate'..." (Letter of 25 July 1836, published in the *Messenger and Advocate* 2:354).

21. Joseph Smith wrote in his article that these were the "views and sentiments I believe, as an individual"; and Oliver Cowdery said, "We speak as an individual and as a man in this matter."

22. While the correlation is most startling in the primary sources, the following more recent studies also demonstrate the extent to which the views were circulated: J. Oliver Buswell, *Slavery, Segregation, and Scripture* (Grand Rapids, 1964); William S. Jenkins, *Pro-Slavery Thought in the Old South* (Chapel Hill: University of North Carolina Press, 1935); Eric L. McKitrick, ed., *Slavery Defended: The Views of the Old South* (Englewood Cliffs, N.J.: Prentice-Hall, 1963); Louis Ruchames, *Racial Thought in America* Vol 1 (Amherst, 1969); H. Shelton Smith, *In His Image, But...: Racism in Southern Religion, 1780-1910* (Durham, N.C.:Duke University Press, 1972); Caroline Shanks, "The Biblical Anti-slavery Argument of the Decade 1830-

1840," *Journal of Negro History*, 15 (1931): 132-157; Charles H. Wesley, "The Concept of Negro Inferiority in American Thought," *Journal of Negro History*, 25 (1941): 540-560. A more limited study that makes a direct comparison to Mormon views is Naomi F. Woodbury, "A Legacy of Intolerance: Nineteenth Century Pro-slavery Propaganda and the Mormon Church Today" (M. A. thesis, University of California at Los Angeles, 1966).

23. For the early history, see Winthrop D. Jordan, *White Over Black: American Attitudes Toward the Negro 1550-1812* (Chapel Hill, N. C.: University of North Carolina Press, 1968; reprint Baltimore: Penguin Books, 1969) pp. 18, 36, and Part I in general; also, David B. Davis, *The Problem of Slavery in Western Culture* (Ithaca, N. Y.: 1966), pp. 450-51. Most of the references cited in note 22 deal with the eighteenth century as well as the nineteenth. Regarding the curse on Ham, the noted anti-slavery evangelist Theodore Weld wrote in 1838, "The prophecy of Noah is the *vade mecum* of slaveholders, and they never venture abroad without it" (as quoted in H. Shelton Smith, *In His Image*, p. 130). It remains a disappointment to me that Hugh Nibley in his recent treatments of the Book of Abraham has not commented on the Ham genealogy or Negro doctrine believed by so many Mormons to be based on this scripture. See, however, his *The World of the Jaredites* (Salt Lake City: Bookcraft, 1952), pp. 160-64.

24. The parenthetical reference, to "Negroes-descendants of Ham," is found in the Manuscript History 19 June 1831. The remark made in 1841 was rather arresting: "I referred to the curse of Ham for laughing at Noah, while in his wine, but doing no harm....[W]hen he was accused by Canaan, he cursed him by the priesthood which he held, and the Lord had respect to his word, and the priesthood which he held, notwithstanding he was drunk, and the curse remains upon the posterity of Canaan until the present day"; (*History of the Church*, 4:445-46). The prophet also modified the account in Genesis to read that Canaan had "a veil of darkness ... cover him, that he shall be known among all men" (Gen. 9:50, *The Holy Scriptures*, Independence, Mo.: Herald House, 1944); the implications of the "Inspired Version" of Genesis may not be as evident as some have suggested, for Joseph Smith characterized the non-Negro Lamanites in very similar terms (2 Ne. 5:21; Jacob 3:5, 8-9; Alma 3:6-9; 3 Ne. 2:14-15; Morm. 5:15).

25. The letter, written 6 Feb. 1835, was published in the *Messenger and Advocate*, 1:82. As the book of Abraham papyri were not in the possession of the Church at this time, the idea that Ham had a black "Canaanite" wife must have been based on the extant Book of Moses (7:8) reference to an antediluvian people of Canaan who became black.

26. All the books cited in notes 22, 23 have references to this belief.

27. Charles B. Thompson, who left the Church after the death of Joseph Smith and subsequently started his own group, claimed that the Negroes ("Nachash") were intelligent subhuman servants who had been taken onto

the Ark among the other animals. Ham's "illicit union with the female" Nachash resulted in "three half-breed sons, Canaan, Mizraim, and Nimrod." Interestingly, Thompson's linguistic pseudo-scholarship was accepted by the prominent Southern slavery advocate, Samuel A. Cartwright, who characterized Thompson as "a star in the East, ... a Hebrew scholar of the first-class," and incorporated his thesis into an article, "Unity of the Human Race Disproved by the Hebrew Bible," published in *De Bow's Review* (Aug. 1860). De Bow published a second article presenting the same claim in the Oct. 1860 issue of his review. Another variant was presented by Joseph F. Smith, while president of the church. He recounted an idea which "he had been told ... originated with the Prophet Joseph, but of course he could not vouch for it," to the effect that Ham's wife was illegitimately pregnant "by a man of her own race" when she went aboard the Ark, and that Cainan [sic] was the result of that illicit intercourse." First Presidency meeting, 18 Aug. 1900, minutes in the Adam S. Bennion papers, Harold B. Lee Library, Brigham Young University, or George Albert Smith papers, University of Utah. Smith was First Counselor at this time but repeated the comment eight years later, as president. See Council Meeting minutes of 26 Aug. 1908, in Bennion or Smith papers.

28. The sum total of the evidence presently available that the Prophet accepted this connection is one parenthetical statement: "In the evening debated with John C. Bennett and others to show that the Indians have greater cause to complain of the treatment of the whites, than the negroes or sons of Cain" (Manuscript History, 25 Jan. 1842; also *History of the Church* 4:501.) There is no known reference in which the Prophet applied the Book of Moses comment that "the seed of Cain were black" (Moses 7:22) to the Negro. In addition to Phelps' letter there were other references to Cain in the mid-1830s. Apostle David Patten reportedly claimed to have "met with a very remarkable personage who had represented himself as being Cain" while on a mission in Tennessee in 1835. Patten, who described the "strange personage" as "very dark," "covered with hair," and wearing "no clothing," appears to have taken the claim seriously, and eventually "rebuked him" and "commanded him to go hence." The account was reported over fifty years later by Abraham Smoot; see Lycurgus Wilson, *Life of David Patten, the First Apostolic Martyr* (Salt Lake City: Deseret News Press, 1904), pp. 45-47. About 1836 a non-Mormon traveller reports being told by a Mormon "... that the descendants of Cain were all now under the curse, and no one could possibly designate who they were ..." see Edmund Flagg, *The Far West or A Tour Beyond the Mountains* ... (New York: Harper & Brothers, 1838), 2:111.

29. From the Council Meeting minutes of 4 June 1879 (Bennion papers), five days after Coltrin related his account: "Brother Joseph F. Smith said he thought Brother Coltrin's memory was incorrect as to Brother Abel being dropped from the quorum of Seventies, to which he belonged, as Brother

Abel has in his possession, (which also he had shown Brother J.F.S.) his certificate as a Seventy, given to him in 1841, and signed by Elder Joseph Young, Sen., and A. P. Rockwood, and a still later one given in this city. Brother Abel's account of the persons who washed and anointed him in the Kirtland Temple also disagreed with the statement of Brother Coltrin, whilst he stated that Brother Coltrin ordained him a Seventy. Brother Abel also states that the Prophet Joseph told him he was entitled to the priesthood."

30. Date of ordination from Andrew Jenson, *Biographical Encyclopedia*, 3:577. The patriarchal blessing is found in Joseph Smith's Patriarchal Blessing Record, p. 88, without date, and is headed, "A blessing under the hands of Joseph Smith, Sen., upon Elijah Abel, who was born in Frederick County, Maryland, July 25, 1808." No lineage was assigned. It is clear that the blessing was given after Abel's ordination, for the Patriarch states, "Thou has been ordained an Elder . . . ."

31. *Messenger and Advocate*, 2:335.

32. Minutes of the Seventies Journal, kept by Hazen Aldrich, 20 Dec. 1836. Abel was one of several ordained by Zebedee Coltrin to the Third Quorum of Seventy. Aldrich and John Young, who with Coltrin were presidents of the seventies, also ordained several seventies that evening. This journal is found in the Historical Department of the Church of Jesus Christ of Latter-day Saints, Salt Lake City; hereafter cited as LDS Church Archives

33. Ibid., 1 June 1839, records: "Elder J. M. Grant communicated to the council a short history of the conduct of Elder Elijah Able [sic] and some of his teachings etc such as teaching that there would be stakes of Zion in all the world, that an elder was a High Priest and he had as much authority as any H.P., that he commanded some of the brethren from Canada to flee from there by such a time saying that if they did not cross the river St. Lawrence then they could not get into the States and that in addition to threatening to [knock] down Elder Christopher Merkley on their passage up Lake Ontario, he publicly declared that the elders in Kirtland make nothing of knocking down one another. This last charge was substantiated by the written testimony of Elder Zenos H. Gurley, most of the charges Elder Grant testified to the truth of and referred to Moses Smith, John and George Beckstead, Robert Burton and Zebedee Coltrin for testimony, for the substantiation of the remainder." No action was reported. "Pres. Joseph Smith Jr. S. Rigdon and Hyrum Smith were also present and most of the twelve."

34. Council Meeting minutes, 4 June 1879, see note 29. Kate B. Carter, *The Negro Pioneer* (Salt Lake City: Daughters of Utah Pioneers, 1965), p. 15, reports that Abel came to Utah in 1847. Jenson, *Biographical Encyclopedia*, 3:577, assumed incorrectly that the certification in 1841 was the date of Abel's initial ordination.

35. Jenson, *Biographical Encyclopedia*, 3:577, states that Abel "was intimately acquainted with the Prophet Joseph Smith"; Carter, *Negro Pioneer*, p. 15, claims, "In Nauvoo he lived in the home of Joseph Smith." See also *History of the Church*, 4:365 for a passing reference to Abel by the Prophet in June 1841.

36. See notes 32 and 113; Coltrin claimed to have been instructed not to ordain Negroes in 1834.

37. L. John Nuttall Journal, 31 May 1879, typescript at Harold B. Lee Library, Brigham Young University, vol. 1, (1876-84), pp. 290-93; a copy is also included in the Council Meeting minutes for 4 June 1879 (Bennion papers). Smoot attributed the second-hand accounts to W. W. Patten, Warren Parrish, and Thomas B. Marsh.

38. In July 1838, the *Elders' Journal*, Joseph Smith, editor, answered the question, "Are the Mormons abolitionists?" with "We do not believe in setting the Negroes free." In 1839, John Corrill published his *Brief History ... of the Church*, with his reasons for leaving, and commented that "the abolition question is discarded by them, as being inconsistent with the decrees of Heaven, and detrimental to the peace and welfare of the community" (St. Louis: "Printed for the author", 1839; pp. 47-48).

39. "There's a feast of fat things for &c," Hymn number 8 in *A Collection of Sacred Hymns for the Church of the Latter Day Saints*, sel. by Emma Smith (Kirtland: F. G. Williams Co., 1835).

40. "Ye Chosen Twelve," by Parley P. Pratt, in *A Collection of Sacred Hymns for the Church of Jesus Christ of Latter-day Saints in Europe*, selected by Brigham Young, Parley P. Pratt, and John Taylor, 1840. This hymn remains in the LDS hymnal in a slightly modified form.

41. *History of the Church*, 2:368-69.

42. "Report of the Presidency" at General Conference, 3-5 Oct. 1840, in *Times & Seasons*, 1:188, or *History of the Church*, 4:213. Though "washing and anointing" was performed in Kirtland, the ordinances presently denied Negroes were not announced until 1841 (sealing) and 1842 (endowments), and were not performed in the Nauvoo Temple until 1846 and 1845, respectively.

43. *Times & Seasons*, 3 (1 March 1842), 722-25; Joseph Smith was then editor. By contrast the Mormon *Northern Times*, published briefly in Kirtland, Ohio, announced in Oct. 1835, that they had received "several communications ... for insertion, in favor of anti-slavery ..." "[t]o prevent any misunderstanding on the subject, we positively say, that we shall have nothing to do with the matter—we are opposed to abolition, and what ever is calculated to disturb the peace and harmony of our constitution and country. Abolition does hardly belong to law or religion, politics or

gospel, according to our ideas on the subject." (9 Oct. 1835) A strongly anti-abolitionist letter had been published in the *Messenger and Advocate* 2 (May 1836): 312-13.

44. Willard Richards and John C. Bennett expressed opinions that were significantly more "liberal" on this subject than had Oliver Cowdery. For a brief discussion of the new directions of anti-slavery, see C. Vann Woodward, *American Counterpoint: Slavery and Racism in the North-South Dialogue* (Boston, 1971), p. 147.

45. *Times & Seasons*, 3 (1 June 1842): 808. This was in specific response to the charge that the letters published in March showed him to be an abolitionist. He referred to himself similarly in July, 1843 (*History of the Church*, 5:498); Dec. 1843 (*General Joseph Smith's Appeal to the Green Mountain Boys—Times and Seasons Extra*); and in Feb. 1844, developed his position at much greater length in his "Views" on government. See note 48.

46. 30 Dec. 1842, in Joseph Smith's Journal, kept by Willard Richards; copy at LDS Church Archives.

47. 2 Jan. 1843, *History of the Church*, 5:217.

48. "Gen. Smith's Views on the Government and Policy of the U. S." See *Times & Seasons*, 5:528-33. He subsequently spoke against slavery on 7 Mar. 1844 (*History of the Church*, 6:243); 14 Apr. 1844 (*Times & Seasons* 5:508-510); and 13 May 1844 (letter published 4 June 1844 in *Times & Seasons*, 5:545). Another indication of his interest in this subject were entries in his history in Feb. 1843, on a John Quincey Adams petition against slavery (*History of the Church*, 5:283), and in May 1843, on the abolition of slavery in the "British dominions in India" (*History of the Church*, 5:379); in November of that year the *Times & Seasons* carried the full text of a Papal Bull "Relative to Refraining from Traffic in Blacks" (*Times & Seasons*, 4:381-2).

49. This idea was expressed 7 Mar. 1844. See *History of the Church* 6:243, and Matthias Cowley, *Wilford Woodruff* (Salt Lake City: Deseret News Press, 1909), p. 203. There is some uncertainty as to what the Prophet planned to do with the freed slaves. At times he spoke of national equalization or equal rights; on this occasion he stated, "As soon as Texas was annexed, I would liberate the slaves in two or three States, indemnifying their owners, and send the negroes to Texas, and from Texas to Mexico, where all colors are alike."

50. Woodward, *American Counterpoint*, p. 153. Just a few days before his death, Joseph Smith published one of his most outspoken comments on slavery, and included an almost sympathetic allusion to the abolitionists. From a letter to Henry Clay, written 13 May 1844, and published 4 June 1844 *Times & Seasons*, 5:545): "True greatness never wavers, but when the Missouri compromise was entered into by you, for the benefit of *slavery*,

there was a mighty shrinkage of *western honor;* and from that day, Sir, the sterling Yankee, the struggling Abolitionist, and the staunch Democrat, with a large number of liberal minded Whigs, have marked you as a *black-leg* in politics...."

51. D&C 130:12-13, dated 2 April 1843.

52. James M. Flake and John H. Redd both report freeing their slaves; Henry Jolly, the third slave owner, also reported that his slaves wanted to stay with him; however, he sold all except one child whose parents had died (see Carter, *Negro Pioneer*, pp. 4-6, 25, 44-45).

53. *Times & Seasons*, 5:508-510.

54. Carter, *Negro Pioneer* and Jack Beller, "Negro Slaves in Utah," *Utah Historical Quarterly* 2 (Oct. 1929): 122-26, provide considerable information on the early Negroes in Utah. The problem of identifying slaves, normally complicated by the use of the term "servant" regardless of a black's legal status, is even more complex during the initial few years in Utah—during which times "slaves" were theoretically at liberty to leave their masters if they chose.

55. Journal History of the Church of Jesus Christ of Latter-day Saints, entries dated 10 and 11 Mar. 1844. The letters were published in the *Millennial Star* some years later 23 (1861): 103-4, 117-19, and most of the text is found in *History of the Church*, 6:256ff, 259ff. Apostle Lyman Wight was among those who signed the letters. The Committee was at least partially correct. The slave holdings of the Cherokee and Choctaw nations together totalled several thousand. The Chickasaw, Creeks, and Seminoles also had Negro slaves. See Wyatt F. Jeltz, "The Relations of Negroes and Choctaw and Chickasaw Indians," *Journal of Negro History*, 33:24ff; and Kenneth W. Porter, "Relations Between Negroes and Indians Within the Present Limits of the United States," *Journal of Negro History*, 17 (1933): 287ff.

56. Letter of January 27, 1855, to *The Northern Islander*, included in *Correspondence of Bishop George Miller...*, Wingfield Watson, comp. (Burlington, Wis., 1916), p. 20. See also Robert B. Flanders, *Nauvoo: Kingdom on the Mississippi* (Urbana: University of Illinois Press, 1965), pp. 290-95.

57. Andrew Jenson, *Encyclopedic History of the Church of Jesus Christ of Latter-day Saints* (Salt Lake City: Deseret News Publishing Co., 1941), p. 870.

58. *Millennial Star*, 23 (1861): 165-67, or *History of the Church*, 6:275-77.

59. His change of opinion was especially marked on this point. In 1836, in addition to arguing that the North had no right to impose its will on the South, he had further characterized the interest of the free states as being based on "the mere principles of equal rights." By 1844 he had obviously reconsidered the importance of equal rights; regarding states' rights, he

advised John C. Calhoun that "God...will raise your mind above the narrow notion that the General Government has no power, to the sublime idea that Congress, with the President as Executor, is as almighty in its sphere as Jehovah is in His." See *Times & Seasons*, (1 Jan. 1844): 395.

60. In Jan. 1844, Mayor Joseph Smith fined two Negroes "for attempting to marry white women" (*History of the Church*, 6:210).

61. Letter of 15 Feb. 1838, as quoted in Carter, *Negro Pioneer*, pp. 3-4.

62. *Elders' Journal*, 1 (Aug. 1838): 59.

63. From a *Nauvoo Neighbor* editorial included in Joseph Smith's History (*History of the Church*, 6:113). A similar parallel was drawn on other occasions (e.g., *Times & Seasons*, 4:375-76).

64. "[T]hey came into the world slaves, mentally and physically. Change their situation with the whites, and they would be like them....Go into Cincinnati or any city, and find an educated negro, who rides in his carriage, and you will see a man who has risen by the powers of his own mind to his exalted state of respectability. The slaves in Washington are more refined than the Presidents, and the black boys will take the shine off many of those they brush and wait on." (*Millennial Star* 20 [1858]: 278; *History of the Church*, 5:217, presents a slightly different version).

Joseph Smith's passing reference to "nigger drivers" or "niggers" (*Times & Seasons*, 4:375-76; 5:395) are less readily evaluated. This epithet is said to have been less derogatory in the early nineteenth century; even then it was without any connotation of racial respect.

65. Of the four Negro Mormons who claimed to have lived in the Prophet's home (Elijah Abel, Jane James, Isaac James, and Green Flake), I have seen the reminiscences only of Jane James. She had arrived destitute in Nauvoo and was taken into the Smith home along with her eight-member family. She eventually became the housekeeper, and lived in the Smith home until the Prophet's death. Her account depicts Joseph Smith as benevolent and fatherly towards her and conveys her great respect for the Prophet (*Young Woman's Journal* 16 [1905]: 551-52; reprinted in *Dialogue* 5 [Summer 1970]: 128-30). On another occasion he is said to have given a Negro a horse to use to purchase the freedom of a relative (*Young Woman's Journal* 17 [1906]: 538). In still another case, Willard Richards, with Joseph Smith's knowledge, hid a Negro who had been beaten for an alleged robbery; subsequently the Prophet spoke out "fearlessly" against the way the case was handled (*History of the Church*, 6:281, 284).

II

66. See the April 1844 conference talk of John Taylor, and a letter from "HOSPES" dated 8 June 1844, both published 15 July 1844 (*Times & Seasons*, 5:577-79, 590); and the conference minutes of 27 May 1844, published 1 Aug. 1844 (*Times & Seasons*, 5:506).

67. "An Epistle of the Twelve to the Church of Jesus Christ of Latter Day Saints, in Nauvoo and all the world," 15 Aug. 1855 (*Times & Seasons*, 5:618-20). Another article in the same issue added, "As a people we will honor the opinions and wisdom of our martyred General; and, as a matter of propriety, we cannot vote for, or support a candidate for the presidency, till we find a man who will pledge himself to carry out *Gen. Smith's view*[*s*] ... as he published them." (*Times & Seasons*, 5:617-18).

68. "A Short Chapter on a Long Subject," *Times & Seasons*, 6 (1 April 1845): 857.

69. "Trouble Among the Baptists," *Times & Seasons* 6 (1 April 1845): 858. Other articles were carried 1 Oct. 1844 (*Times & Seasons*, 5:667-68), 15 April 1845 (*Times & Seasons*, 6:877-78), 1 May 1845 (*Times & Seasons*, 6:889-90), and 1 June 1845 (*Times & Seasons*, 6:916-17, 924). The theme remained evident in Mormon discourses for several decades. See *Journal of Discourses*, 9:5; 10:124; 14:169; 23:85, 296-97.

70. Letter from Brigham Young to Orson Hyde, Journal History, 19 July 1849; see also letter of Willard Richards to Thomas Kane, Journal History, 25 July 1849; and the Journal History entry of 26 Nov. 1849, reporting an interview of Wilford Woodruff and John Bernhisel with Thomas Kane.

71. Letter from John Bernhisel to Brigham Young, Journal History, 7 Sept. 1850.

72. Ibid., 9 Nov. 1850.

73. *Frontier Guardian*, 11 Dec. 1850; also reprinted in the *Millennial Star* 13 (15 Feb. 1851): 63. J. W. Gunnison, who lived in Utah at this time, recorded that "involuntary labor by negroes is recognized by custom; those holding slaves, keep them as part of their family, as they would wives, without any law on the subject." J. W. Gunnison, *The Mormons, or, Latter-Day Saints, in the valley of The Great Salt Lake* ... (Philadelphia: J. B. Lippincott & Co., 1853), p. 143.

74. The figures are my own estimate, based largely on accounts included in Carter, *Negro Pioneer*, pp. 9, 13, 15-33, 38-39, 44; and Beller, "Negro Slaves," p. 125. The official census figures for Utah in 1850 report 50 Negroes, of which 24 were slaves. See *Negro Population 1790-1915* (Washington, D. C.: Department of Commerce, 1918), p. 57.

75. Apostle Charles C. Rich was one of at least eight slaveholders to be sent on the mission to San Bernardino. Most of the "ex-slaves" continued to be "servants" for their masters, and several appear to have returned electively to Utah when the mission was recalled. At least one of the slaveowners, Robert M. Smith of the San Bernardino bishopric, attempted to take his slaves to Texas but was prevented from doing so by the sheriff of Los Angeles County. See W. Sherman Savage, "The Negro in the Westward Movement," *Journal of Negro History*, 25:537-8. Also, Beller, "Negro

Slaves," pp. 124-26; Andrew Jenson, "History of San Bernardino 1851-1938," typescript, LDS Church, p. 10; and Joseph F. Wood, "The Mormon Settlement in San Bernardino 1851-1857," (Ph.D. diss., University of Utah, 1967), pp. 150-52. Apostle John Taylor and N. H. Felt were later cited as informing a "Chicago Paper" that "some slaves had been liberated ... since they were taken to Utah; others remain slaves. But the most of those who take slaves there pass over with them in a little while to San Bernardino [sic]....How many slaves are now held there they could not say, but the number relatively was by no means small. A single person had taken between forty and fifty, and many had gone in with small numbers." *Millennial Star*, 27 Jan. 1855, 17:62-63.

76. "Governor's Message, to the Legislative Assembly of Utah Territory, January 5, 1852," LDS Church Archives. This was the organizational meeting of the legislature.

The Mormons turned down the first two children offered for sale in the winter of 1847-48; when the Indians threatened to kill them if they weren't purchased, one was bought, and the other was killed. Two others brought shortly thereafter were also purchased. H. H. Bancroft, *History of Utah* (1889; reprinted Bookcraft, SLC, 1964): p 278. See also Orson Whitney, *History of Utah* (Salt Lake City: Geo. Q. Cannon & Sons Co, 1892), 1:508-11; Daniel W. Jones, *Forty Years Among the Indians* (Salt Lake City, 1890, 1960 ed), pp. 48-51; several articles in the *Utah Historical Quarterly* 2 (July 1929), 67-90; and Brigham Young's comments (e.g. *Journal of Discourses*, 1:104, 170-71; 6:327-29).

77. Ibid.

78. "An Act in relation to Service," approved 4 Feb. 1852; "A Preamble and An Act for the further relief of Indian slaves and prisoners," approved 7 Mar. 1852.

79. "...the consent of the servant given to the probate judge in the absence of his master ... " The only exception was "in case of a fugitive from labor." A number of slaves had escaped from their Mormon masters enroute to Utah, and Hosea Stout records an episode in which a slave attempted to run away while in Utah. In the latter case his master was tried and acquitted on kidnapping charges after he recaptured the "fugitive." Juanita Brooks, ed., *On the Mormon Frontier: The Diary of Hosea Stout, 1844-1861*, (Salt Lake City: University of Utah Press, 1965), 2:597. Stout adds, "There was a great excitement on on [sic] this occasion. The question naturally involving more or less the Slavery question and I was surprised to see those latent feeling [sic] aroused in our midst which are making so much disturbance in the states."

80. Eugene H. Berwanger, *The Frontier Against Slavery: Western Anti-Negro Prejudice and the Slavery Extension Controversy* (Urbana; University of Illinois Press, 1967).

81. "Message to the Legislature of Utah from Governor Brigham Young," 13 Dec. 1852, in *Millennial Star*, 15:422.

82. *Journal of Discourses*, 2:172 (18 Feb. 1855).

83. *Journal of Discourses* 2:184 (18 Feb. 1855), but a separate discourse from note 82.

84. Ibid., 7:290-91 (9 Oct. 1859). Brigham Young cited the curse on Ham or Canaan on many occasions in addition to those cited in the text: e.g., his 1852 address to the legislature (note 76), "The seed of Canaan will inevitably carry the curse which was placed upon them, until the same authority which placed it there, shall see proper to remove it . . ."; his comments in early 1855 reported in the May 4, 1855, *New York Herald*, p. 8, "You must not think, from what I say, that I am opposed to slavery. No! The negro is damned, and is to serve his master till God chooses to remove the curse of Ham . . ."; an interview with Horace Greeley, 13 July 1859, "We consider [slavery] of divine institution, and not to be abolished until the curse pronounced on Ham shall have been removed from his descendants," in Horace Greeley, *An Overland Journey from New York to San Francisco in the Summer of 1859*, (New York, H. H. Bancroft and Co., 1860), pp. 211-12; also see *Millennial Star*, 21:608-11.

85. The possibility exists that a policy of priesthood restriction had been set forth shortly prior to this time. William Appleby made the following journal entry while travelling in New York 19 May 1847: "In this Branch there is a coloured Brother, An Elder ordained by Elder Wm. Smith while he was a member of the Church, contrary, though[,] to the order of the Church on the Law of the Priesthood, as Descendants of Ham are not entitled to that privilege . . ." William I. Appleby, Journal, LDS Church Archives. However, the question of priesthood entitlement does not appear to have been fully clear to Appleby, for he then wrote to Brigham Young asking "if this is the order of God or tolerated, to ordain negroes to the Priesthood and allow amalgamation. If it is, I desire to know it as I have yet got to learn it"; (Journal History, 2 June 1847). Though the priesthood restriction appears to have been open knowledge in the early 1850s, the first published record of which I am aware was not until April 1852; "To the Saints," *Deseret News*, 3 April 1852. Gunnison, who had resided in Utah in 1851, also referred to the policy in recounting his experiences the following year; *The Mormons*, p. 143.

86. Estimates based largely on Carter, *Negro Pioneer*. The members included Elijah Abel, his wife and four children; Jane James and six children; Francis and Martha Grice; Walker Lewis; a slave, "Faithful John"; and three "servants," Green, Allen, and Liz Flake. The two priesthood holders were Elijah Abel (who had been recertified a seventy at least as late as 1847), and "a colored brother by the name of Lewis" who was ordained by Apostle William Smith (Journal History, 2 June, 1847. The date of the ordination is not given). Two other free Negroes had left the Church by this time. Black Pete, the first known Negro convert, was among those who claimed to receive revelations in

Kirtland prior to leaving the Church. There was also a "big, burley, half Indian, half Negro, formerly a Mormon who has proclaimed himself Jesus Christ . . . " and who had a following of about sixty "fanatics" in Cincinnati (*The Gazette*, St. Joseph, Missouri, 11 Dec. 1846). This may be the William McCairey, or McGarry, who visited the Mormon pioneer camps in the spring of 1847, and "induced some to follow him." See Brooks, *On the Mormon Frontier*, 2:244, and footnote 37. Black Pete was referred to in Mormon discussions on several occasions in later years (e.g., *Times & Seasons*, 3:747; *Journal of Discourses*, 11:3-4); see also Stanley S. Ivins, Notebooks 7:134-5 (Utah State Historical Society) for an additional excerpt on Pete.

87. Matthias Cowley, *Wilford Woodruff* (Salt Lake City, The Deseret News Press, 1909), p. 351.

88. *Journal of Discourses*, 2:142-43, 3 Dec. 1854.

89. Ibid., 7:290-91, 9 Oct. 1859.

90. Ibid., 11:272, 19 Aug. 1866. The belief that Ham's descendants through Canaan were to be servants would also seem to exclude them from the priesthood. This point was not emphasized under Brigham Young; the following observation was made several years later, "Now the priesthood is divine authority to preside, and to say of a race that they shall be servants forever is equivalent to saying that they shall not hold authority, especially divine authority. Hence the curse of Noah necessarily means that the race upon which it rests cannot hold the priesthood." *Liahona, The Elders' Journal*, 5 (1908): 1164-67.

91. The initial quotation is from 3 Dec. 1854 (*Journal of Discourses*, 2:142-43); a comparable statement accompanies virtually every discussion of the curse on Cain during this time. The elaboration which follows in the text is from an explanation attributed to Young by Lorenzo Snow in a Council Meeting, 11 Mar. 1900. The minutes of this meeting are among both the Bennion papers, BYU library, and the George Albert Smith papers, University of Utah library, hereafter GAS. Another explanation has also been attributed to Brigham Young, though indirectly, "to the effect that [Negroes] did not possess sufficient innate spiritual strength and capacity to endure the responsibility that always goes with the priesthood, and to successfully resist the powers of darkness that always oppose men who hold it; and that, were they to be clothed with it, evil agencies would harrass [sic] and torment them, frighten them with spiritual manifestations from a wrong source, and so destroy their rest and peace that the priesthood instead of being a blessing to them would be the reverse." *Liahona, The Elders' Journal*, 5 (1908): 1164-67.

92. *Journal of Discourses*, 2:142-43, 3 Dec. 1854. The prospects seemed equally remote in 1859 (*Journal of Discourses*, 7:290-91), and 1866 (*Journal of Discourses*, 11:272).

Mormonism's Negro Doctrine

93. From a speech to the high priests' quorum in Nauvoo, Sept. 1844. See Joseph Smith Hyde, *Orson Hyde* (Salt Lake City: pub. 1933), p. 56.

94. *The Seer*, 1 (April 1853): 54-56.

95. John S. Lindsay, writing in the *Mormon Tribune*, 23 Apr. 1870, on "The Origin of Races," attributed to "orthodox Mormonism" the teaching that "the black race are such as, at the time of the great warfare in heaven when Lucifer and his hosts were cast out, played an ignoble part, not evincing loyalty on the one hand, nor yet possessing sufficient courage to join with Satan and his band of rebels. To use a homely phrase, now current here, they were '*astraddle the fence*'...." T.B.H. Stenhouse reported essentially the same belief in 1873, attributing it to "the modern prophet." *The Rocky Mountain Saints* (New York: D. Appleton & Co., 1873), pp. 491-92.

96. Journal History, 25 Dec. 1869, citing "Wilford Woodruff's Journal."

97. *Journal of Discourses*, 7:290-91 (9 Oct. 1859). A similar sentiment was implied in the 1852 address to the Utah legislature (see text and note 77), and was repeated on a number of other occasions: "Northern fanaticism [should learn]...that there is but little merit in...substituting their own kindred spirit and flesh to perform the offices allotted by superior wisdom to the descendants of Cain..." Whites, he went on, "should tread the theater of life and action, in a higher sphere," in *Millennial Star*, 15 (July 2, 1853): 422; or, "In the providences of God their ability is such that they cannot rise above the position of a servant, and they are willing to serve me and have me dictate their labor..."; *Journal of Discourses*, 10:190. Not unexpectedly, Utah joined most of the nation in excluding free Negroes from the right to vote or hold office; blacks were also excluded from the Utah militia.

98. *Millennial Star*, editorial, 27 (28 Oct. 1865): 682-83; Brigham Young, Jr., was editor.

99. "From Caucasian to Negro," *Juvenile Instructor*, 3 (1868): 142. The author continues, "The Negro is described as having a black skin, black, woolly hair, projecting jaws, thick lips, a flat nose and receding skull. He is generally well made and robust; but with very large hands and feet. In fact, he looks as though he had been put in an oven and burnt to a cinder before he was properly finished making. His hair baked crisp, his nose melted to his face, and the color of his eyes runs into the whites. Some men look as if they had only been burned brown; but he appears to have gone a stage further, and been cooked until he was quite black." The excerpt is from a series of seven articles, "Man and his Varieties," by "G.R.," which presented an interesting combination of Mormon concepts and nineteenth-century science. Though the author rejects the chain of being, he is willing to rank the races of men with the Caucasian at the top, and the Negro at the bottom. Racial differences are attributed to "climate, variety of food,...modes of life,...combined with the results of the varied religions existing among men," and ("the greatest of all") "the blessing or curse of God." These factors

had led to such diversification since the days of Adam that a permanent race could not longer arise "from people so wide apart as the Anglo-Saxon and Negro ... [a]nd further, ... it is proof of the mercy of God that no such race appears able to continue for many generations." (*Juvenile Instructor*, 3, [1868]: 165).

100. Reference has already been made to the Book of Mormon, and Book of Moses accounts (notes 24, 25, 28). Two contemporary interpretations: "... a black skin ... has ever been a curse that has followed an apostate of the holy priesthood, as well as a black heart ..." (*Times & Seasons*, 6 [1 Apr. 1845]: 857); "we must come to the conclusion that it is not climate alone that has made the Negro what he is [referring to skin color], but must ascribe it to the reason already given: that it is the result of the race suffering the displeasure of Heaven." (*Juvenile Instructor*, 3 [1868]: 166). Brigham Young was equally specific, "Why are so many inhabitants of the earth cursed with a [skin] of blackness? It comes in consequence of their fathers rejecting the power of the Holy Priesthood, and the law of God." (*Journal of Discourses*, 11:272).

101. As late as 1891, "Editorial Thoughts" in the *Juvenile Instructor* (26:635-36) could observe, "It has been noticed in our day that men who have lost the spirit of the Lord, and from whom His blessings have been withdrawn, have turned dark to such an extent as to excite the comments of all who have known them...." More recently, Hugh Nibley has concluded that the "blackness" of the Book of Mormon groups was symbolic, though again he has not referred to the Negro doctrine. See *Since Cumorah* (Salt Lake City: Deseret Book Co., 1967), pp. 246-51.

102. John Campbell (Philadelphia: 1851). The copy from President Young's office is now in the DeGolyer Foundation Library, Southern Methodist University, Dallas, Texas.

103. In addition to the references cited in notes 22 and 23, see also, William Stanton, *The Leopard's Spots: Scientific Attitudes Toward Race in America, 1815-59* (Chicago: University of Chicago Press, 1960); John S. Haller, Jr., *Outcasts from Evolution: Scientific Attitudes of Racial Inferiority, 1859-1900* (Urbana: University of Illinois Press, 1971); and George W. Stocking, Jr., *Race, Culture, and Evolution: Essays in the History of Anthropology* (New York: The Free Press, 1968).

104. Spelling as in original. See Journal History, 29 May 1847. The account originated with William Clayton, official recorder for the 1847 crossing, and is also to be found in Howard Egan's Diary, *Pioneering the West 1846 to 1878* (Richmond, Utah: Howard R. Egan Estate, 1917), p. 57, as well as in various editions of the *Clayton Journal* .

105. *Journal of Discourses*, 3:235, 2 Mar. 1856.

106. For expressions of this sentiment from Young, Kimball, Woodruff,

Hyde, and others, see *Journal of Discourses*, 8:322-24; 9:54-55; 10:15, 46; 12:119-20; and *Millennial Star*, 23:60, 100, 401; 25:540, 805. As to the specific culprits, Young observed in 1864, "The Abolitionists—the same people who interfered with our institutions, and drove us out into the wilderness— interfered with the Southern institutions, till they broke up the Union. But it's all coming out right,—a great deal better than we could have arranged it for ourselves. The men who flee from Abolitionist oppression come out here to our ark of refuge and people the asylum of God's chosen...." See Fitz-Hugh Ludlow, "Among the Mormons," *Atlantic Monthly*, 13 (April 1864): 489.

107. *Journal of Discourses*, 7:290-91, 9 Oct. 1859.

108. Ibid., 10:250, 6 Oct. 1863. For a Mormon view of the Proclamation, see *Millennial Star*, 25:97-101.

109. I am unaware of any published study of Mormon expectations in the Civil War; my understanding derives in part from the following references from Brigham Young, Kimball, Taylor, Hyde, Pratt, and others: *Journal of Discourses*, 5:219; 8:322-24; 9:5, 7, 142-43; 11:26, 38, 106, 154; and *Millennial Star*, 23:52, 300, 396; 24:158, 456; 25:540; 26:836; 27:204-5; as well as *Deseret News*, 10 July, 1861; 26 Mar. 1862. Boyd L. Eddins, "The Mormons and the Civil War" (M.A. thesis, Utah State University, 1966), deals with this question to some extent. Fitz-Hugh Ludlow, "Among the Mormons," p. 489, reported after a visit to Utah in early 1864, "I discovered, that, without a single exception, all the saints were inoculated with a prodigious craze, to the effect that the United States was to become a blighted chaos, and its inhabitants Mormon proselytes and citizens of Utah within the next two years—the more sanguine said, "next summer."

110. Orson Pratt, *Millennial Star*, 28:518. Pratt held the same opinion five years later, in 1871 (*Journal of Discourses*, 14:275).

111. *Journal of Discourses*, 11:269 (19 Aug. 1866). The preceding year, Heber Kimball reviewed the situation, and came to a similar conclusion: "'Thou shalt not interfere with thy neighbor's wife, nor his daughter, his house, nor his man servant, nor his maid servant.' Christ said this; but our enemies don't believe it. That was the trouble between the North and the South. The Abolitionists of the North stole the niggers and caused it all. The nigger was well off and happy. How do you know this, Brother Heber? Why, God bless your soul, I used to live in the South, and I know! Now they have set the nigger free; and a beautiful thing they have done for him, haven't they?" From a talk 24 Sept. 1865, reported in the *New York Daily Tribune*, 10 Nov. 1865, p. 8. In fact, while Brigham Young had believed that Negroes were justifiably condemned to servitude, he had also spoken out repeatedly against the abuses of slavery and encouraged slaveowners to treat the blacks "like servants, and not like brutes." (See *Journal of Discourses*, 1:69; 2:184; 10:111, 190, 250.) Even so, President Young's view of states' rights led him to conclude, "If we treated our slaves in an oppressive manner," it would still be

"none of [the] business" of the President or Congress, and "they ought not to meddle with it" (*Journal of Discourses*, 4:39-40).

112. Brigham Young wrote Thomas Kane in 1869 that the constitution of the State of Deseret had been amended 4 Feb. 1867, to eliminate the words "free, white, male" from voting requirements by a vote of "14,000 for, & 30 against." (26 Oct. 1869, in Brigham Young papers, LDS Church Archives.)

III

113. John Nuttall Journal 1 (1876-84): 290-93, Typescript, BYU library. The interview took place 31 May 1879. A corrected copy of the account is included in the minutes of the council meeting of 4 June 1879 in the Bennion papers.

114. Minutes of the Council of Twelve, 4 June 1879 in the Bennion papers. An extensive excerpt from these minutes has been included in note 29. This subject had been discussed the previous week, 28 May 1879, though the minutes of that meeting are not among the Bennion or the George Albert Smith papers.

115. Ibid

116. Though not theoretically synonymous, temple marriages or sealings were generally equated with Mormon plural marriages, and thus the former received considerable attention in the years prior to the Manifesto. Angus M. Cannon, one-time Salt Lake Temple president, in denouncing the candidacy of a man who "has not the courage" to live up to gospel principles, observed: "I had rather see a colored man, who is my friend here, sent to Washington, because he is not capable of receiving the priesthood, and can never reach the highest celestial glory of the kingdom of God. This colored man could go and stand upon the floor of Congress as the peer of every man, there, and would be able to say conscientiously that he had not accepted the doctrine of plurality , because he could not . . ." *Salt Lake Tribune*, 5 Oct. 1884. Several years later the Church received national publicity when a patriarch speaking at a funeral remarked that as Elijah Abel was the only Negro to have received the Melchizedek priesthood, he was the only one of "his race who ever succeeded in gaining entrance within the pearly gates." The report, from the hostile *Tribune* (1 Nov. 1903) was probably inaccurate in some parts. Nonetheless, when the story was picked up by Eastern papers, the Church felt it necessary to issue denials on two occasions through the *Deseret News*. In both cases, however, the editors avoided comment on the subtlety of Mormon theology which allowed the belief that a Negro could go to heaven as part of his "salvation" but could not attain the highest degree of glory therein ("exaltation") because of the priesthood restriction. See *Deseret News*, "Salvation for the Negro," 28 Nov. 1903; and "Negroes and Heaven," 17 Dec. 1903, both included in the *Journal History* for those dates.

117. In practice Negro women would have been excluded from sealings

regardless, as the husband would not have held the priesthood. However, many single women have received their endowments. Later the blacks were described as ineligible for the "blessings of the Priesthood," an expression encompassing the priesthood and temple restrictions, but somehow without reference to the other ordinances requiring the priesthood for which the Negroes were eligible.

118. See Council Meeting minutes, 26 Aug. 1908, Bennion papers (or GAS papers).

119. Ibid

120. See Council Meeting minutes, 4 June 1879, Bennion papers.

121. Recounted in Council Minutes, 2 Jan. 1902, Bennion papers (or GAS papers).

122. Jenson, *Biographical Encyclopedia*, 3:577. While on his mission, Abel reportedly "was not authorized to confer... the holy priesthood...";. First Presidency letter to David McKay, 16 Mar. 1904.

123. Council Minutes 22 Aug. 1895, Bennion (and GAS) papers. On this occasion Joseph F. Smith stated that Abel "had been ordained a Seventy and afterwards a High Priest." I have found no evidence for the latter claim. A previous appeal to Wilford Woodruff by "Aunt Jane" was reported in Cowley, *Wilford Woodruff*, p. 587. An appeal to John Taylor is recorded in the "Gardo House Office Journal" for 20 Mar. 1883, included in the Bennion papers. Jane James's appeal to Wilford Woodruff in 1895 was denied, but she was later offered a remarkable alternative to her desires. George Q. Cannon, First Counselor to Woodruff, suggested that while she was not eligible for the traditional ceremonies, a special temple ceremony might be prepared—to adopt her into the family of Joseph Smith "as a servant" (she having been the Prophet's housekeeper). With the approval of President Woodruff this was done, and Jane James thereby became the first black knowingly allowed into the Mormon temple since Elijah Abel had been anointed in Kirtland, Ohio, nearly fifty years before. This special dispensation was not so major a concession as it may appear, as true "exaltation" was still impossible without the traditional ordinances. This fact was not lost on Sister James; and though she was apparently satisfied for a time, she shortly renewed her plea to participate in the regular temple ceremonies. See Council minutes for 2 Jan. 1902, and 26 Aug. 1908, in Bennion (or GAS) papers.

124. Council minutes, 22 Aug. 1895, Bennion (or GAS) papers.

125. Council minutes, 11 Mar. 1900, Bennion (or GAS) papers. Cannon had joined the Church in 1840 but was not ordained an apostle until sixteen years after the Prophet's death, in 1860.

126. Council minutes, dated 16 Dec. 1897 in Bennion papers (dated 15 Dec. 1897 in the GAS papers). During Taylor's presidency, 8 Mar. 1888, Utah

passed an anti-miscegenation law prohibiting marriages between a "negro" or "mongolian" and a "white person."

127. "Shall I tell you the law of God in regard to the African race? If the white man who belongs to the chosen seed mixes his blood with the seed of Cain, the penalty, under the law of God is death on the spot." Brigham Young, 8 March 1963 (*Journal of Discourses* 10:110); see also Young's address to the legislature, 16 Jan. 1852, in Wilford Woodruff's Journal for a more graphic discussion. Most of Young's discussions of the curse on Cain emphasized that it would not be lifted until all of the "other children of Adam" had received their entitlement.

128. Council minutes, 18 Aug. 1900, Bennion (or GAS) papers. Cannon was then First Counselor to Snow.

129. Council minutes, 22 Aug. 1895, Bennion (or GAS) papers. By 1908 this policy had been reversed, and a temple sealing was approved in a comparable case.

130. Council minutes, 16 Dec. 1897, Bennion papers. See also note 123.

131. *Journal History*, 13 Feb. 1849, for the original inquiry; Council minutes of 11 Mar. 1900 reveals the question in Snow's mind as to the author of the policy. There are two versions of these minutes which should be compared. The Bennion and GAS papers have virtually identical accounts, but George F. Gibbs, secretary to the First Presidency, reported a slightly different version in a private letter to John M. Whitaker, 18 Jan. 1909 (Whitaker papers, University of Utah library). The latter account suggests that Snow believed the explanation of the policy could have been based on the "personal views" of Brigham Young.

132. Council minutes 2 Jan. 1902, Bennion (or GAS) papers.

133. Council minutes, 26 Aug. 1908, Bennion (or GAS) papers. A more extensive excerpt: "In this connection President Smith referred to Elijah Abel, who was ordained a Seventy by Joseph Young, in the days of the Prophet Joseph, to whom Brother Young issued a Seventies certificate; but this ordination was declared null and void by the Prophet himself. Later Brother Abel appealed to President Young for the privilege of receiving his endowments and to have his wife and children sealed to him, a privilege President Young could not grant. Brother Abel renewed his application to President Taylor with the same result; and still the same appeal was made to President Woodruff afterwards who of course upheld the position taken by Presidents Young and Taylor...." Compare this with Smith's earliest account, quoted in note 29.

134. In addition to George Q. Cannon, Apostle Franklin D. Richards had also attributed Church policy ultimately to Joseph Smith (Journal History, 5 Oct. 1896). Richards, who joined the Church in 1838, was ordained an apostle in 1849; there is no indication from his remarks that he was claiming

first-hand information. Joseph Smith's history was also published about this time, and it contained the lone direct quote by the Prophet relating the Negro to Cain [but] without reference to the priesthood; (*History of the Church,* 4:501).

135. *Improvement Era,* 11:465-66, as quoted in *Gospel Doctrine,* vol. 1, pp. 234-45, the Melchizedek Priesthood Quorum Manual, 1970-71. President Smith allowed for an alternative which appears more applicable to the situation he described in the Council Meeting: "To prevent a person, for cause, from exercising the rights and privileges of acting in the offices of the priesthood may be and has been done, and the person so silenced still remains a member of the Church, but this does not take away from him any priesthood that he held."

136. First Presidency letter from Joseph F. Smith, Anthon H. Lund, and Charles W. Penrose to Milton H. Knudson, 13 Jan. 1912, Bennion papers. The Presidency wrote "The Prophet Joseph Smith is said to have explained it in this way...", Cannon was not referenced, and the statement on miscegenation was deleted. A question remains as to the specific timing of these developments. Though Joseph F. Smith is not known to have "explained" the situation with Elijah Abel prior to 1908, he had accepted Joseph Smith as the original author of the priesthood policy at least as early as 1904. That year the First Presidency wrote, without reference: "the Prophet Joseph taught the doctrine in his day that the seed of Cain would not receive the priesthood..." (Letter to David McKay, 16 Mar. 1904, copy in my possession).

137. "The Negro and the Priesthood," *Improvement Era,* 27 (April 1924): 564-65.

138. *The Contributor,* 6:296-97; Roberts's italics. Erastus Snow in 1880 discussed the priesthood restriction on the descendants of Cain and the passage of the curse through the Flood in a manner suggestive of the Pearl of Great Price account, but he does not present nearly so developed a case as Roberts. His explanation was attributed to revelation ("as revelation teaches"), which presumably referred to the Book of Abraham, as no other "revelation" has ever been cited on the subject (*Journal of Discourses,* 21:370).

139. *Juvenile Instructor,* 26 (15 Oct. 1891): 635-36.

140. Council minutes for 11 Mar. 1900, and 18 Aug. 1900, both in Bennion (or GAS) papers. In the latter meeting, "President Cannon read from the Pearl of Great Price showing that negroes were debarred from the priesthood...."

141. "Are Negroes Children of Adam?" *Millennial Star* 65 (3 Dec. 1903): 776-78.

142. "The Negro and the Priesthood," *Liahona, The Elder's Journal* 5 (18 Apr. 1908) 1164-7.

143. E.g., Council minutes, 26 Aug. 1908; letter from Joseph F. Smith and Anthon H. Lund to Rudger Clawson, 18 Nov. 1910, both in Bennion papers.

144. Letter of 13 Jan. 1912, from Joseph F. Smith, Anthon H. Lund, and Charles W. Penrose, to Milton H. Knudson, in the Bennion papers. A similar sentiment was included in another letter, dated 1 May 1912, to Ben E. Rich (Bennion papers), "The Pearl of Great Price gives particulars on this point that are very pertinent to the subject (See Abr. 1:21-27). These texts show that while men of the negro race may be blessed of the Lord both temporally and spiritually... yet they are not eligible to the Priesthood." Orson Whitney also included the Pearl of Great Price explanation in his *Saturday Night Thoughts* on doctrine in 1921, and several years later Joseph Fielding Smith began his extensive discussions of the subject.

145. These first two statements were based on the Book of Moses, revealed to Joseph Smith in December 1830 and published August 1832. The remainder of the argument derives from the Book of Abraham which was first published in 1842. The two books were combined into the Pearl of Great Price in 1851.

146. The specific verses most widely cited:

> "Cain rose up against Abel, his brother, and slew him." (Moses 5:32; Gen. 4:8); "And I the Lord set a mark upon Cain..." (Moses 5:40; Gen. 4:15); "the seed of Cain were black" (Moses 7:22); "the people of Canaan... shall go forth in battle array..." (Moses 7:7); "a blackness came upon all the children of Canaan" (Moses 7:8); "Egypt being first discovered by a woman, who was the daughter of Ham, and the daughter of Egyptus" (Abr. 1:23); "Pharaoh, the eldest son of Egyptus, the daughter of Ham" (Abr. 1:25); "the king of Egypt was a descendant from the loins of Ham, and was a partaker of the blood of the Canaanites by birth" (Abr. 1:25); "and thus the blood of the Canaanites was preserved in the land" (Abr. 1:22); "and... from Ham, sprang the race which preserved the curse in the land" (Abr. 1:24); "[Pharaoh was] cursed... as pertaining to the priesthood" (Abr. 1:26).

The "complete" version of the Pearl of Great Price argument can be found in published sources after 1903 (e.g., *Millennial Star*, 65:776-78) and can be pieced together from earlier discussions after 1884.

147. The term *Canaan* or *Canaanite* appears six times in the book of Abraham. The first two are the well-known, "Now this king of Egypt was a descendant from the loins of Ham, and was a partaker of the blood of the Canaanites by birth. From this descent sprang all the Egyptians, and thus the blood of the Canaanites was preserved in the land" (Abr. 1:21-22). In the third instance Abraham records, "Therefore I left the land of Ur, of the Chaldees, to go into the land of Canaan..." (Abr. 2:4). The remaining three references also speak of this land, "I... came forth in the way to the land of Canaan..."; "As we journeyed... to come to the land of Canaan...";

"...and we had already come into the borders of the land of the Canaan-ites,... the land of this idolatrous nation" (Abr. 2:15-16, 18). The last four of these references relate ultimately to the son of Ham, Canaan, and the people traditionally descended from him. Except for its convenient use in the priest-hood argument, there is no apparent reason for relating the first two uses of "Canaanite" to a different group by the same name who lived before the Flood, and who were not otherwise mentioned by Abraham. Another particu-larly weak point in the Pearl of Great Price argument is the importance which must be attributed to the spellings of *Cainan* and *Canaan*. Not only is it essential that there be separate antediluvian and post-flood "Canaans," but more importantly a clear distinction must be maintained between the "good" people and land of "Cainan" from whence came the prophet Enoch and the "bad" people of "Canaan" incorporated into the cursed lineage. The spellings in the current Pearl of Great Price are consistent and permit a distinction to be made. However, previously published versions and the original manuscripts on which these were based demonstrate that there is a significant question about the correctness of the present spellings. Variations were evident throughout the nineteenth century (which explains the frequent "incorrect" spellings found in the Council minutes during that time), and the earliest manuscripts suggest that Enoch may well have come from the land of "Canaan." While it is not practical to include a full discussion of this problem at present, it should be clear that the history of these works seri-ously undermines any argument based on a particular spelling being correct. See Richard P. Howard, "Variants in the Spelling of Canaan (Cainan) in the Original Manuscripts of the 'Inspired Version' of the Bible, as found in Genesis, Chapters 6 and 7," typescript, Library-Archives, Reorganized Church of Jesus Christ of Latter Day Saints, Independence, Missouri, or my own unpublished "Compilation on the Negro in Mormonism," Appendix I, HBL Library Special Collections, BYU.

148. The correlation surely was apparent much earlier. Orson Pratt seems to have had reference to the Book of Abraham in 1853 when he wrote, "...African negroes or [those] in the lineage of Canaan whose descendants were cursed, pertaining to the priesthood" (*The Seer*, 1:56). Similarly, the *Juvenile Instructor* series on "Man and His Varieties" in 1868 included in the section on "The Negro Race" the comment, "We are told in the Book of Abraham...that Egypt was first discovered by a woman, who was a daugh-ter of Ham, the son of Noah. This was probably the first portion of Africa inhabited after the flood." See also note 138.

149. "The Negro and the Priesthood," *Liahona, The Elders' Journal*, 5 (1908): 1164-67.

150. *Journal of Discourses*, 20:310-13 (6 Oct. 1879). Three years later Erastus Snow carried this sentiment one step further: "The extreme excesses perpetrated under [the system of slavery in the Southern States], in many particulars, were very great wrongs to mankind, and very grievous in the

sight of heaven and of right-thinking people. And changes were determined in the mind of Jehovah, and have been affected . . . " (*Journal of Discourses*, 23:294, 8 Oct. 1882). Though Joseph Smith's "Views" in opposition to slavery had been dropped rather quickly after his death, they were resurrected during the Civil War at a time when the Union was considered "hopelessly and irremediably broken" with the suggestion that the rejection of the Prophet's plan was in part responsible for the current state of affairs (*Millennial Star*, 25 [14 Feb. 1863]: 97-101). After the death of Brigham Young the "Views" were cited more frequently. Erastus Snow, for instance, referred to the proposals on slavery on two occasions in 1882, as "the voice of the Lord through the Prophet Joseph Smith." (*Journal of Discourses*, 23:91) and as "the true policy and counsel of heaven to our nation" (ibid, 23:296-97).

151. ". . . disenfranchisement of a class, on the ground that it is not entitled to human rights because of the color of the skin, cannot be justified by any arguments from the Scriptures." See "The Colored Races," *Deseret Evening News*, 14 Mar. 1908, in Journal History of this date; also, the earlier editorials, e.g., "Status of the Negro," 17 May 1900; "Political Rights of Negroes," 8 May 1903; "The Negro Problem," 9 Sept. 1903.

152. Frank H. Eastmond, "Slavery and Apostacy," *Millennial Star*, 76 (23 Apr. 1914): 269-71.

153. "The Negro Problem," editorial, 12 May 1903. The editor quoted at length the "pertinent remarks" from a Southerner who said, in part, "I cannot say that I believe in the doctrine 'that education ruins the negro,' for while it may unfit him in a sense for being a hewer of wood and a drawer of water, it should, if education means anything, force him to an intellectual condition wherein he should more firmly realize his position and recognize the inherent restrictions of his race in regard to the social conditions of mankind." Similarly, the *News*, some fifteen years earlier, had reported a projection of Negro population growth that would have reached 96,000,000 in 1960, and observed that it "is not cheering to Anglo-Saxons to contemplate subjugation to the African race. "Two years later the projections had proved ill-founded, and the *News* reported that the Negro "forebodes no numerical danger to the country." (4 Jan. 1888; 22 July 1891, both included in the Journal History).

154. William Benjamin Smith, *The Color Line*. The thesis of this author was that social equality would lead to intermarriage, and "that the comingling of inferior with superior must lower the higher is just as certain as that the half-sum of two and six is four." The quotation was included in B. H. Roberts, *Seventy's Course in Theology, First Year*, Outline History of the Seventy and A Survey of the Books of Holy Scripture (Salt Lake City: Deseret Book, 1907, reprinted 1931).

155. *Times and Seasons*, 6 (1 Apr. 1845): 857. With other Mormon leaders, Taylor had denounced both "Southern fire-eaters" and "rabid abolitionists" in the days before the Civil War, but his less restrained remarks were more

often directed at the latter, with whom he had greater familiarity. Horace Greeley, for instance, was "a great man to talk about higher law, which means, with him, stealing niggers ... they need not be afraid of our stealing their niggers ..." (*Journal of Discourses*, 5:157; see also *Journal of Discourses*, 5:119).

156. E.g., *Journal of Discourses*, 18:200; 22:304.

157. Ibid, 22:302, 28 Aug. 1881; 23:336, 29 Oct. 1882. There is some basis for this idea in remarks delivered by Brigham Young to the Utah Territorial Legislature, 16 Jan. 1852, recorded in Wilford Woodruff's diary of that date.

158. Conference address, 7 Apr. 1887, reported in *Millennial Star*, 51:339.

159. Cowley, *Wilford Woodruff*, p. 587, from Wilford Woodruff's journal.

160. The question, posed to Brigham Young, was made the day after Snow was ordained an apostle. Journal History, 13 Feb. 1849.

161. Council minutes, 16 Dec. 1897, in Bennion papers.

162. E.g., Council minutes, 11 Mar. 1900, in Bennion (or GAS) papers.

163. Council minutes, 26 Aug. 1908, in Bennion (or GAS) papers.

164. For comparison, the state of Virginia extended its legal definition of "a colored person" in 1910, to include "every person having one-sixteenth or more of negro blood," and further, in 1930, to include "every person in whom there is ascertainable any negro blood." Woodward, *In His Image*, p. 86, reports that the 1930 Federal census enumerators were instructed to count as Negroes any person of mixed blood, "no matter how small the percentage of Negro blood." For another indication of Apostle John Henry Smith's different perspective on race, see Carter, *Negro Pioneer*, p. 57.

165. Council minutes, 11 Mar. 1900, in Bennion (or GAS) papers.

166. Council minutes, 2 Jan. 1902, in Bennion (or GAS) papers. The "doctrine" described had actually provided a theoretical model which should have allowed people with Negro ancestry to be ordained to the priesthood. Brigham Young had taught that not only could an individual "extract all of the blood" of a particular lineage from his parents, but that it was also possible for such a lineage to be "purged" from the individual's blood: "Can you make a Christian of a Jew? I tell you, nay. If a Jew comes into this Church, and honestly professes to be a Saint, a follower of Christ, and if the blood of Judah is in his veins, he will apostatize. He may have been born and bred a Jew, speak the language of the Jews, and have attended to all the ceremonies of the Jewish religion, and have openly professed to be a Jew all his days; but I will tell you a secret—there is not a particle of the blood of Judaism in him, if he has become a true Christian, a Saint of God; for if there is, he will most assuredly leave the Church of Christ, or that blood will be purged out of his veins. We have men among us who were Jews, and became converted from Judaism. For instance, here is Brother Neibaur; do I

believe there is one particle of the blood of Judah in his veins? No, not so much as could be seen on the point of the finest cambric needle, through a microscope with a magnifying power of two millions..." (*Journal of Discourses*, 2:143; 11:279). Presumably a negro would have been susceptible to a similar purge of the blood of Cain.

167. "Extract from George F. Richards' Record of Decisions by the Council of the First Presidency and the Twelve Apostles," in the GAS papers. The entry is not dated; the following entry was from 8 Feb. 1907. Compare note 164. In 1913 Dr. Booker T. Washington delivered an address at the University of Utah, attended by "practically every one of the General Authorities." Afterwards Bishop John Whitaker asked Washington, in a private conversation, "If perchance under discussion on some negro problem the question arose as to how a negro would vote if only one drop of negro blood run [sic] in his veins which way would that drop of blood vote on a question, white or black?" Whitaker writes, "Without hesitation he said, 'If there was one drop of blood in a person and such a question arose, it would always vote with the negro.' I was struck with his ready answer, showing he had thought out almost every conceivable connection [between] white and black. And I have been told that pure white blood through intermarriage with any other blood runs out in four generations. I am told that negro blood will persist up to eight generations. There seems to be something in that accursed blood that will not yield to white blood..." (John M. Whitaker, Daily Journal, 27 Mar. 1913, University of Utah library).

168. It is surprising that this idea has not appeared in the explanations of how the "pure" Negro lineage was transmitted through the Flood. See note 27.

169. The millennialist expectations at that time lent a certain urgency to the call of the Church to carry the gospel to every nation, kindred, tongue, and people. As the Civil War approached, the universal obligation came to be viewed more symbolically. Wilford Woodruff, in 1855, observed that "we have preached... in France, Italy, Germany, and the States of the German Confederacy; and it has been preached in the British Isles, in North and South America, and the Society and Sandwich Islands, and to China, and we have even sent them to the dark regions of Asia and Africa... two of our brethren... have been to those countries. Chauncey West has been through that country... he has cleared his skirts of those people among whom he travelled, and he has cleared this people, for they have been commanded to preach this Gospel to all the nations of the earth." (*Journal of Discourses*, 9:226). Three years later the missionaries were recalled from abroad as Johnston's army moved on Utah. At this time Orson Pratt wrote, "Now, the Lord moves upon the hearts of the First Presidency to say... 'It is enough: come home. Your testimony is sufficient.'" (*Journal of Discourses*, 6:201). By 1860, Brigham Young could say that "my brethren have said enough to

warn the whole world. This frees our garments." (*Journal of Discourses*, 8:147).

170. Council minutes, 26 Aug. 1908, in Bennion (or GAS) papers. Anthon H. Lund, writing "on behalf of First Presidency," had given the same advice the previous month. Letter of 11 July 1908 to H. L. Steed in my possession. A remarkably different philosophy had been developed at length in a *Deseret Evening News* editorial just five months before: ". . . And how do we know that the disciples of the Apostles did not go both to China and to the interior of Africa? To assert that they did not do so, should not be done without sufficient evidence. There is no reason to believe, against tradition that their labors were confined to the Mediterranean coast lands . . . But, without going any further into this, it seems to us that the commission given by the Lord to His Apostles embraced every human being. For He commissioned them to preach the gospel to 'every creature.' If that means anything, it means that neither color, nor ignorance, nor degeneration is a bar to salvation. No one is so black that he is not one of God's creatures." ("The Colored Races," 14 Mar. 1908).

171. Letter from B. A. Hendricks reported in Council minutes, 10 Nov. 1910, in Bennion (or GAS) papers. Hendricks described the blacks as "good honest people."

172. Letter from Joseph F. Smith and Anthon Lund, 18 Nov. 1910, in Bennion papers. They continued, "But at the same time where honest-hearted Negroes who perchance hear the gospel preached, become pricked in their hearts and ask for baptism, it would not be becoming in us to refuse to administer that ordinance in their behalf." A decade prior, George Q. Cannon had made a point of the fact that "Enoch in his day called upon all people to repent save it were the descendants of Cainan [sic]"; Council minutes, 18 Aug. 1900, in Bennion (or GAS papers).

173. President Smith's remark is found in the Council minutes, 10 Nov. 1910. The mission president was informed via a letter from Joseph F. Smith and Anthon H. Lund to Rudger Clawson, 18 Nov. 1910, both among the Bennion papers. The letter continued, "But in thus answering we do not wish President Hendricks [of the South African Mission] or his successors in office to encourage the Negro saints of South Africa to emigrate to Zion in order that they may be in a position to do temple work." Nor did they wish a gathering to be preached to the whites.

174. First Presidency letter from Joseph F. Smith, Lund, and Charles Penrose, to M. Knudson, 13 Jan. 1912, in Bennion papers. The letter also reported that "there is no written revelation going to show why the negroes are ineligible to hold the priesthood, the Prophet Joseph Smith is said to have explained." See notes 124, 136, and text.

175. First Presidency letter from Smith, Lund, and Penrose, to Ben Rich,

1 May 1912, in Bennion papers. The suggestion that negroes had been committed to Cain's lineage in the preexistence and were perhaps electively remaining in that line attributed by Lorenzo Snow to Brigham Young (see note 91 and text) had not necessarily implied a "neutral" performance on their part. See Matthias Cowley's account of Snow's belief to this effect, reported in a talk at the L.D.S. University Branch, Chicago, 4 Oct. 1925, typescript, LDS Church Archives.

IV

176. See, for example, letters of Heber J. Grant to H. L. Wilkin, 28 Jan. 1928; of Grant, Anthony W. Ivins, and Charles W. Nibley to Don Mack Dalton, 29 Nov. 1929; of Grant, J. Reuben Clark, Jr., and David O. McKay to Graham Doxey, 9 Feb. 1945; and of George Albert Smith, Clark, and McKay to Francis W. Brown, 13 Jan. 1947; and of Smith, Clark, and McKay to Virgil H. Sponberg, 5 May 1947; all found among the Bennion papers.

177. In 1947 the First Presidency wrote, "The rule of the Church as heretofore followed has been set forth by the early Church leaders. You will find a discussion thereof in Brother Joseph Fielding Smith's book, 'The Way to Perfection,' chapter 16." Letter of 13 Jan 1947 to Francis Brown, Bennion papers.

178. Joseph Fielding Smith, *The Way to Perfection* (1931; reprinted ed., Salt Lake City: Deseret Book Co., 1970), pp. 103, 111. Smith deals directly with the Negro doctrine in Chapters 7, 15, and 16. He had previously published two short articles on the subject, "The Negro and the Priesthood," *Improvement Era*, 27 (April 1924): 564-65 and "Salvation for the Dead," *Utah Genealogical and Historical Magazine*, 17 (1926): 154.

179. Smith quoted Brigham Young's statement on neutrality and would also have been aware of his father's opinion as he was an apostle when Joseph F. Smith expressed himself on the subject. *The Way to Perfection* also included Roberts' *Contributor* article. More recently, Orson Whitney had dealt with the related problem of a curse on Canaan, and "the unsolved problem of the punishment of a whole race for an offense committed by one of its ancestors." He concluded, "It seems reasonable to infer that there was a larger cause, that the sin in question was not the main issue. Tradition has handed down something to that effect, but nothing conclusive on the question is to be found in the standard works of the Church. Of one thing we may rest assured: Canaan was not unjustly cursed, nor were the spirits who came through his lineage wrongly assigned. 'Whatsoever a man soweth, that shall he also reap.' Or, putting it inversely: Whatsoever a man reaps, that hath he sown. This rule applies to spirit life, as well as to life in the flesh." *Cowley & Whitney on Doctrine* (Salt Lake City Bookcraft, 1963), pp. 313-14, from a series of articles by Whitney written in 1918-1919.

180. *The Way to Perfection*, p. 43. For Smith the restrictions extended beyond the priesthood policy—Cain "because of his wickedness... became the father of an inferior race..." (p. 101).

181. Ibid., pp. 43-44, 105-6. Since the argument was being advanced that blacks were coming from their "sin" in the preexistence to a penalty in this life, it is not exactly clear how the term "innocent" is being applied. Smith references *Doctrine and Covenants* 93:38.

182. Ibid., pp. 43-44.

183. A representative progression: "it is highly probable" (Orson Pratt, 1853); "It seems reasonable to infer" (Orson Hyde, 1918-19); "It is a reasonable thing to believe..." (Joseph Fielding Smith, 1924); "few will doubt" (Joseph Fielding Smith, 1931); "it is very probable that in some way, unknown to us, the distinction..." (Joseph Widstoe, 1944); "Is it not just as reasonable to assume" (Harold B. Lee, 1945); "Your position seems to lose sight of the revelation of the Lord touching the preexistence of our spirits, the rebellion in heaven, and the doctrine that our birth in this life and the advantages under which we may be born, have a relationship in the life heretofore" (First Presidency, 1947); "Accepting this theory of life, we have a reasonable explanation of existent conditions in the habitations of man" (David O. McKay, 1947); "Under this principle there is no injustice whatsoever involved in this deprivation as to the holding of the priesthood by the Negroes" (First Presidency statement, 1949).

184. An extreme of a sort was achieved 28 Aug. 1947 when the Quorum upheld a decision by John Widtsoe denying a temple recommend to a "sister having one thirty-second of negro blood in her veins" (one black great-great-great grandparent). Widtsoe did question "whether in such cases the individual... might be recommended to the temple for marriage," but previous policy prevailed. Council minutes, 28 Aug. 1947, in Bennion papers. See note 164.

185. Council minutes, 29 Oct. 1936, Bennion papers. By 1950 at least sixteen such cases involving either the priesthood or admission to the temple had come to the attention of the Quorum or First Presidency, exclusive of such groups as those found in Brazil; additional cases are also reported from other sources.

186. Council minutes, 30 Jan. 1947, Bennion papers.

187. Ibid., 9 Oct. 1947.

188. See the "South African Mission Plan," Dec. 1951, pp. 45-46, LDS Church Archives.

189. Most Mormons associated the Polynesians with the Lamanites (e.g., *Juvenile Instructor* 3:145-46) rather than Cain or Ham; however, there were exceptions. See *Juvenile Instructor* 3:141-42, and *Dialogue* 2 (Autumn 1967). 8, letter from Gary Lobb.

190. First Presidency letter from George Albert Smith, Clark, and McKay, to Francis W. Brown, 13 Jan. 1947, Bennion papers.

191. See Wallace R. Bennett, "The Negro in Utah," *Utah Law Review*, Spring 1953; "Symposium on the Negro in Utah," held 20 Nov. 1954, by the Utah Academy of Sciences, Arts, and Letters, at Weber College; or David H. Oliver, *A Negro on Mormonism* (USA, Salt Lake City, D. H. Oliver 1963).

192. E.g., J. Reuben Clark, *Improvement Era* 49 (Aug. 1946): 492. "It is sought today in certain quarters to break down all race prejudice, and at the end of the road, which they who urge this see, is intermarriage. That is what it finally comes to. Now, you should hate nobody; you should give to every man and every woman, no matter what the color of his or her skin may be, full civil rights. You should treat them as brothers and sisters, but do not ever let that wicked virus get into your systems that brotherhood either permits or entitles you to mix races which are inconsistent." The following year Clark is also cited on this matter in a Council meeting. "President Clark called attention to the sentiment among many people in this country to the point that we should break down all racial lines, as a result of which sentiment negro people have acquired an assertiveness that they never before possessed and in some cases have become impudent." (Council minutes, 9 Oct. 1947, Bennion papers).

193. See Bennett, "Negro in Utah."

194. Letter from the First Presidency (Smith, Clark, McKay), 5 May 1947, to Virgil H. Sponberg, in Bennion papers.

195. See note 192; also Harold B. Lee's KSL address 6 May 1945, "Youth of a Noble Birthright," (Typescript in LDS Church Archives); and First Presidency letter of 17 July 1947, to Lowry Nelson, copy at the Brigham Young University library.

196. Of the three instances cited in note 195, Clark stated, "Biologically, it is wrong"; Lee invoked the "laws of heredity and the centuries of training"; and the First Presidency characterized intermarriage as "a concept which has heretofore been most repugnant to most normal-minded people." These arguments were, of course, secondary to the doctrinal objections. In 1939 Utah extended its anti-miscegenation statute to prohibit a "white" from marrying a "Mongolian, a member of the malay race or a mulatto, quadroon, or octoroon."

197. First Presidency letter (from Presidents Smith, Clark, and McKay) to Ezra T. Benson, 23 June 1942, in Bennion papers. A similar problem was resolved in 1936 by a branch president in Cincinnati, Ohio, by ruling that a "faithful" Negro family "could not come to Church meeting." See Mark E. Petersen, "Race Problems—As They Affect the Church," address delivered at Brigham Young University, 27 Aug. 1954, Typescript LDS Church Archives.

198. First Presidency letter (from Presidents Smith, Clark, and McKay) to Lowry Nelson 17 July 1947, copy at Brigham Young University library.

199. First Presidency statement, 17 Aug. 1949, copy at LDS Church Archives; also in Bennion papers, and elsewhere. William E. Berrett, in "The Church and the Negroid People," pp. 16-17, conveys the incorrect impression that this statement was issued in 1951; see Berrett's supplement to John J. Stewart, *Mormonism and the Negro* (Orem, Utah, Community Press, 1967).

200. Even with the genealogical advances having progressed to the point where several million men can be vicariously ordained in the temples each year, it will still require centuries to provide this opportunity for the billions of men who have been ineligible for the priesthood on other than racial grounds.

V

201. Conference address reported in the *Deseret News*, 6 Oct. 1963; a slightly different version appeared in the December 1963 *Improvement Era*. In March 1965, pressure was again brought to bear on the Church to issue a statement in conjunction with civil rights legislation then pending in Utah. After several hundred marchers demonstrated in front of Church offices, the *Deseret News* carried an editorial, "A Clear Civil Rights Stand," which reprinted Brown's remarks as a "concise statement given officially" on the subject, which was both "clear and unequivocal" (*Deseret News*, 9 March, 1965). Though Apostle Mark E. Petersen has been singled out for his extensive, unequivocally segregationist remarks in 1954 (see note 197), he had not strayed significantly from the sentiments expressed by other Church leaders in the preceding few years. Just three months before, the First Presidency had "directed" their secretary, Joseph Anderson, to respond to a correspondent, "that the Church is opposed on biological and other grounds, to intermarriage between whites and negroes, and that it discourages all social relationships and associations between the races, as among its members, that might lead to such marriages..." (Letter of 4 May, 1954, from Anderson to Chauncey D. Harris, copy in my possession). The presidency also believed that "all men, without regard to race or color" were entitled to "full civil rights and liberties, social, economic, and political, as provided in the Constitution and laws."

202. First Presidency statement, 15 Dec. 1969, "by Hugh B. Brown, N. Eldon Tanner" (*Church News*, 10 Jan. 1970, p. 12). President McKay, who was gravely ill at the time, died 18 Jan. 1970.

203. "Church to Open Missionary Work in Nigeria," *Deseret News*, 1 Jan. 1963.

204. As early as 1946, Council minutes report correspondence from Nigeria which "pleads for missionaries to be sent... and asks for literature regarding the Church." See Council minutes of 24 Oct. 1946, and 9 Oct. 1947, both in

Bennion papers. *Time* magazine ("The Black Saints of Nigeria," 18 June 1965) reported that Lamar Williams was sent to Nigeria in 1959 to investigate the situation; Henry D. Moyle appears to date this to 1961 in a talk late that year ("What of the Negro?," 30 Oct. 1961, copy at LDS Church Archives, though he seems to err in identifying the country involved as South Africa.

205. A Nigerian student attending school in California learned of the planned mission, and sent a copy of John J. Stewart's *Mormonism and the Negro* to the *Nigerian Outlook*, along with his analysis of Church beliefs on the negro. The *Outlook* published the letter, excerpts from the book, and an editorial, "Evil Saints," which demanded that the Mormons not be allowed into the country. See *Nigerian Outlook*, 5 Mar. 1963, photocopy at Brigham Young University library.

206. Information obtained largely in an interview with Lamar S. Williams, who had been set apart as the presiding elder over the Nigerian Mission. Two derivative groups of the original Church of Jesus Christ of Latter Day Saints, both of whom ordain blacks to the priesthood, have also been involved with Nigerian "Mormons." The Church of Jesus Christ (Monongahela, Pennsylvania), who trace their origins to William Bickerton and Sidney Rigdon and accept the Book of Mormon, have had a mission to Nigeria for nearly twenty years. The Reorganized Church of Jesus Christ of Latter Day Saints also opened a mission to Nigeria in the mid-sixties. Both groups have ordained Nigerian elders.

207. Information obtained from a principal in the case who had interceded on behalf of the person involved (the latter previously had been denied the priesthood because of his black ancestry).

208. Information obtained from a former temple president who possesses a copy of the authorization signed by President McKay.

209. This point was made public by President Harold B. Lee, in an interview reported in the *Salt Lake Tribune*, 24 Sept. 1972, which reported, "President Lee said skin color is not what keeps the Negro from the priesthood. It [is] strictly a matter of lineage and involves only African Negroes. In comparison, he noted, dark or black islanders, such as Fijians, Tongans, Samoans, or Maoris, are all permitted full rights to the priesthood." Another policy change which had no contemporary impact, but which would have posed an interesting problem for nineteenth century literalists, was the decision to stop segregating negro and white blood in the Church hospitals' blood banks. This decision, prompted by Public Health Service rulings and affecting many hospitals nationally, has no doubt resulted in many instances wherein priesthood holders have had several drops of "Negro blood" in their veins, at least for a few weeks.

210. As early as 1924, McKay had published a short article, "Persons and Principles," criticizing the hypocrisy of "pseudo-Christians" who preached "universal Brotherhood" and then showed prejudice towards Negroes and

others in their daily lives. See *Millennial Star*, 86 (31 Jan. 1924): 72.

211. Quoted in a letter from Sterling McMurrin to Llewelyn R. McKay, 26 Aug. 1968, copy in my possession. An excerpt has been published in Stephen G. Taggart, *Mormonism's Negro Policy: Social and Historical Origins* (Salt Lake City University of Utah Press, 1970), p. 79; see also *Salt Lake Tribune*, 15 Jan. 1970, "Educator Cites McKay Statement...."

212. The remarks were not recorded for several hours after the interview, and the original notes have reportedly been lost. However, Llewelyn McKay has stated that he showed McMurrin's letter to President McKay and that the prophet verified the account. See Taggart, *Mormonism's Negro Policy*, p. 79, and *Salt Lake Tribune*, 15 Jan. 1970, "Educator Cites McKay Statement of No Negro Bias in LDS Tenets." There has been no official response by the Church to Llewelyn's claim; a senior apostle has said privately that the verification came only because of President McKay's debilitated condition.

213. First Presidency statement, 17 Aug. 1949; McKay was then Second Counselor. Moyle, "What of the Negro?", reported that the statement was reaffirmed in 1961.

214. Letter of 3 Nov. 1947, published in Llewelyn R. McKay, *Home Memories of President David O. McKay* (Salt Lake City: Deseret Book Company, 1956), pp. 226-31; or Berrett, in Stewart, *Mormonism and the Negro*, 18-23.

215. First Presidency statement, 15 Dec. 1969.

216. The Genesis Group, organized in Salt Lake City in October 1971 was designed to provide the Church auxiliary programs, except Sunday School, for black members in the Salt Lake Valley. The group had a "group presidency" and officer and teachers drawn from the black membership in the area.

217. See "Lee Says Complete Status for Negroes in LDS Priesthood Only Matter of Time," *Salt Lake Tribune*, 24 Sept. 1972. For an indication of President Lee's views in 1945, see his "Youth of a Noble Birthright," note 195.

218. First Presidency statement, 15 Dec. 1969.

219. See note 214.

Elijah Abel and the Changing
Status of Blacks
Within Mormonism

Newell G. Bringhurst

After 1973 the most extensive research into the origins of Mormon teachings on blacks was that of Newell Bringhurst, who completed a doctoral dissertation on the subject in 1975. The Mormon History Association awarded this essay, carried in Dialogue *in 1979, the Best Article Award. Bringhurst here traces the circumstances and fate of several early black Mormons in the context of the emerging church teachings on race. In the process he incorporates most of the new information he had uncovered which bears directly on the origin of Mormonism's Negro doctrine. This essay originally appeared in* Dialogue *12 (Summer 1979).*

On the surface it was just another regional conference for the small but troubled Cincinnati branch of the Church of Jesus Christ of Latter-day Saints on a summer day in June 1843. Not unlike other early branches of the Church, the Cincinnati congregation had a number of problems, including internal dissension and just plain "bad management." Presiding over this conference was a "Traveling High Council" consisting of three Mormon apostles.[1] As the visiting council probed the difficulties plaguing the Cincinnati Saints, its attention was drawn to the activities of Elijah Abel, a unique member of the branch. Abel, a black Mormon priesthood holder, found himself under fire because of his visibility as a black Mormon. Apostle John E. Page maintained that while "he respects a coloured Bro, wisdom forbids that we should introduce [him] before the public." Apostle Orson Pratt then "sustained the position of Bro Page" on this question. Apostle Heber C. Kimball also expressed concern about this black priesthood holder's activities. In response, Abel "said he had no disposition to force himself upon an equality with white people." Toward the end of the meeting, a resolution was adopted restricting Abel's activities. To conform with the established "duty of the 12 [Apostles]...to ordain and send men to their native country Bro Abels [sic] was advised to visit the coloured population. The advice was sanctioned by the conference. Instructions were then given him concerning his mission."[2]

This decision represents an important turning point not only for Elijah Abel but for all Mormon blacks. For the first time race was used as a criterion for limiting the activities of a black Latter-day Saint. Until 1843, Abel had suffered no known racial discrimination despite his status as one of Mormonism's few black members. His membership in the Church went back to 1832 when he was baptized by Ezekiel Roberts.[3]

Abel was born on July 25, 1810 in Maryland and later migrated to Mormonism's headquarters in Kirtland, Ohio.[4] Within four years of his conversion, he was ordained an elder in the Melchizedek Priesthood.[5] By June 1836, he was listed, along with a number of other Mormon priesthood holders, as a duly licensed "minister of the gospel."[6] As a member in good standing, he was promoted in the Melchizedek Priesthood to the rank of seventy in December 1836[7] and received a patriarchal blessing in the same year. This ordinance, performed by Joseph Smith, Sr., father of the Mormon prophet, proclaimed that Abel was "ordained an Elder and annointed to secure thee against the power of the destroyer." In this blessing were apparent allusions to Abel's unusual status as one of Mormonism's few black members. In contrast to his white fellow Saints who were often declared descendants of a particular biblical lineage—usually Joseph or Ephraim—Abel was not assigned such a lineage. Instead, he was proclaimed "an orphan." Finally, this blessing promised, "Thou shalt be made equal to thy brethren, and thy soul be white in eternity and thy robes glittering."[8]

Like many of his white male priesthood brethren, Abel served as a missionary for the Church during the late 1830s. The field of Abel's missionary labors included New York State and Canada. Little is known about his success as a missionary, but his activities did generate controversy. According to one account,... Abel was accused by the non-Mormon residents of St. Lawrence County, New York, of murdering a woman and five children. "Handbills were pasted up in every direction... and a great reward was offered for him." Apparently Abel was successful in refuting these charges, leaving the community "unmolested."[9] While in Canada, Abel also ran into difficulties—this time with his fellow Saints. He was challenged on "some of his teachings, etc." Abel proclaimed "that there would be Stakes of Zion in all the world, that an elder was a High Priest and he had as much authority as any H.P." He was also accused of "threatening to knock down" a fellow elder. Abel reportedly rationalized this behavior, declaring that "the elders in Kirtland make nothing of knocking down one another." The topic of Abel's behavior came up in a meeting of church leaders, which included Joseph and Hyrum Smith and Sidney Rigdon as well as the quorum of Seventies, but no disciplinary action was taken.[10]

Abel had not been the only black Mormon to create controversy within the Church during the 1830s. "Black Pete," through his activities in Kirtland as a self-styled "revelator," attracted notoriety both within and outside Mormonism.[11] Unfortunately, little is known about his background. According to one account, Pete migrated to Ohio from Pennsylvania where he had been born to slave parents.[12] After his arrival in Ohio, Pete joined the Mormon movement in late 1830 or early 1831. This "man of colour" was described in two other accounts as "a chief man, who [was] sometimes seized with strange vagaries and odd conceits."[13] On at least one occasion Pete fancied he could "fly" and "took it into his head to try his wings; he accordingly chose the elevated bank of Lake Erie as a starting-place, and, spreading his pinions, he lit on a treetop some fifty feet below, sustaining no other damage than the demolition of his faith in wings without feathers."[14]

There is some confusion over Pete's other activities among the Saints. According to one reminiscence Pete "wanted to marry a white woman" but Joseph Smith could not get any "revelations" for him to do so.[15] According to another, however, Pete was active at a time when Joseph Smith and other church authorities were not around. Whatever the case, the Mormon prophet brought forth in February 1831 a revelation condemning false revelators such as Black Pete. Smith was told that only certain individuals "appointed unto you" were authorized "to receive revelations" (D&C 43:3-6). Thereafter, several of the self-appointed revelators, possibly including Pete, were "tried for [their] fellowship" and "cut off" from the Church.[16]

Despite the controversy caused by the Mormon activities of both Black Pete and Elijah Abel, Latter-day Saint leaders did not establish a subordinate ecclesiastical place for black people within Mormonism during the 1830s. The number of free blacks casting their lot with the Saints was very small. According to Apostle Parley P. Pratt, "one dozen free negroes or mulattoes never have belonged to our society in any part of the world, from its first organization [in 1830] to this date, 1839."[17] As for the secular status of black slaves in Missouri and the slaveholding South—regions of increased Mormon activity during the 1830s—the Church in 1835 officially adopted a strong antiabolitionist position which assented to the servile conditions of these blacks.[18] At the same time, concerned Latter-day Saints maintained a basic dislike for slavery as a viable institution for themselves. This attitude, originally articulated in the Book of Mormon but muted during the 1830s, was still evident throughout this period. By expressing antipathy for both slavery and antiabolitionism, in turn or even concurrently, the Saints were able to avoid internal divisions over slavery and to minimize Mormon involvement in the increasingly acute national controversy.[19]

Thus, in 1839 when Elijah Abel migrated from Kirtland to Nauvoo, Illinois, he was still accepted in full fellowship both within the Church and the larger community. As an active Latter-day Saint, Abel participated in at least two baptisms for the dead following his arrival in Nauvoo.[20] He earned his livelihood as a carpenter and joined with six others who described themselves as "the House Carpenters of the Town of Nauvoo." In February 1840 the group published a small "book of prices" which outlined the uniform rates to be charged by these Nauvoo carpenters.[21] In addition, Abel, according to his own recollections, was "appointed" by Joseph Smith "to the calling of an undertaker in Nauvoo."[22] In this occupation, Abel was kept busy by the appallingly high number of deaths from malaria and other diseases during the early years of Nauvoo's settlement.[23]

While in Nauvoo, Abel apparently had close contact with the Joseph Smith family. According to one account, Abel was "intimately acquainted" with the the Prophet and lived in his home.[24] Abel recalled being present at the bedside of Patriarch Joseph Smith, Sr. "during his last sickness" in 1840. The following year Abel, along with six other Nauvoo Mormons attempted to rescue Joseph Smith after his arrest for earlier difficulties in Missouri.[25]

In 1842 Abel moved for unknown reasons from Nauvoo to Cincinnati, where he continued to labor as a carpenter.[26] While in Cincinnati he married a black woman, Mary Ann Adams, and by the time of his migration from Cincinnati to Salt Lake City in 1853, he was the father of three children.[27] Just six months before the June 1843 conference that attempted to limit Abel's visibility, Joseph Smith apparently alluded to him in a positive way. The Prophet declared, "Go to Cincinnati . . . and find an educated negro, who rides in his carriage, and you will see a man who has risen by the powers of his own mind to his exalted state of respectability."[28]

Abel continued to remain active in the affairs of the Cincinnati branch. In June 1845, for example, "Elder Elijah Able [sic] preferred a charge against" three women for their failure to attend church meetings and for "speaking disrespectfully of the heads of the Church."[29] Nevertheless, the Mormon status of Elijah Abel and all black Latter-day Saints deteriorated after 1840 despite their faithful activity.

In addition to Abel, other Mormon blacks found themselves in conspicuous situations during these years. One such member was Walker Lewis, a barber in Lowell, Massachusetts. Little is known of Lewis's background other than that he was apparently ordained an elder by William Smith, the younger brother of the Mormon prophet.[30] As with Abel, Lewis's role or place within Mormonism was not initially questioned by church officials. Various Mormon apostles visiting Lowell as late as 1844-45 seemed to accept Lewis's priesthood status.[31] One of these visitors, Apostle Wilford Woodruff, merely observed in November 1844 that "a coloured Brother who was an Elder"—presumably Lewis—manifested his support for the established church leadership during this time of great internal division.[32] By 1847, however, Lewis's status within the Church was challenged by William L. Appleby who was in charge of Mormon missionary activity in the eastern states. During a visit to Lowell in 1847, Appleby encountered Lewis and in a terse letter to Brigham Young expressed surprise at finding a black ordained to the priesthood. Appleby asked the Mormon leader if it was "the order of God or tolerated, to ordain negroes to the priesthood . . . if it is, I desire to know it as I have yet got to learn it." Unfortunately by the time Appleby's letter arrived at Winter Quarters, Young was on his way to the Great Basin with the first group of Mormon settlers and thus was unable to reply in writing to Appleby's question.[33]

However, by 1849, Brigham Young was willing to assert that all Mormon blacks were ineligible for priesthood ordination. Young's 1849 statement—one of the earliest known declarations of black priesthood denial—came in response to a question posed by Apostle Lorenzo Snow concerning the "chance of redemption . . . for the African." Young replied:

> The curse remained upon them because Cain cut off the lives [sic] of Abel, to prevent him and his posterity getting ascendency over Cain and his generations, and to get the lead himself, his own offering was not being accepted of God, while Abel's was. But the Lord cursed Cain's seed with blackness and prohibited them the priesthood, that Abel and his progeny might yet come forward, and have their dominion, place, and blessings in their proper relationship with Cain and his race in the world to come.[34]

Brigham Young's decision to deny blacks the priesthood was undoubtedly prompted by several factors. Among the most important may well have been the controversy generated in 1846-47 by the flamboyant activities of William McCary, a half-breed Indian-black man referred to variously as the "Indian," "Lamanite," or "Nigger Prophet."[35] The descriptions of McCary are vague and often conflicting, making it difficult to determine his exact activities and relationship to the Latter-day Saint movement. McCary's origin and occupation are not known. The earliest known account, written in October 1846, claims that Apostle Orson Hyde while at a camp near Council Bluffs, Iowa, "baptised and ordained . . . a Lamanite Prophet to use as a tool to destroy the churches he cannot rule."[36]

By late October 1846, McCary shifted his base of operation east to Cincinnati. The Cincinnati *Commercial* described the exploits of "a big, burley, half Indian, half Negro, formerly a Mormon" who built up a religious following of some sixty members "solemnly enjoined to secrecy" concerning their rites due to their apparent practice of plural marriage.[37] McCary "proclaimed himself Jesus Christ" showing his disciples "the scars of wounds in his hands and limbs received on the cross"; and performed "miracles with a golden rod."[38] The blessing that he conferred upon his followers reflected at least some knowledge of Latter-day Saint ritual. "Accept this blessing in the name of the Son, Jesus Christ, Mary, the mother, God our Father, our Lord. AMEN. It will preserve yours, yourself, your dead, your family through this life into [the] celestial kingdom, your name is written in the Lamb's Book of Life, AMEN."[39]

It is not clear whether McCary had any contact with Elijah Abel or any of the other Cincinnati Saints upholding the leadership claims of Brigham Young and the Twelve. Whatever the case, McCary's Cincinnati-based movement was short-lived. By mid-November his following had dwindled to thirty, and by February 1847, McCary himself had left Cincinnati.[40]

McCary returned west to Winter Quarters, Nebraska, joining the main body of Saints under the leadership of Brigham Young in their temporary encampment. Young and others initially welcomed McCary into the Mormon camp where he was recognized as an accomplished musician, entertaining the encamped Saints during the months of February and March 1847.[41] The Saints might have had other uses in mind for McCary. In a somewhat ambiguous statement, John D. Lee, a follower of Young, said that the black Indian "seems to be willing to go according to counsel and that he may be a useful man after he has acquired an experimental knowledge," and he advised his fellow Saints to "use this man with respect."[42] By late March 1847, however, McCary had fallen from Mormon favor. What he did to offend Brigham Young is not clear but at a "meeting of the twelve and others" summoned to consider this matter "McCary made a rambling statement, claiming to be Adam, the ancient of days, and exhibiting himself in Indian costume; he also claimed to have an odd rib which he had discovered in his wife. He played on his thirty-six cent flute, being a natural musician and gave several illustrations of his ability as a mimic."[43] Following this March 1847 meeting, Church leaders expelled McCary from the Mormon camp at Winter Quarters. Subsequently, Apostle Orson Hyde preached a sermon "against his doctrine."[44]

This was not the end of McCary's Mormon involvement, although his subsequent activities are even more difficult to trace.[45] It appears, however, that McCary remained active in the area around Winter

Quarters and proceeded to set up his own rival Mormon group drawing followers away from Brigham Young.[46] According to a July 1847 account, the "negro prophet" exerted his influence by working "with a rod, like those of old."[47] By the fall of 1847, McCary was teaching and practicing racial miscegenation in which McCary had a number of women "seald to him in his way which was as follows, he had a house in which this ordinance was preformed his wife . . . was in the room at the time of the proformance no others was admited the form of sealing was for the women to go to bed with him in the daytime as I an informed 3 diforant times by which they was seald to the fullest extent." McCary's activities and this "Sealing Ordinance" caused a negative reaction among those Latter-day Saints in the surrounding community not involved with his sect, particularly the relatives of McCary's female disciples. One irate Mormon wanted "to shoot" McCary for trying "to kiss his girls." But McCary, sensing the impending storm, "made his way to Missouri on a fast trot."[48]

While the whirlwind generated by McCary's activities upset Brigham Young and other church leaders, the decision to deny blacks the priesthood was probably prompted as much, if not more, by the exposure of the Latter-day Saints to a large number of blacks—both slave and free— following the Mormon migration to the Great Basin. This region's black population of 100 to 120 individuals, who arrived during the years 1847-49, stood in sharp contrast to the twenty or so blacks that had lived in Nauvoo during the Mormon sojourn there.[49] The sudden appearance of these Great Basin blacks—a significant proportion of whom were slaves—helped to encourage Brigham Young and other church leaders to clearly define both their secular and ecclesiastical status and that of black people generally. In response, Latter-day Saint leaders not only prohibited blacks from holding the priesthood but also adopted through the Utah territorial legislature a set of antiblack laws that limited the rights and activities of free blacks and gave legal recognition to the institution of black slavery in the territory.[50]

A final factor not to be overlooked as influencing the 1849 Mormon decision to deny blacks the priesthood was the intensification of Mormon antiblack attitudes during the 1840s. The Latter-day Saints became more prone to associate blackness, black counter-figures, and indeed black people with a widening circle of opponents and enemies.[51] While this tendency was certainly evident before Joseph Smith's death, it became increasingly prominent after Brigham Young's emergence as the leader of the Saints who migrated West. As Lester E. Bush, Jr. has suggested, Brigham Young was more willing than Joseph Smith to embrace certain antiblack racial concepts and practices prevalent in American society. This, in turn played a crucial role in the emergence of Mormon black priesthood denial by 1849.[52]

When Elijah Abel migrated from Cincinnati to Utah in 1853, he found that his status within Mormonism had been undermined. While no effort was made to declare Abel's priesthood authority "null and void" (despite later suggestions to the contrary), Abel was prohibited from participating in certain temple ordinances considered essential for full Mormon salvation. When Abel "applied to President Young for his endowments . . . to have his wife and children sealed to him," the Mormon president "put him off" because, according to one account, participation in these ordinances was "a privilege" that the Mormon president "could not grant."[53] This refusal was ironic in light of Abel's willingness to contribute his time and labor to the construction of the Salt Lake Temple.[54]

Despite these difficulties, Elijah Abel tried to make the best of his situation. By 1857 he was listed as a member of the Mill Creek Ward in Salt Lake City where he, his wife, and his oldest son, Maroni, were rebaptized like so many other Saints during the "Mormon Reformation" of 1857.[55] In 1877, "Bro Elijah Abel was notified that he was still a member of the Third Quorum" of Seventies.[56] In the meantime Abel's family continued to grow. At least four daughters and one son were born during the years 1856-69.[57] Throughout most of the period, Abel continued to support himself and his family as a carpenter.[58] In addition, for a brief period in 1859, he and his wife managed the Farnham Hotel in Salt Lake City.[59] Abel also resided for a very short time during the early 1870s in Ogden, where according to the recollections of one old-time resident the Abel family "went around from ward to ward . . . putting on minstrel shows."[60]

The period 1855-77 was also marked by difficulty and disappointment for Elijah Abel. On at least two occasions, in 1855 and again in 1864, Abel was listed as delinquent in paying his taxes.[61] Also in 1864 Abel's son Maroni "was charged before Alderman Clinton with stealing a shaving knife from an emigrant on the Public square."[62] The Abel family was plagued with further heartache in 1871 when Maroni died while still in his early twenties.[63] Six years later Abel's wife Mary Ann died of pneumonia at the relatively young age of 46, leaving the aging black priesthood holder to care for himself.[64]

Despite these difficulties, Abel once again renewed his application for his temple endowments to John Taylor, who by 1880 had succeeded Brigham Young as Church president. Taylor submitted Abel's request to the Council of the Twelve which rendered "a decision unfavorable to Brother Abel."[65]

Abel was not the only black Mormon trying to secure temple ordinances during this period. Like Abel, Jane Manning James petitioned church leaders on several occasions for her endowments and sealings. The background and experiences of Jane Manning dramatized the changing and, indeed, deteriorating place of blacks within Mormonism.[66] Manning was also a long-time member of the Church. She joined the Mormon movement during the early 1840s while a resident of Wilton, Connecticut. Following her conversion she and eight members of her immediate family migrated to Nauvoo in 1853. Upon her arrival in the Mormon community, Manning became "a member of Joseph Smith's household" where she stayed until "shortly before" the Mormon prophet's death. Just before the Mormon abandonment of Nauvoo, she married Isaac James, a free black Mormon who had lived in Nauvoo since 1839.[67] Jane Manning James and her family were among the earliest Saints to migrate west, arriving in the Great Basin in 1847. Like so many Great Basin Mormons, the James family engaged in farming and achieved a fair degree of success. However, Jane and her husband had separated by late 1869 or early 1870.[68] Possibly as a result of this separation, Jane became concerned about her future salvation. Realizing the importance of temple ordinances for future exaltation, she petitioned for the right to receive her sealings and endowments. This was done in a number of requests submitted to various Latter-day Saint leaders, including John Taylor and Joseph F. Smith, throughout the late nineteenth and early twentieth centuries.[69] In the most interesting of these requests, James asked to be "sealed" to Walker Lewis, the black Mormon elder who had lived in Lowell, Massachusetts, during the 1840s. According to James, "Brother Lewis wished me to be sealed to Him."[70] These requests were rejected by Church authorities.[71]

As for Elijah Abel, even though he failed to secure his long-sought temple ordinances, he continued to be accepted as a member of the Third Quorum of Seventies as late as 1883.[72] In fact, during that same year Abel, then an elderly man in his early seventies, was appointed to serve a mission for the Church. He was set apart by Apostle Joseph F. Smith and sent to Ohio and Canada.[73] Abel's missionary activities, however, were cut short by ill health, and he returned to Utah in early December 1884. Two weeks later he died of "old age and debility."[74] His motives for going on a mission at such an advanced age is a mystery, especially at a time when his status as well as that of blacks in general had deteriorated. Perhaps he was motivated by a desire to demonstrate his "full faith in the Gospel" and thereby obtain long-sought temple endowments and sealings before his death.

The story of Elijah Abel and his activity in the Church is significant for several reasons. First, Abel's changing status was a microcosm of what happened to all Mormon blacks during the nineteenth century. Up until the 1840s, Mormon blacks were accepted in full Mormon fellowship including the right to receive the priesthood. However, by 1849 this was no longer the case; Mormon black priesthood denial was recognized as a churchwide practice. Even though Abel "got in under the wire" in receiving the priesthood, he and all other black Mormons were unable to participate in temple ordinances considered essential for full Mormon salvation.

Abel was significant for a second reason. Despite the parallels between Abel and other black Mormons, he was unique because of his status as one of Mormonism's few known black priesthood holders. Because of his unusual status, Abel was the only known black Mormon to fulfill not one but three missions for the Church: full-time missions in the 1830s and 1880s and a local mission in 1843. In addition, at least two of Abel's descendants were apparently allowed to hold offices in the priesthood despite their black ancestry.[75] The unique status of Abel and his descendants was further underscored by the fact that they apparently did not interact with other Great Basin blacks or really consider themselves a part of Utah's small but growing black community during the late nineteenth and early twentieth centuries. The Abels stood apart from other well-known black Mormons, including Jane Manning James, Samuel Chambers and Edward Leggroan.[76] In fact, it has been suggested that by the early twentieth century Abel's descendants had managed to "cross the color line" and "pass for white."[77]

Despite these developments, Abel's race remained an issue that Latter-day Saints had to deal with during the late nineteenth and early twentieth centuries. In 1879, while Elijah Abel was still alive, his status as a black priesthood holder figured prominently in the efforts of certain Latter-day Saints to trace the origins of priesthood denial back to Joseph Smith. One of the leaders of this movement, Zebedee Coltrin, conceded that "Brother Abel was ordained a seventy because he had labored in the [Nauvoo] temple." But Coltrin maintained that when Joseph Smith learned of Abel's black lineage "he was dropped from the quorum and another was put in his place."[78] However, Apostle Joseph F. Smith felt that "Coltrin's memory was incorrect as to Brother Abel being dropped from the quorum of Seventies to which he belonged" since Abel had in his possession two certificates attesting to his status as a Seventy; the first "given to him in 1841" and a "later one" issued in Salt Lake City.[79] Abel spoke up in his own defense, stating that he had been ordained a Seventy back in 1836 by none other than Zebedee Coltrin! In addition, Abel stated "that the Prophet Joseph told him he was entitled to the priesthood."[80] John Taylor tried to reconcile the conflicting views of Abel, Apostle Smith, and Coltrin by suggesting that Abel had "been ordained before the word of the Lord was fully understood." Abel's ordination, therefore, was allowed to stand.[81] By 1908, Joseph F. Smith, then president of the Church, abandoned the position he had taken in 1879 that Elijah Abel's priesthood authority had been recognized by the Mormon Prophet.

According to Smith, even though Abel had been "ordained a seventy . . . in the days of the Prophet Joseph Smith . . . this ordination was declared null and void by the Prophet himself" when he became aware of Abel's black lineage.[82] Smith's later view of Abel's relationship to Joseph Smith fit in with the widespread Mormon belief that it was Joseph Smith, not Brigham Young who had fostered the practice of black priesthood denial.[83] This "rewriting of the Mormon past" was also reflected in the way Elijah Abel was presented in Andrew Jenson's *Latter-day Saint Biographical Encyclopedia* (1920). According to Jenson, Abel was ordained to the priesthood because "an exception" was "made in his case with regard to the general rule of the Church" against black ordination.[84] By 1955 even this qualified view of Abel's place as a Mormon priesthood holder was denounced by Apostle Joseph Fielding Smith. In response to a private inquiry, Smith rejected Jenson's account of Abel, suggesting that there were *two* Elijah Abels in the early Church—one white and the other black. Jenson had confounded the "names and the work done by one man named Abel . . . with the name of the Negro who joined the Church in an early day.[85]

At about the same time Joseph Fielding Smith was trying to bury the ghost of Elijah Abel once and for all, other individuals brought Abel back into the limelight through their efforts to probe the origins of black priesthood denial and the changing role of blacks within the Church.[86] By the late 1960s and early 1970s, the unique status of Abel figured prominently in studies on the Mormon-black issue written by Dennis L. Lythgoe, Stephen G. Taggart and Fawn M. Brodie.[87] However it was Lester E. Bush's seminal *Dialogue* article that really underscored the unusual relationship to the often contradictory twists and turns of Mormonism's policy toward its black members.[88] It would be nice to believe that the publicity given the history of Elijah Abel and his unique Mormon ordeal had some effect in undermining the historical justification for black priesthood denial. Whatever the case, the bringing forth of the June 1978 revelation abandoning black priesthood denial has restored Mormon blacks to the position of equality that they occupied during the 1830s when Elijah Abel joined the Church.

NOTES

The author wishes to express his deep appreciation for the suggestions and information provided by the following individuals: Lester E. Bush, Jr., associate editor of *Dialogue* ; H. Michael Marquardt of Sandy, Utah; Noel Barton of the LDS Church Genealogical Society; and William G. Hartley of the LDS Church Historical Department. Without the assistance of these individuals this article would not have been possible. In addition, a summer grant-in-aid provided by Indiana University at Kokomo made it possible for me to examine certain crucial materials in the Historical Department Archives of the Church of Jesus Christ of Latter-day Saints in Salt Lake City.

1. The three included John E. Page, Orson Pratt, and Heber C. Kimball. Lorenzo Snow, an apostle (1849) and later church president, was also a member of this "Traveling High Council."

2. "Minutes of a conference of the Church of Jesus Christ of Latter-day Saints held in Cincinnati, June 25, 1843," LDS Church Archives.

3. Andrew Jenson, *Latter-day Saint Biographical Encyclopedia*, 4 vols. (Salt Lake City: Andrew Jenson History Co., 1920) 3:577.

4. According to "Joseph Smith's Patriarchal Blessing Record," 88, recorded by W. A. Cowdery, LDS Church Archives, Abel was born in 1808. In other census and church records, the 1810 birth date is used. There is some confusion about in which Maryland county Abel was born. According to Abel's patriarchal blessing, he was born in Frederick County but the "Mill Creek Ward Record of Members," no. 1913, p. 63, LDS Church Archives, lists Abel's birthplace as Hancock, Washington County, while the "LDS Missionary Record" books A & B, 6176, pt. 1860-1906, p. 75 (1883), microfilm 025,664, LDS Church Archives, lists Abel's birthplace as Hancock County. Finally, Abel's obituary in the *Deseret News* 26 Dec. 1884 lists his birthplace as simply Washington County.

5. The exact date of Abel's ordination as an elder is not clear. Abel's 26 Dec. 1884 *Deseret News* obituary says that he "was ordained an Elder as appears by certificate dated March 3d, 1836." It is possible that Abel had been ordained before this date since "certificates of ordination" were frequently issued after the date of original ordination.

6. *Latter Day Saints Messenger and Advocate* (Kirtland, Ohio) June 1836.

7. Minutes of the Seventies Journal, kept by Hazen Aldrich, 20 Dec. 1836, LDS Church Archives.

8. "Joseph Smith's Patriarchal Blessing Record," 88, as cited in Lester E. Bush, "Compilation on the Negro in Mormonism," pp. 16-17; copy of unpublished manuscript in possession of author.

9. Eunice Kenney, "My Testimony of the Latter Day Work," unpublished manuscript, 1885?, LDS Church Archives.

10. Minutes of the Seventies Journal, 1 June 1839.

11. As indicated by articles in newspapers, not only in Ohio, but as far away as New York and Pennsylvania. See *Ashtabula Journal* (Ashtabula, Ohio), 5

Feb. 1831, taken from *Geauga Gazette* [n.d.]; *Albany Journal* (Albany, New York), 16 Feb. 1831, reprinted from Painesville Gazette [n.d.] and *The Sun* (Philadelphia) 18 Aug. 1831, taken from the *A.M. Intelligencer* [n.p., n.d.].

12. *Naked Truth About Mormonism* (Oakland, Calif.), January 1888, quotes a statement of Henry Carroll, 18 Mar. 1885, on Black Pete's background.

13. *Ashtabula Journal*, 5 Feb. 1831 and *Albany Journal*, 16 Feb. 1831.

14. *The Sun*, 18 Aug. 1831. Also see *Ashtabula Journal*, 5 Feb. 1831. Later recollections have Pete chasing "a ball that he said he saw flying in the air" or "revelations carried by a black angel." See *Times and Seasons* (Nauvoo, Illinois), 1 Apr. 1842 and George A. Smith, *Journal of Discourses*, 15 Nov. 1865, 11:4.

15. *Naked Truth*, Jan. 1888.

16. This according to a later recollection in the *Times and Seasons*, 1 Apr. 1842.

17. Parley P. Pratt, *Late Persecutions of the Church of Latter-day Saints* (New York: J. W. Harrison, 1840), 28.

18. As outlined in "A Declaration of Belief regarding Governments and Laws in General" approved by a general assembly of the Church 17 Aug. 1835 which stated in part, "We do not believe it right to interfere with bond-servants ... to meddle with or influence them in the least to cause them to be dissatisfied with their situations in this life ... such interference we believe to be unlawful and unjust, and dangerous to the peace of every government allowing human beings to be held in servitude." This declaration was included as part of the Doctrine and Covenants (ultimately section 134:12); which was canonized in 1835.

19. For one view outlining the development of Mormon antiabolitionist-antislavery attitudes during the 1830s see Lester E. Bush, "Mormonism's Negro Doctrine: An Historical Overview," *Dialogue* 8 (Spring 1973): 12-15. Also see Warren A. Jennings "Factors in the Destruction of the Mormon Press in Missouri, 1833," *Utah Historical Quarterly* 15 (Winter 1967) pp. 56-76; Dennis L. Lythgoe, "Negro Slavery and Mormon Doctrine," *Western Humanities Review* 21 (Autumn 1967) pp. 327-38; and Stephen L. Taggart, *Mormonism's Negro Policy: Social and Historical Origins* (Salt Lake City, Utah: University of Utah Press, 1970).

20. See "Elijah Abel bapt for John F. Lancaster a friend," as contained in Nauvoo Temple Records Book A100, LDS Church Archives. Also see two other entries in this same record: "Delila Abel bapt in the instance of Elisha [sic] Abel. Rel son. Bapt 1840, Book A page 1" and "Delila Abel Bapt. in the instance of Elijah Abel 1841, Rel. Dau. Book A page 5."

21. See Elijah Abel Papers, LDS Church Archives, for a description of this

pamphlet which was printed according to an "Agreement," 20 Feb. 1840, between E. Robinson and D. C. Smith—the Nauvoo town printers—and "Elijah Abel, Levi Jackson, Samuel Rolf, Alexander Badlam, Wm. Cahoon, Wm. Smith and Elijah Newman." Robinson and Smith agreed "to Print for Abel, Jackson & Co., small pamphlet of 200 copies 'Book of Prices of Work adopted by the House Carpenters of the Town of Nauvoo' to be paid upon in labor or putting up a building when called upon." The sum agreed upon was $58. I have not had the opportunity to look at the original but according to this reference the "original is in the possession of Mrs. Alfred M. Henson, St. George."

22. As recorded in "Minutes of First Council of Seventy, 1859-1863," 5 Mar. 1879, p. 494, LDS Church Archives.

23. As noted by W. Wyl, *Mormon Portraits* (Salt Lake City: Tribune Printing and Publishing Co., 1886), pp. 51-52.

24. Kate B. Carter, *The Negro Pioneer* (Salt Lake City Daughters of Utah Pioneers, 1965), p. 15; Jenson, *Biographical Encyclopedia*, p. 577. It is somewhat unclear what Carter meant by "living in the home" of Joseph Smith. It seems unlikely that Abel resided with the Smith family itself. Probably Abel lived in the Nauvoo House, a hotel/guesthouse run by the Smith family. In addition, Isaac Lewis Manning and his sister Jane Manning James were described as "servants" of Joseph Smith who both "lived for many years in the household of Joseph Smith." See Carter, *Negro Pioneer*, pp. 9-13.

25. Joseph Smith, Jr., *History of the Church*, ed., B.H. Roberts, 7 vols. (Salt Lake City: Deseret Book Co., 1908) 4:365 (6 June 1841).

26. As noted in the *Cincinnati City Directories* for 1842, Charles Cist, comp. Genealogical Society of Utah (GS) microfilm 194,001 and for 1849-50, GS 194,002.

27. As indicated by 1850 U.S. Census, 10th Ward, Cincinnati, Hamilton County, Ohio, 26 Aug. 1850 and 1860 U.S. Census, 13th Ward, Salt Lake City, pp. 5:217.

28. *History of the Church*, 4:217 (2 Jan. 1843).

29. "Minutes of a special Conference of the Cincinnati [sic] branch of the Church... held at Elder Pugh's on the 1st day of June, 1845," *Times and Seasons* (1 June 1845), 5:916.

30. William L. Appleby to Brigham Young, 2 June 1847; also noted in William L. Appleby, Journal, 19 May 1847, LDS Church Archives. There is, however, some confusion over *who* actually ordained Lewis. According to the recollections of Jane Elizabeth James, "Parley P. Pratt ordained Him an Elder." See Jane E. James to Joseph F. Smith, 7 Feb. 1890, as cited in Henry J. Wolfinger, "A Test of Faith: Jane Elizabeth James and the Origins of the Utah Black Community," Clark Knowlton, ed., *Social Accommodation in*

Utah, American West Center Occasional Papers Salt Lake City: University of Utah, 1975, p. 145. Also through an error committed by the compilers of the Journal History, 2 June 1847, LDS Church Archives, the impression that Walker Lewis was a member of the Mormon branch at Batavia, New York was created. Such a false impression was obtained because Appleby's letter describing Walker Lewis was mailed to Brigham Young from Batavia, New York. However, the contents of both this letter and Appleby's journal show Lewis to be a resident of, and member of the church at Lowell, Massachusetts.

31. See Wilford Woodruff to Brigham Young, 16 Nov. 1844. Woodruff in his journal, LDS Church Archives, during late 1844 and early 1845 made note of his numerous visits to Lowell and the areas around Lowell. Both Apostles Brigham Young and Ezra T. Benson visited these same areas during 1844-45 but reported nothing unusual in the ethnic or racial qualities of Mormon priesthood holders.

32. Woodruff to Young, 16 Nov. 1844. According to Ezra T. Benson to Brigham Young, 22 Jan. 1845, LDS Church Archives, the particular difficulties in the Lowell Branch came about as a result of church finances and the collection of funds.

33. Appleby to Young, 2 June 1847; also noted in Appleby, Journal, 19 May 1847. When Young finally had a chance to respond to Appleby's inquiry following his return from the Great Basin to Winter Quarters in the fall of 1847, Appleby was present at Winter Quarters. Therefore, Young and/or other church leaders were able to respond to any questions that Appleby had on this matter. As for Walker Lewis, little is known about his activities after 1847. However, by 4 Oct. 1851, Lewis had journeyed to the Great Basin where he received a patriarchal blessing at the hands of John Smith. It is interesting to note that Lewis was assigned the lineage of Cainan. "Historian's Office Patriarchal Blessings," vol. 11, p. 326 as noted in Patriarchal Blessing Index, CR5001 #64, LDS Church Archives. Lewis's assigned lineage stood in sharp contrast to the "orphan" status assigned Elijah Abel some fifteen years earlier. But the lineage of "Cainaan" had been assigned to Mormon blacks as early as 1843. See references to patriarchal blessings given by Hyrum Smith to Jane Manning and Anthony Stebbins as noted by Patriarchal Blessing Index, CR5001 #64.

34. Manuscript History of the Church, 13 Feb. 1849, LDS Church Archives.

35. McCary's name was spelled a number of different ways: "McGarry," "McCairey," "McCarry," McCarey" as well as "McCary." In one source he was referred to as "Wm. Chubby," Juanita Brooks ed., *On the Mormon Frontier: The Diary of Hosea Stout* 1844-1861, 2 vols. (Salt Lake City: University of Utah Press, 1966), entry for 8 Mar. 1848, 1:304. In *The True Latter Day Saints Herald* (Cincinnati, Ohio), March 1861, he was referred to as "Mr. Williams the imposter." For uniformity and simplicity of spelling I will refer to him as William McCary.

36. *Voree Herald*, Oct. 1846. According to the *True Latter Saints Herald*, March 1861, the agreement between Hyde and McCary was made in Nauvoo, Illinois, where Hyde "married" McCary "to a white sister."

37. Cincinnati *Commercial*, 27 Oct.1846.

38. Ibid. As indicated by a warning in the *Commercial* cautioning the citizens of this city to "Lookout for more sensuality in open daylight, in your families, and almost before your eyes, all under the cloak of sanctity."

39. Ibid, 17 Nov. 1846.

40. *Zion's Revelle* (Voree, Wisc.), 25 Feb. 1847. Despite the short-lived nature of McCary's Cincinnati activities they were noted by newspapers as far away as Illinois and Missouri. See *Nauvoo New Citizen*, 23 Dec. 1846 and *The Gazette* (St. Joseph, Missouri), 11 Dec. 1846.

41. Brooks, ed., *On the Mormon Frontier*, 2:244; John D. Lee, Journal, 27 Feb. 1847, LDS Church Archives.

42. Lee, Journal, 27 Feb. 1847. Young possibly had one or more of the following uses for McCary's talents: (1) to dupe or mislead his Mormon rivals, (2) to be an interpreter among the Indians as the Saints traveled west, (3) to entertain the Saints on their westward trek with his talents as a mimic and ventriloquist.

43. Manuscript History of the Church, 26 March 1847. According to other accounts this "coolored man [sic] . . . showed his body to the company to see if he had a rib gone" and demonstrated his talents as a ventriloquist by passing himself off as the ancient Apostle Thomas—throwing his voice and claiming that "God spoke unto him and called him Thomas." See Wilford Woodruff, Journal, 26 Mar. 1847, LDS Church Historical Department; *The True Latter Day Saints Herald*, March 1861. A brief mention of the confrontation between McCary and church leaders is also contained in Willard Richards, Journal, 26 Mar. 1847, LDS Church Archives.

44. Lorenzo Brown, Journal, 27 Apr. 1847, LDS Church archives; Lee, Journal, 25 Apr. 1847.

45. According to one account, McCary joined the dissident Mormon apostle Lyman Wight, then on his way to Texas. See Lee, Journal, 7 May 1847 and the *Latter-day Saints Millennial Star* (vol. 11) (1 Jan. 1849), p. 14, which notes the interaction between Wight and the "Pagan Prophet." Other accounts, however, suggest that McCary joined Charles B. Thompson, the leader of a minor Mormon schismatic sect based initially in Missouri and later in Iowa. In this regard see my "Forgotten Mormon Perspectives: Slavery, Race, and the Black Man as Issues Among Non-Utah Latter-day Saints, 1844-75," *Michigan History*, 61 (Winter 1977): 357-70. Finally, it has been suggested that McCary traveled "South to his own tribe." See Lorenzo Brown, Journal, 27 April 1847.

46. *Ibid.*, Nelson W. Whipple, Journal, 14 Oct. 1847, LDS Church Archives; Brooks, *On the Mormon Frontier*, 1:244, fn 37, and 1:304, (25 Apr. 1847).

47. *Zion's Revelle*, 29 July 1847.

48. Whipple, Journal, 14 Oct. 1847.

49. These are my own compilations as derived from a number of sources including: Carter, *Negro Pioneer*; Wolfinger, "Test of Faith," and Jack Beller, "Negro Slaves in Utah," *Utah Historical Quarterly*, 2 (1929): 123-26. It is worth noting that the total number of blacks within Utah as compiled from these sources is considerably greater than the official U. S. Bureau of the Census, totals of 24 black slaves and 26 free blacks, 25 reputed for 1850, *The Seventh Census of the United States: 1850* (Washington, D. C., pub. 1853), p. 993.

50. For two discussions of the forces leading to the enactment of these measures see Lester E. Bush, Jr., "Mormonism's Negro Doctrine," pp. 22-29 and Dennis L. Lythgoe, "Negro Slavery in Utah," *Utah Historical Quarterly* 39 (1971): 40-54.

51. Newell G. Bringhurst, "An Ambiguous Decision: The Implementation of Mormon Priesthood Denial for the Black Man—A Reexamination," *Utah Historical Quarterly* 46 (1978): 45-64.

52. Bush, "Mormonism's Negro Doctrine," pp. 22-29.

53. Council Meeting Minutes, 2 Jan. 1902, George A. Smith Papers, (hereafter GAS Papers), University of Utah library, Salt Lake City; Council Meeting Minutes, 12 Aug. 1908, Adam S. Bennion Papers, Harold B. Lee Library, Brigham Young University, Provo, Utah.

54. Salt Lake Temple Time Book, Dec. 1853, June and July 1854, LDS Church Archives.

55. Mill Creek Ward Record of Members, #1913, pp. 63, 69, LDS Church Archives.

56. First Quorum of Seventies Minute Book, 6 June 1877, LDS Church Archives.

57. This according to U. S. Bureau of the Census, *1860 Census*, 13th Ward, Salt Lake City, Utah, #80S313, and *1870 Census*, Ogden, Weber County, 16 July 1870, p. 44.

58. *Salt Lake City Directory*, 1869, 1874, p. 14.

59. *Valley Tan*, (Salt Lake City), 26 Apr. 1859; *Deseret News*, 27 Apr. 1859.

60. Mrs. Annie Hermine Chardon Shaw, Federal Writer's Project, pp. 1 & 5, Manuscript File, Utah State Historical Society, Salt Lake City, Utah.

61. *Deseret News*, 30 Nov. 1855; 5 Feb. 1862.

62. Ibid., 27 July 1864.

63. Ogden City Cemetery Records, GS 979,228/01, vol. 220, pt. 1, give Maroni's date of death as 20 Oct. 1871.

64. *Deseret News*, 28 Nov. 1877, and Salt Lake City Death Records, 1848-84, GS 8,099, p. 203.

65. Council Meeting Minutes, 2 Jan. 1902, Bennion Papers.

66. For an excellent description of Jane E. Manning James' life and activities see Wolfinger "Test of Faith," pp. 126-147. Also see her autobiographical "Life Sketch of Jane Elizabeth Manning James," LDS Church Archives, and printed in Wolfinger, pp. 151-56.

67. Wolfinger, "Test of Faith," pp. 129-30.

68. Ibid., pp. 130-34.

69. Ibid., pp. 150-51.

70. Jane E. James to Joseph F. Smith, 7 Feb. 1890 as cited in Ibid., p. 149.

71. Church officials allowed Jane James to "be adopted into the family of Joseph Smith as a servant" through a "special" temple ceremony prepared for that purpose. See minutes of a Meeting of the Council of the Twelve Apostles, 2 Jan. 1902, GAS Papers.

72. Third Quorum of Seventy, Minutes, 1883-1907, 10 Dec. 1883, LDS Church Archives.

73. Missionary Records, 6175, pt. 1, 1860-1906, p. 75, 1883, LDS Church Archives.

74. Jenson, *Biographical Encyclopedia*, 3:557; *Deseret News*, 26 Dec. 1884.

75. This according to the findings of Jerald and Sandra Tanner, *Mormons and Negroes* (Salt Lake City, Utah, Modern Microfilm Co., 1970), pp. 12, 16, which contains documentary evidence indicating that Enoch Abel, a son of Elijah Abel, was ordained an elder on 10 Nov. 1900. and that a grandson, Elijah Abel, was ordained a priest on 5 Jul. 1934 and an elder on 29 Sept. 1935. The Tanners also suggested that Elijah Abel's other surviving son, also named Elijah, may have been ordained to the priesthood.

76. This is my own tentative conclusion based on an examination of various secondary works which describe the interaction and, indeed, intermarriage between members of Utah's black community. See: Wolfinger, "Test of Faith," Carter, *Negro Pioneer*, and William G. Hartley, "Samuel D. Chambers," *New Era* 4 June 1974: 47-50.

77. Tanner and Tanner, *Mormons and Negroes*, p. 18.

78. L. John Nuttall, Journal, 30 May 1879, Brigham Young University Library. Coltrin also recalled that: "In the washing and Annointing of Bro

Abel at Kirtland I annointed him and while I had my hands upon his head, I never had such unpleasant feelings in my life—and I said I never would again Anoint another person who had Negro blood in him. unless I was commanded by the Prophet to do so [sic]."

79. Council Meeting, 4 June 1879, Bennion Papers.

80. Ibid.

81. Ibid.

82. Minutes of a Council Meeting, 26 Aug. 1908, Bennion Papers.

83. This important development is described in Bush, "Mormonism's Negro Doctrine," pp. 31-34.

84. 3:577.

85. Joseph Fielding Smith to Mrs. Floren S. Preece, 18 Jan. 1955, S. George Ellsworth Papers, Utah State University, Logan.

86. The first to do this was L. H. Kirkpatrick, "The Negro and the LDS Church," *Pen*, 1954, pp. 12-13, 29.

87. Lythgoe, "Negro Slavery and Mormon Doctrine," Taggart, *Mormonism's Negro Policy*, and Brodie, *Can We Manipulate the Past?* (First Annual American West Lecture, University of Utah, Salt Lake City, 3 Oct. 1970).

88. Bush, "Mormonism's Negro Doctrine," pp. 16-17, 31-34.

The Fading of the Pharaohs' Curse: The Decline and Fall of the Priesthood Ban Against Blacks in the Mormon Church

Armand L. Mauss

The recent history of Mormon teachings and policies on blacks had never received the same detailed anaysis as had the earlier periods, an oversight which loomed larger after the priesthood revelation of 1978. Armand Mauss corrected that deficiency in 1981 with a detailed and descriptive analysis of the final years of the priesthood ban. He finds clear developments that anticipated the revelation and documents a surprisingly complex picture of Mormon responses to the challenges of the race question. In the process, he documents his view that the policy change was related far more closely to internal Mormon developments than to external pressure from critics. This essay originally appeared in Dialogue 14 *(Autumn 1981).*

* * * * *

Now Pharaoh, being of that lineage by which he could not have the right of priesthood, notwithstanding... would fain claim it from Noah through Ham... [Noah] blessed him with the blessings of the earth, and... wisdom, but cursed him as pertaining to the priesthood.[1]

When President Spencer W. Kimball announced to the world on 9 June 1978 a revelation making Mormons of all races eligible for the priesthood, he ended a policy that for 130 years denied the priesthood to those having any black African ancestry. Now, just three years later—in a day when Eldredge Cleaver is talking about joining the Church—it is easy to forget the major changes that led to this momentous announcement.

The history of the policy of priesthood denial can, of course, be traced back to the middle of the last century. Most Mormons have assumed that it is even older, much older, having been applied against the ancient Egyptian pharaohs. In this article I shall not be concerned with the full sweep of this history, on which a considerable body of scholarly literature already exists,[2] but rather with the final stage, or "decline and fall," starting around the end of World War II.

The first stirrings of this final stage might be seen in the 1947 exchange of letters between Professor Lowry Nelson, a distinguished Mormon sociologist, and the First Presidency of the Church.[3] The latter's remarks to Nelson, who questioned the validity of church policy on race, are important because they were the first official (though not public) church utterance on the race subject for a long time. Following the traditional rationale, the Presidency explained the policy on blacks in terms of differential merit in the premortal life; stated that the priesthood ban was official church policy from the days of Joseph Smith onward; and raised, with great misgivings, the specter of racial intermarriage.[4]

Two years later, the First Presidency issued its first general and public statement on the priesthood policy. This letter went beyond the earlier private one in its theological rationale, and included references to the black skin as indicating ancestry from Cain. It elaborated further upon the notion of differential merit in the preexistence, and held out the prospect that the ban on blacks could be removed after everyone else had had a chance at the priesthood.[5] Apparently based upon *The Way to Perfection*, the 1931 distillation by Joseph Fielding Smith of the cumulative racial lore since Brigham Young, this well-known letter expressed the position held, with rare exception and certainly without embarrassment, by Mormon leaders until very recent times.[6] The durability of that position, however, was to prove more apparent than real.

The Gathering Clouds of the 1950s

David O. McKay became president of the Church early in 1951. He was to preside over the stormiest two decades in the entire history of the Mormon-black controversy. In retrospect, President McKay would seem to have been an almost inevitable harbinger of change, not only because of the civil rights movement emerging... in the nation itself, but even more so because of his own personal values. As early as 1924, Apostle McKay had attacked anti-Negro prejudice and the "pseudo-Christians" who held it; and, in a widely republished personal letter written in 1947, he had shown himself remarkably free of the traditional notions about marks, curses, and the like, referring instead to faith in God's eventual justice and mercy.[7] Close personal friends, as well as members of his own immediate family, have affirmed that from early in his presidency, McKay believed that the restrictions on blacks were based not on "doctrine" but on "practice."[8] One might well take the inference from such statements, that he considered the way clear to a change in the policy by simple administrative fiat, rather than by special revelation. Why, if the reports of those close to him are true, no such change came during his administration, remains one of the unanswered questions of this period.[9]

President McKay does, however, seem to have taken some initiatives to reduce the *scope* of the priesthood ban to more parsimonious dimensions and concomitantly to expand the missionary work of the Church considerably among the darker-skinned peoples of the earth. These initiatives took two principal (and related) forms: (1) the transfer of entire *categories* of people from "suspect" to "clear" as far as lineage was concerned; and (2) the transfer, in *individual* cases, of the "burden of proof" of clear lineage from the candidate to his priesthood leaders (i.e., to the Church).

It is difficult to be certain just when the "burden of proof" was shifted, and the shift may well not have occurred at the same time everywhere in the Church. Until 1953, at least, it was apparently incumbent upon suspect candidates for the priesthood to clear themselves genealogically before they could be ordained or given temple recommends. This was certainly the case in places like South Africa and parts of Latin America, where the risk of black African ancestry was especially high.[10] Such a policy obviously would place many converts in a kind of "lineage limbo" until they could be "cleared," and deny the Church the badly needed leadership contributions of these potential priesthood holders. It was just such a predicament that prompted President McKay to investigate the situation first-hand in a visit to the South African Mission early in 1954. Immediately after that visit, the burden of genealogical proof was shifted to the mission president and priesthood leaders in that mission.[11]

There is reason to believe that the visit and subsequent policy deliberations on South Africa provoked more than a passing concern on President McKay's part over the broader implications of the traditional racial restrictions in a church increasingly committed to worldwide expansion. It was in the spring of 1954, just after his return from South Africa, that President McKay had his long talk on this general subject with Sterling M. McMurrin, and at very nearly the same time, one of the Twelve reported that the racial policy was undergoing reevaluation by the leadership of the Church.[12] Just how serious the deliberations of the General Authorities were at this time we are not yet in a position to know. Only a year later, however, during an extended visit to the South Pacific, President McKay faced the issue again in the case of Fiji, where emigre' Tongans had settled in fairly large numbers and had intermarried to some extent with the native Fijians.

The Church had been inconsistent over the years in its policy toward Fijians, and as recently as 1953 the First Presidency defined them as ineligible for the priesthood. President McKay, however, was convinced by his visit to Fiji and by certain anthropological evidence that the Fijians should be reclassified as Israelites. He subsequently issued a letter to that effect which not only removed the doubt hanging over the Polynesian converts of mixed blood in Fiji, but also opened up a new field for missionary work. In 1958, a large chapel was completed in Suva, Fiji, and the first Fijians received the priesthood.[13] The Negritos of the Philippines had been cleared much earlier, and the various New Guinea peoples were also ruled eligible for the priesthood in the McKay administration.[14] An important doctrinal implication of extending the priesthood to all such "Negro-looking" peoples was to emphasize that the critical criterion was not color *per se*, but lineage (from "Hamitic" Africa).[15]

The situation in Latin America was far more complicated; and nowhere were the complications more pervasive and vexing than in Brazil. Categorical clearances of this or that population group, as in Fiji or New Guinea, could not feasibly be made in Latin America, nor, in the absence of apartheid, could the "burden of proof" of clear lineage be transferred to the Church with as little relative risk as in South Africa. That transfer thus seems to have taken place somewhat later in Latin America than elsewhere.[16] The Spanish and Portuguese *conquistadores* had had few qualms about miscegenation; and countries like Brazil had had such an extensive admixture of both Indian and African Negro ancestry as to make any reliable lineage "clearance" a practical impossibility. This problem was well known to Church leaders and may have been a factor in the postponement of proselyting among the Portuguese-speaking native populations in Brazil. Until World War II, proselyting in both Brazil and Argentina was directed largely at Germans and other European emigre' peoples. The first converts in South America were actually Italians, though they were soon joined by equal numbers of Spanish-speaking converts in Argentina. However, in Brazil, where racial mixture was especially extensive, proselyting was mostly confined to Germans until the outbreak of war, when the Brazilian government outlawed German-based organizations. Only then did the proselyting efforts of the Church shift to the Portuguese-speaking Brazilians.[17]

When proselyting finally began in earnest among the latter, strenuous efforts had to be made to identify, well before baptism, those converts who might be genealogically suspect. Such efforts included a special lesson for investigators near the end of the standard lesson series in which the topic of lineage and access to the priesthood was discussed in a larger doctrinal and historical context. Investigators were urged to look through family photo albums, often in the presence of the missionaries, for evidence of ancestors who might have shown indications of African ancestry. Similar "screening" efforts were employed in various other Latin American countries, and the lineage lesson developed in Brazil was widely adopted with various local modifications in several Latin American missions.[18] The mission presidents, however, were given a great deal of autonomy by the General Authorities in the application of the priesthood ban to specific cases.

It is not difficult to imagine the potential for grief that would follow such screening policies, the more so because of their ultimate operational futility. To make matters worse, there was considerable variation among mission presidents in how meticulously the screening was enforced, so that even in the same mission an incoming president of conservative bent might inherit from his more liberal predecessor a number of problematic cases of priests or elders of obviously suspect lineage. Even with *bona fide* screening efforts of the most meticulous kind by all parties concerned, there was a constant potential for *post hoc* discoveries of ineligible lineage as the Saints in Brazil and elsewhere took seriously their genealogical obligations. When such discoveries were made, the mission presidents again had a great deal of autonomy in deciding how they were to be resolved or whether they had to be referred to the General Authorities for resolution.

These resolutions themselves tended to have an inconsistent, *ad hoc* quality from one time or mission to another. Sometimes there really was no resolution; the case was either ignored or treated with benign procrastination. In other cases, the hapless holders of both Hamite lineage and priesthood office were notified that their right to exercise the priesthood had been "suspended" (or some synonym thereof). An intermediate resolution in some cases was to "suspend" an elder for all formal ecclesiastical purposes but permit him to continue his exercise of the priesthood within his own home (including administrations to the sick). With the eventual transfer by 1960 of the burden of genealogical proof from the Saints and investigators to missionaries and priesthood leaders, the incidence of *post hoc* discovery greatly increased. Nevertheless, the missionary harvest in Latin America only grew more bountiful than ever. Meanwhile, in North America itself, a number of cases long awaiting ordination or temple privileges were cleared under President McKay's new policy on burden of proof.[19]

All such deliberations, adaptations, and reformulations of the church racial policy during the 1950s remained unobserved by the membership and public at large, of course. Dr. Lowry Nelson, apparently not satisfied with the outcome of his earlier correspondence with the First Presidency, went public in 1952 with an article in *The Nation* that reiterated some of the thoughts he had expressed in his 1947 letter.[20] Having earlier responded to Nelson and others, however, the presiding brethren remained largely aloof from public controversy. A few General Authorities and other well-intentioned brethren attempted during these years to offer their own explanations and interpretations of Church doctrines and policies on race, primarily for internal consumption.[21] On the whole, the statements by church leaders in this period, like their less public struggles over policy applications, showed a certain consistency with the traditional and operative lore of the times, including a special concern for the problems presented by intermarriage.[22] Outside the Church, meanwhile, the nation itself was just beginning to discover its own racial problems and as yet paid little attention to the Mormons. Indeed, as late as 1957, when Thomas F. O'Dea published his insightful sociological study, *The Mormons*, he saw no reason to mention Mormonism's "Negro problem," even in his section on "Sources of Strain and Conflict."[23]

The Stormy Sixties

Like most Americans, Mormons were somewhat taken by surprise at the civil rights movement. Treating blacks "differently" had become so thoroughly normative in the nation that even the churches generally did not question it until the 1950s, at the earliest.[24] Prior to that time, the public schools, the military, and nearly all major institutions of the nation were racially segregated. Accordingly, rumblings about racism among the Mormons were rare and continued so until the 1960s.

The arrival of the New Frontier, however, was accompanied by an accelerating and increasingly successful civil rights movement, which not only produced a long series of local, state, and federal antidiscrimination edicts, but which also rendered increasingly untenable and ridiculous a number of traditional racial ideas held by Mormons and others. The racial policy of the Church was soon attacked by spokesmen of liberal Christianity, who at length had discovered racism in the land;[25] it was attacked by the Utah branch of the NAACP;[26] it was attacked by important and nationally syndicated journalists;[27] and it was even attacked publicly by certain prominent Mormons.[28] Other internal critics, while agreeing with the official church stance that revelation was the only legitimate vehicle for change, still questioned the historical basis for the priesthood ban against the blacks, and especially the folklore that had traditionally been marshalled to support it.[29]

As external criticism grew, the reaction among the Saints was one of uncertainty and some dismay. Cherishing a heritage of persecution and discrimination of their own, like Jews, Mormons had never been accustomed to thinking of themselves as the offenders in matters of civil rights. Yet church leaders and spokesmen actually had very little to say to their critics. When they responded at all, they fell back on a formal and legalistic position: However unpopular the Mormon policy might be in the rest of the nation, it was nobody else's business, for it was an internal ecclesiastical matter. It was not a civil rights issue, because it had nothing to do with constitutional guarantees of secular, civil equality. Since non-Mormons did not agree that the Mormon priesthood was the exclusively valid one anyway, why did they care who got to hold it? Nor were Mormon blacks complaining. Thus, the continued harassment of the Mormon Church over its priesthood policies actually constituted interference and infringement, under the First Amendment, of the civil rights of *Mormons*.[30]

To say that the world did not accept the Mormon definition of the situation would be a bit of an understatement. The America of the 1960s was not the place or time to try to convince anyone that any aspect of race relations was purely a private matter. The cacophony of criticism and recrimination directed against the Church intensified steadily and finally spent itself, only at the end of the decade, in a great crescendo. As the decade started, George Romney's 1962 gubernatorial campaign in Michigan gave critics in the media and in the civil rights movement a handy and legitimate occasion to raise questions about the carryover of racist religious doctrines into political behavior. However, Romney's terms as governor were so progressive in civil rights matters that the issue was left dormant. It arose again during the 1968 presidential primaries, but this time Romney's campaign was aborted early, in part, some have claimed, to avoid putting any more pressure on the Church.[31]

The Utah chapters of the NAACP played a conspicuous role in the public pressures felt by the Church during these years. A plan for demonstrations at Temple Square during the October 1963 General Conference was called off only after private negotiations between President Hugh B. Brown and local NAACP representatives. President Brown's unequivocal statement in advocacy of civil rights, at the opening Sunday session of the conference, was apparently one outcome of these negotiations.[32] Similar statements, repeated at subsequent conferences or other public occasions, did not long suffice, however, to dampen the NAACP animus. Under its auspices, pickets marched through downtown Salt Lake City to the old Church Office Building in early 1965 to demand church support for civil rights measures pending in the state legislature; and later in the same year the Ogden and Salt Lake branches of the NAACP introduced a resolution at the organization's national meeting strongly condemning the Church, and calling, in particular, for Third World countries to deny visas to Mormon missionaries.[33]

One such country, Nigeria, had already anticipated the NAACP call. The emergence of the Nigeria story in the midst of all the bad publicity of the time introduced an incredibly ironic note. In response to initiatives from interested Nigerians dating back as far as 1946, the Church had been sending literature and exchanging letters, without much enthusiasm, until 1959, when a representative from Salt Lake City was sent to evaluate the situation. It was discovered that certain self-converted Nigerians had organized branches of the Church on their own authority and had thereby generated a pool of potential Mormon converts amounting to several thousands. Early in 1963, half a dozen missionaries were set apart for service in Nigeria that would have included not only proselyting but also the construction and operation of schools and hospitals—then an unprecedented aspect of Mormon missionary work. Before the missionaries could be dispatched, however, the Nigerian government got wind of the traditional racial doctrines and policies of the Church and refused to grant visas. Negotiations over the matter between the government and the Church continued for several years but came to naught as the outbreak of civil war in Nigeria rendered the issue moot for the time being.[34] The ironic emergence and outcome of these developments, however, should not distract us from the more important point that the commitments made by the Church under President McKay to a country in black Africa represented a distinct softening of the traditional policy of nonproselytization in such countries.

The Nigerian developments again occasioned some serious deliberations among the First Presidency in 1962 and 1963 over the feasibility of dropping, at least partially, the ban against blacks in the priesthood. President Brown, then second counselor, urged on his two colleagues that the traditional policy be modified to grant blacks at least the Aaronic Priesthood, pointing to the sudden need for local leadership that had developed in Nigeria. President Henry D. Moyle, then first counselor, approved of this idea. So did President McKay himself, in principle, though he had qualms that such a piecemeal change might only exacerbate the already serious problem of intermarriage in various places.[35] For whatever reasons, these deliberations did not produce a policy change at that time, but they may well have been the basis for the optimism about change that President Brown expressed publicly on more than one occasion in 1963.[36] On the other hand, President McKay's own expressed pessimism a year later may have been a reflection of a more realistic awareness on his part of the opposition to policy change that still obtained among some of the Twelve. A hint of that opposition surfaced very briefly around General Conference time in April 1965, when President Brown and Elder Benson were found to be in public disagreement.[37]

On an official level, though, the presiding brethren seemed at least to stand together on the declarations in President Brown's 1963 General Conference statement. That statement, of course, did not even mention the church priesthood policy; it simply upheld the emergent civil rights doctrine of the nation. Critics both in and out of the Church seemed unwilling to let the brethren off that easily. As the decade drew to a close, the Church was forced to fend off more serious attacks, first on the book of Abraham (the only scriptural precedent for priesthood denial), and then on Brigham Young University, discussed below. During this period, President Brown moved once again for an administrative decision to drop the priesthood ban. Presumably he was joined by President Tanner, his nephew and colleague in the First Presidency. Throughout the latter part of 1969, Brown strove vigorously to win the concurrence of President McKay, whom he knew to share his view that the priesthood ban could properly be ended administratively. However, McKay was by then fading fast toward his death the next January, and he was not often physically capable of sustained deliberations. The decision-making process this time was complicated not only by President McKay's condition, but also by the fact that the First Presidency had by that time temporarily acquired five counselors, rather than the usual two.[38]

While we cannot be sure just how much resistance President Brown encountered among the rest of the General Authorities, the other counselors in the First Presidency at that time were Joseph Fielding Smith, Alvin R. Dyer, and Harold B. Lee, all of whom were on record with conservative views on the race question.[39] In any case, the public statement that ultimately issued from all these deliberations was not an announcement of an end to the priesthood ban against blacks, as President Brown and Tanner had proposed, but rather the letter of 15 Dec. 1969, which, while promising eventual change, actually only reaffirmed the traditional policy.[40] As in 1963, President Brown may have allowed his optimism in the deliberations to spill over into his public utterances, for he was widely quoted in the press during December 1969, as intimating imminent change.[41] The change was not yet to come, however, and President McKay died on 18 Jan. 1970, thereby dissolving the entire First Presidency. A week later, the new president of the Church, Joseph Fielding Smith, assured the world at a formal news conference that his views on church policy and doctrine had "never been altered" and that no changes should be expected.[42]

Anticlimatic as this episode may seem, it would be a mistake to overlook the significance of the document it produced. The December 1969 statement of the First Presidency (signed only by Presidents Brown and Tanner "for" the First Presidency) dealt with the theological basis of the priesthood ban for the first time in twenty years. This portion of the statement is notable for its parsimony: While referring back vaguely to a premortal life, it said nothing about that life, nothing about the war in heaven, or about any differential merit having implications for mortality. It said nothing about Cain or Ham or marks or curses or perpetual servitude. It relied almost entirely on the simple claim that the Church had barred Negroes from the priesthood since its earliest days "for reasons which we believe are known to God, but which He has not made fully known to man." Thus, in its first official statement on the controversy in nearly a generation, the Church chose to set aside almost the entire doctrinal scaffolding that had bolstered its priesthood policy toward blacks for more than a century.[43]

The last doctrinal resort, presumably in support of the traditional priesthood ban, was the book of Abraham, which contained the only passage in all of Mormon scripture relating explicitly to a lineage denied access to the priesthood—"the Pharaohs' curse," as it were. The acquisition by the Church late in 1967 of a critical fragment from the papyrus, upon which Joseph Smith had based his translation of the book of Abraham, gave rise to a vigorous controversy starting in 1968 over the authenticity of the translation. Though the various partisans in the controversy spent their ammunition in rather a short period of time, there was never a conclusive resolution except for a general agreement that Joseph Smith's rendering of at least the fragments in question had not been even approximately a literal one. While such a disclosure might seem to impeach the doctrinal authenticity of "the Pharaohs' curse," there is as yet no reason to believe that it affected the thinking of President Brown or any of his colleagues. Indeed, it seems rather surprising in retrospect that the implications of the book of Abraham controversy for the traditional priesthood policy entered only occasionally and peripherally into the literature of that controversy, which seemed almost totally preoccupied instead with the more fundamental issue of Joseph Smith's claims to the gift of translation and to the prophetic mantle more generally.[44]

As the end of the decade approached, the Church was beginning to appear unassailable and impervious to all forms of outside pressure. The priesthood policy on blacks could not be changed, it was repeatedly explained, without a revelation from the Lord; and it began to appear that the greater the outside clamor for change, the less likely would be the revelation. Then the civil rights movement found a vulnerable secondary target. Brigham Young University began late in 1968 to encounter increasingly hostile demonstrations during athletic contests, chiefly in Colorado, Wyoming, New Mexico, Arizona, and California. At least two prestigious universities, Stanford and the University of Washington, severed athletic relations with BYU altogether amidst much publicity and controversy, even though investigations by both the Western Athletic Conference and a University of Arizona delegation had exonerated the Mormon school of any discriminatory practice.[45] It soon became clear that this treatment of its showplace university, whether fair or not, had struck a sensitive Mormon nerve, and the Church began to fight back as it had never done while the issue was strictly an ecclesiastical or theological one. In a rare counterattack, evidently intended to forestall the rupture in athletic relations with the University of Washington, BYU President Ernest L. Wilkinson (doubtless with the approval of Church authorities) placed a full-page ad in major Washington newspapers on 1 April 1970. Entitled, "Minorities, Civil Rights, and BYU," the advertisement strikes one as a very persuasive (if futile) public relations piece.[46]

Concomitant with the campaign against BYU and probably stimulated by it was the rise of a brief spell of collective jitters in Utah (mainly Salt Lake City) over rumors of impending black "invasions" and violence. It is difficult to assess the magnitude or intensity of this episode. Some people apparently acquired a kind of "siege mentality" as the public campaign against the Church and BYU intensified during the late 1960s. This mentality expressed itself in a number of ways: vigilante-type groups, called "Neighborhood Emergency Teams" (NETs) were formed in some areas for the "protection" of the citizens from the expected black onslaught;[47] a folk prophecy attributed to John Taylor, which predicted open warfare and bloodshed in the city streets, was retrieved and reinterpreted to give credence to current rumors; humor at the expense of blacks apparently became more common and more vicious; and rumors were circulated about attacks by blacks, in California and elsewhere, on the occupants of cars with Utah license plates.[48] White mob action, ironically, must have seemed for a time a more realistic prospect in Utah than black mobs ever were!

It is difficult to know how much exaggeration went into accounts of this period by the press and other observers. A Louis Harris poll taken in Utah during 1971, however, found Mormons far more likely than others in the state to give some credence to the existence of "a black conspiracy to destroy the Mormon Church."[49] One apostle during this period privately expressed fear for the physical safety of Church leaders, and another was already well known to have tied the civil rights movement to the international communist conspiracy.[50] Nevertheless, it must be emphasized that both Church authorities and civil authorities actively opposed the incipient vigilantism of that hectic time, and it did not last long.[51] Nor is there reason to believe that it had much effect on the Saints outside Utah. While it surely must be counted as a troubling and embarrassing episode in Mormon-black relations, it does seem to have been limited in time and scope, so one must be cautious in attributing to it any general significance for "the Church" or for "the Mormons."[52]

It is ironic that the "twenty years of tempest" just recounted coincided almost exactly with the presidency of David O. McKay. It is difficult to think of a president in the history of Mormonism who more personified the very antitheses of racism and social conflict; yet these will always stand as the traits that most marked his regime to the outside world. The storm began largely unnoticed behind a mountain range of ecclesiastical privacy, as President McKay and his colleagues struggled with the implications of adapting race policies developed in the isolation of Utah to the anomalies of exotic places. However expedient those adaptations may have seemed at the time, they were to prove ultimately unsatisfactory, not only in faroff places, but in North America, as well.[53]

The national civil rights movement soon blew the storm out into the plains of public visibility and scrutiny. There it buffeted the brethren with blasts in the media from all quarters, including Nigeria; with pickets, protests, and political pressure; with assaults on BYU and the book of Abraham; and ultimately with a vexing outbreak of mob mentality among the faithful in the heartland. Then, as unexpectedly as it had arisen, the worst of the storm seemed to die with President McKay in early 1970. By the end of spring that year, nothing more was heard from pickets, protestors, vigilantes, or athletic disruptions. Through it all, the maddening Mormon policy on blacks had stood unchanged. Or had it? A closer look reveals that the policy had been stripped to its bare bones, both theologically and operationally. More change was yet to come.

Respite and Reconciliation

The outstanding developments of the 1970s were the respite granted the Mormon Church over the race issue by its critics, black and white; the reconciliation between the church and the blacks, in particular; and the revelation, late in the decade, ending the discriminatory ban. The civil rights movement in the surrounding society had begun to peak. A less supportive national government had come to power, many of the movement's objectives seemed to have been accomplished, and other minorities were now laying claim to some of what the blacks had won for themselves. Accordingly, critics inside and outside the Church backed off noticeably. It was as though they had all decided to give up on the obstinate Mormons and concentrate on other violations of the national equalitarian ethos (one of which, the women's issue, would soon be haunting the Mormons).

When Joseph Fielding Smith succeeded David O. McKay as president of the Church, there was some speculation about the presumably reactionary stance that he might take on racial matters. However, the aged incoming president never publicly reiterated the ideas he had expressed in his more vigorous years. Indeed, in several ways the Church began during his administration to show increasing awareness and sensitivity about race relations generally and relations with blacks in particular.[54] In late 1972, for example, when the Church was preparing to construct its new high-rise center in New York City, black residents of the area and black members of the city planning commission objected to the construction on the grounds that it would serve as a symbol of racism in an otherwise integrated neighborhood. The Church responded with public assurances about its planned relationships with the neighborhood, even offering to compensate a local black resident who felt that the value of his property had been somewhat compromised, and gave guarantees of nondiscriminatory employment practices on the construction site. Black opposition thereupon faded rapidly.[55]

Not all such confrontations were so amicably settled. A scheduled tour of the Tabernacle Choir to New England in 1974 had to be cancelled because of protests from black clergymen in the region.[56] In the same year, the Church inadvertently ran afoul of the Boy Scouts of America through a new organizational arrangement that had the effect of integrating its scout troops more closely with the Aaronic Priesthood groups. The Church and the BSA had earlier agreed on this change, but neither had anticipated the barring of black youths from positions of scout leadership in Mormon troops. (Actually, all non-Mormons in those troops were also barred.) The Church was soon confronted by an NAACP suit over the matter, and corrective action was very fast in coming.[57] The Church clearly was more responsive now.

At the same time, however, the Church was as insistent as ever that policy change relating to the priesthood itself would still have to come through legitimate channels, and it tolerated little dissent from the inside over this issue. Two active (and theretofore loyal) brethren attracted considerable publicity, one in 1976 and the other in 1977, through certain dramatic gestures of dissent; both were promptly excommunicated for their efforts.[58] Toward the outside, though, there seemed to be an increasingly conciliatory posture on racial matters. It was as though, with the pressure off, the Church could afford to be less defensive about the integrity of its procedures for legitimate change.

Much of the Church's more amicable relationship with the outside world during the 1970s may have been attributable to the initiative of the new Public Communications Department formed in August 1972 with Wendell J. Ashton as its first managing director. Of course, the Church had had public relations efforts before: There had been a Church Information Service and a press secretary. For special public relations projects, a professional firm would be retained. The new PCD, however, was an all-purpose, comprehensive, integrated public relations arm of the Church, with seven separate divisions staffed mainly by professionals and with literally thousands of representatives located in the stakes and missions.[59] One of its earliest division heads (and now PCD managing director) was Heber G. Wolsey, who had been in charge of public relations at BYU during the sensitive time there a couple of years earlier.[60] One of the missions specifically assigned to the PCD from the beginning was "improving the image of the Church." This was to be done, furthermore, not merely by reacting to criticism from the outside (the usual policy in the past), but by taking the initiative at given opportunities.[61]

In line with this new public relations enterprise and policy, Wendell

Ashton himself began to appear on the national media (e.g., an NBC Special Report in 1973) and to field in a low key but sophisticated way some tough questions on the race policy and other matters.[62] The more embarrassing (from a PR standpoint) doctrinal baggage omitted in the 1969 First Presidency statement remained firmly out of the public arena. It was the PCD itself, furthermore, that arranged for President Kimball to appear on NBC's morning *Today Show* in 1974, where again he was faced with some rather blunt questions on the race policy, women's roles and the family.[63] Whether entirely through PCD initiatives or not, the public image of the Church by the mid-1970s had greatly improved compared to a decade earlier. Criticism on the black issue, in particular, was far less frequent. The polemics of the sixties were replaced with more restrained and informed critiques.[64]

Nowhere was this new relaxed public relations posture more evident than in Mormon initiatives toward blacks during the 1970s. In retrospect, it seems clear that the Church, near the beginning of the decade, launched a deliberate and sustained campaign to build bridges with blacks, both inside and outside the Church. If it was not yet ready to end the priesthood ban, it at least felt the need to come to know more blacks better, and to remove the aura of "the cursed" or "the forbidden" that had accumulated in the consciousness of most white Mormons. It is scarcely possible for outsiders to appreciate the fundamental significance of this development, however gradually it may have occurred; it was, indeed, second in significance only to the later bestowal of the priesthood itself.

A few examples will suffice. Significant efforts to cultivate ties with outside blacks seem to have centered largely on BYU. During the 1969-70 controversy over BYU's athletic ties with other schools, it was already apparent that the Mormon university was recruiting black athletes, many of whom were put in a very difficult position by the hostile pressures from the other schools and from the black community more generally.[65] Nevertheless, the recruiting efforts continued, eventually bringing several black athletes to BYU, some Mormon and some not, and most on athletic scholarships.[66] Nor were BYU's efforts all athletic. During the summer of 1971, a black man and wife from Los Angeles were both presented with doctoral degrees from the BYU College of Education.[67] In March 1976, BYU students elected their first black student body vice-president.[68] In 1977, the renowned author of *Roots*, Alex Haley, was a commencement speaker at BYU; and in early 1978, Senator Edward Brooke was a special speaker at the university on the subject of relations with South Africa. During his speech (obviously well researched for a Mormon audience), the Senator disgressed extensively toward the end for a discussion of Mormon-black relationships in the United States. His comments were remarkable partly for the candor which he felt free to use in reference to the Mormon position on blacks but mainly for the conciliatory tone which provided the context for that candor. This was all in stark contrast to the hostile terms and the demands for immediate policy change which had characterized the comments of the Utah NAACP in 1965, or the Black Student Union indictment of BYU in 1969-70.[69] Even off campus, BYU students participated significantly in such things as fund-raising activities for black churches in Salt Lake City, thereby earning the appreciation of a prominent black minister, who, while clearly expressing his disagreement with the Church's teachings, was nevertheless "glad that we could get together to show people that we're not going to kill one another about it."[70]

Perhaps even more remarkable, however, was the new Mormon stance toward its own blacks. After more than a century of having been nearly "invisible," Mormon blacks began to receive attention and promotional coverage in Church publications and social circles. *The Church News* had ignored almost entirely things black (or Negro) until 1969. The Index to the *Church News* for the period 1961-70 shows only one listing on the topic from July 1962 to January 1969, but several a year thereafter. Black singers began to appear with increasing frequency in the Tabernacle Choir, and one of these, a recently converted contralto, was also appointed to the BYU faculty.[71] Feature articles about Mormon blacks began to appear in Church magazines.[72] Blacks began to participate more conspicuously and perhaps more frequently in some of the lesser temple rituals (e.g., baptisms for the dead). One elderly black woman who had been a Mormon in the Washington, D.C., area for seventy years was featured in a widely viewed television documentary about the new temple there.[73] Several black Mormons published small books during this period describing their experiences as converts and members in rather positive terms. Though all privately published, these books gained fairly wide circulation among Mormons.[74] Other Mormon blacks freely submitted to interviews with the media in which they generally defended the Church.[75]

Of special significance was the creation of the Genesis Group late in 1971, an enterprise still very much alive a decade later.[76] This group was organized as a supplement, not a substitute, for the regular church activities of Mormon blacks in their respective Salt Lake area wards. Led by a group presidency, their program consists of monthly Sunday evening meetings, plus Relief Society, MIA, choir and other auxiliary and recreational activities. With a potential membership of perhaps 200, its participation levels have ranged between about twenty-five and fifty, consisting disproportionately of women, middle-aged and older people, and high school-educated skilled and semi-skilled workers.[77] About half are partners in racially mixed marriages, and the most active members are (with a few important exceptions) blacks converted to Mormonism in adult life, rather than life-long members from the old black families of Utah.[78]

The Genesis Group was organized mainly on the initiative of the small band of faithful black Mormons who became its leaders. Three of them approached the Quorum of Twelve with a proposal for an independent black branch to be led by a few blacks ordained to the priesthood on a trial basis—a proposal, in effect, for a racially segregated branch. The main rationale was that the unique predicament and feeling of Mormon blacks called for more intensive fellowship and mutual support than their residential dispersion would normally allow. While the presiding brethren were not yet willing to go as far as an independent branch, they were very willing to sponsor the kind of group that eventually resulted from these negotiations, irregular though the Genesis Group surely was.[79]

A special committee of three apostles was appointed to organize the new group and oversee it, though eventually it was placed directly under stake jurisdiction.[80] It is not clear just what future the apostles envisioned for the Genesis Group, but to its members it represented the beginning of a whole new era for Mormon blacks, and they chose its name accordingly. While leaders of the group were not ordained to the priesthood, they had the distinct impression—whether on adequate grounds or not—that their organization was a step in the direction of eventual priesthood ordination; and they believed, furthermore, that such an expectation was shared by leading members of the Twelve.

The official mission given the Genesis Group at its inception, however, consisted mainly of the reactivation or proselyting of blacks in the area. Early on, the group inevitably acquired other functions: (1) It came to serve as a kind of unofficial speakers' bureau for wards and stakes in the area seeking more association with Mormon blacks and more acquaintance with their feelings; this, in turn, contributed to the growing visibility of blacks in Utah church circles. Also (2) the group provided a vehicle for mutual support, counseling, and fellowship among Mormon blacks themselves, and a legitimized forum for the expression of aspirations, frustrations, or even bitterness. There was, of course, the inherent risk that the Genesis Group might move into a more militant form of consciousness-raising. It is a comment on the loyalty of the group members that such did not happen despite occasional outbreaks of acrimony.

Since the end of the priesthood ban, the mutual support function of the group has perforce been expanded to include the counseling and fellowshipping of new black converts from around the nation (by telephone and mail) who are having trouble with both the historical and the residual racism they may have encountered on joining the Church. One would expect that such activities will become less burdensome as racism recedes, and more black converts join such thriving branches as the one recently organized in the Watts area of southern California.[81] Meanwhile, the Genesis Group has been rendering the Church and its black members a unique and selfless service.

We are not yet in a position to know what cumulative impact the events of the 1970s may have had behind the closed doors of the highest councils of the Church. We have already noted that the relentless public pressures of the 1960s do not seem to have been sustained into the next decade—not that there was a lack of vexing incidents: the 1972 confrontation with New York City blacks; the cancellation of the Tabernacle Choir tour and the run-in with the Boy Scouts in 1974; and the highly publicized excommunications and related harassments of 1976 and 1977. These tended to be separate and *ad hoc* in nature, however, and usually could be brought to closure in a limited time with limited public relations damage, unlike the endless and orchestrated barrage of the 1960s.

The external and public episodes of the 1970s are thus not as likely as the internal developments in the Church to provide the explanation for the decline and fall of the priesthood ban on blacks. When the historical documents are made available, we are likely to see the year 1974 emerge from the data as the crucial year of no return, the year, that is, when the decline of the priesthood ban entered a steeper phase and its end became not only inevitable but imminent. It is not merely that 1974 was the year that Spencer W. Kimball assumed the presidency (actually on 30 Dec. 1973). To be sure, President Kimball was to play the most critical role in ending the ban, but it is unlikely that he saw himself in that role as he took office. His 1974 interview on the *Today Show* makes it clear that while he was praying about the matter, he did not think change was imminent.[82] Still, he was praying about it, and, ultimately, in a manner that Bruce R. McConkie implies may have been unprecedented.[83] Certainly by the time the historic revelation came in mid-1978, President Kimball had been agonizing over the issue for some time.[84]

For just how long we are not sure. However, he could not long have remained unmindful of the consequences of the decision made during his very first year as president in 1974 to build a temple in Brazil. By that time, there were four missions, nine stakes, and 41,000 Latter-day Saints in Brazil alone.[85] It was a matter of grave concern to the mission presidents and regional representatives who had served recently in Brazil, which they surely must have communicated to President Kimball and his colleagues, that racial intermixing for hundreds of years in that country was making the issue of priesthood eligibility an impossible tangle.[86] It seems unbelievable that a decision would deliberately have been made to build a temple in the most racially mixed country on the continent without a concomitant realization (or a rapidly emerging one) that the priesthood ban would have to be ended. It is in this sense that 1974 was a year of no turning back, and that is why Jan Shipps and others are probably correct in seeing the eventual revelation of 1978 as far more the product of internal pressures like Brazil than of external pressures from public relations.[87]

The quicksands of the lineage-sorting enterprise also were brought forcibly to the attention of some members of the Quorum of the Twelve by another development in the mid-1970s. While this development fortunately remained an internal one, it could easily have become public, with a high potential for scandal. For some time there had been a group of trained genealogists—full-time church employees—who assumed responsibility for reviewing complicated lineage problems referred from around the Church. These genealogists reported directly to a member of the Twelve and made recommendations about priesthood eligibility in hard cases. From an internal ecclesiastical point of view, the arrangement made perfectly good sense: few church leaders at either the local or general level felt that they had the expertise to make crucial judgments about lineage in individual cases.

The existence of this screening process became problematic when the Church became aware of proposed legislation pending in Congress which would have prevented access to the 1900 census records stored under the control of the U.S. Archivist. The Church was interested in this legislation because the 1900 census contained information of critical value to genealogists. (Such data were of great interest also to the University of Utah medical school, a major center for the study of family disease histories.) The problem grew more complicated, however, when the head of the Bureau of the Census opposed release of the data because he believed it an invasion of privacy for the Church to use census information for genealogical purposes which ultimately led to "bizarre" temple ceremonies vicariously involving people who were not even Mormons. As the bill moved through committee hearings, certain black members of Congress also opposed the bill because of the priesthood ban on blacks. In such a context, the outside discovery of a church group specializing in black lineage identification would have not only scuttled the Church's legislative efforts but also have created a major public relations embarrassment.[88]

As things turned out, the three or four year tug-of-war in Congress over the access issue ended indecisively and eventually became moot with the automatic expiration of statutory and regulatory restrictions on the archival census data in question. However, in 1976 the hazards of the Church's group of lineage specialists were brought quietly to the attention of certain members of the Twelve. Some friction among the Brethren subsequently developed, for the lineage screening program, it seems, was a surprise even to some of the Twelve, and approval for the enterprise was not universal among them. Exactly what ensued thereafter is not clear, but the sensitive screening program at the headquarters level does seem to have been dropped, for an official letter from the First Presidency eventually transferred to stakes and missions the final determination of "whether or not one does have Negro blood."[89]

Revelation and Aftermath

In the spring of 1978, as the new revelation waited in the wings, there was no inkling of its pending dramatic entrance to center stage. The charged deliberations of the presiding brethren during the weeks immediately preceding had obviously been carried on in great secrecy, preventing the preliminary rumors that had been "leaked" during earlier and abortive deliberations in 1963 and 1969. Yet, as we have seen, the new revelation was not as sudden a reversal of the status quo as it may have seemed. The stage had clearly been set. Many trends had merged into a common strain toward greater parsimony and ever greater limitation on the impact and implications of the traditional priesthood ban. These trends had the effect of preparing both the leaders and the membership of the Church for the new revelation.

First, there was the gradual constriction of the scope of the ban *within* the Church, a casting of the net less broadly, as it were. Whole categories of people were moved out from under the ban, as in the South Pacific. The burden of proof in the case of dubious lineage was shifted from the questionable family or individual to the priesthood leaders and the Church, not only in North American but also in South Africa and even in the hopelessly mixed countries of Latin America. A certain looseness at the boundaries of the ban was also apparent in the decentralization and delegation of the decision-making about priesthood eligibility, at first partially and then (by February 1978) totally. Another way of seeing this trend would be to say that by the time Spencer W. Kimball became president, there were far more categories and situations among mankind eligible for the priesthood than had been the case when David O. McKay had assumed the presidency.

Then there was a corresponding trend toward reducing the implications, or damage, as it were, deriving from the priesthood ban in the *external* relationships of the Church with the world. First, starting in the early 1960s, the Church increasingly attempted to strip the priesthood policy of any social or civic implications, embracing the civil rights doctrines of the nation and eventually putting the Church behind progressive legislation in Utah. Every official statement from 1963 on emphatically denied that the internal church policy provided any justification for opposition to civil rights for all races. At least equally important was the deliberate and rapid public redefinition during the 1970s of blacks, Mormon or otherwise, as acceptable and desirable associates and equals. A new media image for blacks always had been part of the thrust of the civil rights movement as a whole in America, but for Mormons, the most salient medium was ultimately their religion, and particularly its public and official posture. As long as the black man appeared to be regarded by Mormon leaders as *persona non grata*, or even as "the invisible man," Mormons would probably keep their distance, despite a formally proper equalitarian stance in civic affairs. The new message seemed to be, then, that the priesthood ban justified neither the denial of civil rights nor the apprehensive social avoidance of black people.

The third important expression of the trend toward parsimony was the gradual discarding of the traditional theological justifications for priesthood denial. This evolution is obvious from a systematic comparison of official Church statements across time: the First Presidency letters of the 1940s (so reminiscent of the nineteenth century lore distilled by Joseph Fielding Smith in 1931); their counterparts in the 1960s, either avoiding theology altogether or espousing only "reasons which we believe are known to God, but which He has not made fully known to man"; and finally the stark declaration by the Public Communications director of the Church (presumably on behalf of the First Presidency), on the eve of the new revelation, that "any reason given . . . [for priesthood denial] . . . except that it comes from God, is supposition, not doctrine."[90]

With the doctrinal scaffolding thus removed, the priesthood ban itself reduced in scope to the bare minimum, and a new visibility and identity created for blacks in the Mormon milieu, all that was left of the residue of racism was a restrictive policy of priesthood eligibility under increasing strain. The public announcement of its demise was dramatic but not elaborate—scarcely 500 words long. It began by citing the expansion of the Church in recent years, and then alluded briefly to the expectations expressed by some Church leaders in earlier years that the priesthood would eventually be extended to all races. Most of the brief statement, however, was devoted to legitimating the policy change by reference to direct communication with Deity, which the prophet and his two counselors "declar[ed] with soberness" that they had experienced "after spending many hours in the upper room of the temple supplicating the Lord for divine guidance." After these strenuous efforts, the Lord's will was revealed, for he "by revelation has confirmed that the long-promised day has come when every faithful, worthy man in the Church may receive the holy priesthood . . . without regard for race or color."[91]

The optimistic (if unsupported) observation of Arrington and Bitton may be true, that the new revelation "was received, almost universally, with elation."[92] Some credence for that observation may be found in a systematic survey of Salt Lake City and San Francisco Mormons more than a decade ago, which found that more than two-thirds of the sample were ready to accept blacks into the priesthood or at least did not oppose it.[93] If one can accept the proposition that Mormon public opinion had been well prepared for changes in the status and image of blacks, then widespread acquiescence in the new policy would be expected, the more so in a religion stressing the principle of modern revelation.

At the same time, however, in parts of the Mormon heartland, at least, there was a period of discomfiture that expressed itself in the circulation of some rather bad jokes at the expense of our newly enfranchised black brothers and sisters.[94] And it may well be awhile yet before most white Mormons, at least in North America, will be free of traditional reservations about serving under black bishops or watching their teenagers dance with black peers at church social events. In all such matters, one can hope that we follow the compelling example of the Saints in New Zealand, where "Mormons are the most successful of all churches in the implementation of a policy of integration ... This applies to the absolute numbers of Maoris who are in meaningful interaction with Pakehas [whites] in face-to-face religious groups ... [as well as to] ... their effectiveness in reaching and moulding their members into cohesive communities ..."[95]

The public relations build-up on blacks was greatly intensified in the year immediately following the new revelation and has only partly slackened since then. The first rush of publicity had to do with the rapid ordination and advancement of many faithful Mormon blacks into the ranks of the priesthood, into stake presidencies and high councils, into the mission field and into regular temple work for themselves and for their dead.[96] Besides the coverage of these events in Church publications, Salt Lake City's Sunday evening television talk show, *Take Two*, in early June, 1978, featured the entire presidency of the Genesis Group, by then fully ordained, who presented a very upbeat image in expressing their own feelings and in answering numerous "call-in" phone questions.[97] Interest apparently has remained high also in stories about conversions of American blacks to Mormonism: The *Church News* carried a major feature article on this subject in 1979, and another firstperson account published in 1980 has sold well in bookstores around Utah.[98] Appearances at BYU by Eldredge Cleaver in February and July of 1981, together with the highly publicized prospects that he might join the Mormon Church, introduced a note of ultimate irony into the continuing Mormon-black detente.[99] [He was baptized 11 Dec. 1983.]

At least as much publicity has been lavished on the burgeoning (if belated) proselyting efforts among black populations in Africa and elsewhere. It seemed especially appropriate and symbolic that the first new missions to be opened, just weeks after the new revelation, were in Nigeria and Ghana, where the proselyting efforts of fifteen years earlier had been so tragically aborted. The two mature and experienced missionary couples first sent to West Africa in 1978 literally exhausted themselves baptizing eager new members of the Church. After only a year, they had baptized 1,707 members into five districts and thirty-five branches of the Church in Nigeria and Ghana.[100] Meanwhile, the rapid growth of the Church already under way in Latin America and the Pacific Islands continued with much publicity toward the day of the dedication of the Brazilian temple late in 1978. The Church was clearly making up for lost time in all such areas, and it was anxious for the world to know it.

Apart from these developments, it seems fair to add that the new revelation has provoked neither the wholesale departure of die-hard traditionalists from the Church, as one had heard predicted occasionally, nor the thundering and triumphant return of marginal Mormon liberals, who had long become accustomed to citing the priesthood ban on blacks as the major "reason" for their disaffection. Those disposed to apostatize over the ending of the ban seem already to have done so over the Manifesto of 1890, for polygamous fundamentalists offered the only apparent organized opposition to the new priesthood policy (as just another "retreat" from orthodoxy)[101]. The liberals, for their part, scarcely had time to notice that their favorite target had been removed before they were handed a new one in the form of the ERA controversy. Mormon intellectuals, whether liberal or not, have reacted predictably with a number of publications (like this one) offering post-mortems on the whole Mormon/black controversy.[102] Commentators outside the Church generally have shown only mild interest in the new revelation; in fact, it was old news within a few days.[103]

Reflections

If the Church, then, has reacted to the new revelation mainly with white acquiescence and black conversion, does that mean that all is well in Zion? The answer depends upon how much we care about certain unresolved historical and ecclesiastical issues. Some of these, of course, have been lingering in the minds of concerned Mormons for decades, as many of us have struggled to understand and somehow explain (if only to ourselves) the anomaly of the pharaohs' curse in the Lord's church. Even the change in policy evokes reflections and questions for the loyal but troubled mind: (1) Why did we have to have a special revelation to change the traditional policy toward blacks; and, if it was going to come anyway, why didn't it come a decade earlier? (2) Since the policy was changed by revelation, must we infer that it also was instituted by revelation? (3) How can we distinguish *authentic doctrine* in the Church from authoritatively promulgated *opinion*? (4) Now that the era of the pharaohs' curse is over, how should we deal with it in our retrospective feelings?

There is obviously no point in debating whether a revelation from the Lord "really" occurred. The committed Mormon will take the proposition for granted, while the secular and the cynical will reject it out of hand. In practical terms, it makes little difference whether the Lord or the prophet was the ultimate source of the revelation, for we are obliged as much to seek understanding about the mind of the one as of the other. It is clear from the reflections of President Kimball and other participants in the revelational process that they all shared a profound spiritual experience, one which swept away life-long contrary predispositions.[104] This experience was apparently a necessity if the priesthood ban ever were to be dropped, if for no other reason than that all earlier attempts to resolve the problem at the *policy* level had bogged down in controversy among the brethren. Only a full-fledged revelation defined as such by the president himself would neutralize that controversy and bring the required unanimity among the First Presidency and the Twelve. Moreover, for years nearly all the General Authorities who had spoken publicly on the priesthood ban had been clear in stating that it could be changed only by direct and explicit revelation.

Why didn't the revelation come earlier, before all the public relations damage was done? This is much too complex a question to be answered by the facile conventional wisdom of Church critics that the obstinately backward Mormons finally got their "revelation" when the progressive forces of the outside world applied sufficient pressure.[105] Such an "explanation" betrays ignorance of the complex dynamics operating within the Church during the 1960s and 1970s and of certain crucial Mormon ecclesiastical imperatives. Furthermore, it ignores the several years' respite from external pressure which the Church had generally enjoyed before 1978 and which, indeed, gave the new revelation much of its quality of surprise.

Prophets in the Mormon tradition do not sit around waiting for revelations. Like Church leaders at all levels, they grapple pragmatically with the day-to-day demands and problems that go with their callings, presumably striving to stay as close as possible to the promptings of the Holy Spirit on a routine basis. They are not infallible, and they sometimes make mistakes. They carry the initiative in their communication with Deity, and when they need special guidance they are supposed to ask for it. Even this inquiry is often a *petition for confirmation* of a tentative decision already produced by much individual and collective deliberation (D & C 9:7-8). That means that prophets are left to do a lot on their own; it means, too, that receiving a special revelation may depend on previously identifying an appropriate solution.

All of this leads to the point that the timing of the new revelation on priesthood eligibility was dependent in large part on the initiative of President Kimball himself, who had to come to a realization that the

Church had a serious problem; then he had to "study ... out in his mind" a proposed solution to the problem and only then petition the Lord for confirmation of the proposal.[106] Bruce R. McConkie, a direct participant in the process of collective affirmation that followed President Kimball's own solitary spiritual sojourn, described the president's approach very much in these terms, strongly implying furthermore, that he was the first president of the Church to have taken the black problem that far. If so, we already have much of the explanation for the timing of the end of the pharaohs' curse.

Given the relatively restrained role of Deity in the revelational process just described, we are then entitled to wonder just what were the considerations that brought President Kimball to frame his proposal and petition the Lord for its confirmation.

I have argued that *inside* pressures from *outside* Utah were probably more compelling than *outside* pressures from *inside* Utah. Brazil was not the only consideration, of course, but it was surely the most immediate and weighty of the Third World examples. When the 1974 decision was made to build a temple in Brazil, the realization among the brethren must have developed rapidly, if indeed it was not there to start with, that the priesthood ban would be untenable and unmanageable. This point has been noted not only by so astute an outside observer as Jan Shipps, but also explicitly by Apostle LeGrand Richards and implicitly by Bruce R. McConkie and by President Kimball himself.

The exact timing of the revelation ending the "Negro issue" for the Church, however it is best explained, was providential in a public relations sense as well. Damage to the public image of the Church could probably have been averted altogether only by dropping the priesthood ban before it became a public issue. One viable chance for that, and maybe the last one, was lost when the First Presidency failed to reach consensus in 1954. Once the NAACP and other civil rights partisans took up the issue in the early 1960s, the Church could not have changed the Negro policy without resurrecting from polygamy days the specter of a pressure-induced "revelation on demand." Even with the pressure off in the late 1970s, critics of the Church made cynical comments in that vein but with much less credibility. Had the new revelation come a decade earlier, at the height of the political agitation, there would have been little room for anything but a cynical interpretation of how the prophetic office is conducted. It seems certain that to most Mormons, maintaining the integrity and charisma of that office was a more important consideration than either racial equality or societal respectability. There could be no reenactment in Mormon vestments of the assault of *aggiornamento* upon the papacy.[107] It seems understandable, then, that the timing of the new revelation should have fallen well after the apex of the civil rights movement, but before a temple opened in Brazil.

There is no known record of any revelation in this dispensation that either denies the priesthood to blacks or ties them to the lineage of the pharaohs. Nor is there any record that the Church had a policy of priesthood denial in the lifetime of Joseph Smith. There is much evidence that the policy developed after Brigham Young took charge of the church.[108] Was that policy established by revelation? We may never know, but it is not necessary to believe so. There is an especially relevant biblical precedent suggesting that ecclesiastical policies requiring revelation for their *removal* do not necessarily *originate* by revelation. The controversy over circumcision among the New Testament apostles offers us a parallel problem of "racial discrimination." If Jesus had given some priority in the teaching of the gospel "to the Jew first, and also to the Greek," he certainly never instituted the requirement of circumcision before baptism for the Gentiles, as some of his early apostles apparently believed. In spite of Peter's vision about "unclean meat," which should have settled the question, it is clear from Paul's epistles that the circumcision controversy in the early church lasted for many years.[109] We may well wonder why the Lord "permitted" a racially discriminatory policy to survive so long in either the ancient or the modern church, and what circumstances finally brought about his intervention. It does seem plausible, however, that both the ancient and the modern instances could have had strictly human origin. An open admission of this realization may be the best way to start dealing with the black issue in Mormon history. There is no reason for even the most orthodox Mormon to be threatened by the realization that the prophets do not do everything by revelation and never have.[110]

The changing definitions surrounding the black man in Mormon history raise the question, as few other issues have, of just what is authentic doctrine in the Church? That we had an official policy or practice of withholding the priesthood from blacks cannot be denied. The doctrinal rationale supporting that policy, however, is quite a separate matter. Note, in this connection, that the revelation of June 1978 actually changed only the policy and did not address any doctrine at all, except indirectly by overturning a common belief that priesthood for the blacks could come only in the next life. It is against this background that Presidents McKay and Brown and like-minded colleagues seem to have been correct all along (though perhaps beside the point) in considering the priesthood ban a policy and not a doctrine.

Yet the question of authentic doctrine remains. As we have seen, the flow of doctrinal commentary from the days of Brigham Young, reflected in the First Presidency letters of the late 1940s, is clearly followed by an ebb thereafter to the doctrinal nadir of April 1978, when a spokesman for the Church declared, in effect, that there wasn't any doctrine on the

subject at all. In their private beliefs, however, not all of the brethren
followed the lead of the First Presidency in this process of doctrinal
devolution. Perhaps the most perplexing case in point is Elder McConkie,
who, a few weeks after the June, 1978, revelation, counseled us to forget
doctrines expounded earlier by himself and others who had spoken "with
limited understanding," but then chose to retain virtually all the old
Negro doctrines in the 1979 revision of his authoritative reference book![111]

In the quest for authentic doctrine, I find it useful to employ a
typology or "scale of authenticity," which I have derived from empirical
induction, rather than from anything formal. It is thus an operational
construct, not a theological one, not synonymous with "truth" in any
ultimate, objective sense. The nature of "truth," even in an LDS doctrinal
context, is an altogether different epistemological issue. By "authentic"
here, I a mean only that a claim can legitimately be made that a given
doctrine or policy had divine origin. At the top of this scale is a category of
complete or ultimate authenticity, which I call *canon doctrine*, following
conventional Christian terminology. This would include both doctrines
and (for these purposes) policy statements which the prophets represent
to the Church as having been received by direct revelation and which are
subsequently accepted as such by the sustaining vote of the membership.
The four standard works of the Church (with recent addenda) obviously
fall into this highest category of authenticity, but it is difficult to think of
anything else that does.

A secondary category, nearly as important, is *official doctrine* (and,
again, policy). Included here are statements from the president or from
the First Presidency, whether to priesthood leaders or to the world as a
whole; also church lesson manuals, magazines, or other publications
appearing under the explicit auspices of the First Presidency. General
Conference addresses in their oral form would not routinely be included
here, or, if so, only tentatively, given the revisions that they have frequently
undergone before being allowed to appear in print. There is no assumption
of infallibility here, but only that the legitimate spokesmen for the Church
are expressing its official position at a given point in time. "Official"
positions or doctrines may be subsequently changed, repudiated, or
proved wrong but are still official at the time they are promulgated.

The third category of authenticity I would call *authoritative doctrine*.
Here would fall all of the other talks, teachings and publications of
authorities on Mormon doctrines and scriptures, whether or not these are
published by a Church press like Deseret Book. The presumption of
authoritativeness may derive either from the speaker's high ecclesiastical
office (e.g., Bruce R. McConkie), or from his formal scholarly credentials
and research (e.g., Hugh Nibley), or from both (e.g., James E. Talmage).

The lowest (least authentic) category is *popular doctrine*, sometimes called "folklore." This is to some extent a residual category, but it clearly includes the apocryphal prophecies that often circulate around the Church, common beliefs such as that temple garments offer protection from physical injury, and a host of other notions having either local or general circulation. Occasionally a popular doctrine will be considered subversive enough by the General Authorities to warrant official condemnation, but usually folklore flourishes unimpeded by official notice.

Now obviously a particular doctrine can be found in all four categories simultaneously. In fact, such would ideally be the case for canon doctrine, so the "authenticity scale" I have recommended may have a cumulative property in many cases. Indeed, it is rare for a doctrine in a given category not to have some "following" in the lower categories. What becomes crucial for us to determine, however, is how high up the scale is the primary source of a given doctrine or policy. This is a determination rarely made or even considered by most church members, who therefore remain very susceptible to folklore, as well as to doctrines that may be authoritative or even official for a time but which later prove erroneous.

Let us take the traditional "Negro doctrines" as a case in point: These seem to have begun at the level of folklore in the earliest days of the Church, imported to a large extent from the traditional racist lore in Christianity more generally.[112] It is not clear from surviving records how often these doctrines received authoritative endorsement by church leaders during the lifetime of Joseph Smith, but there is little reason to believe they ever became official. By 1850, though, they seem to have been elevated to the official level, if only because President Brigham Young taught them in his official capacity. Most of them were still officially embraced by First Presidency letters in the late 1940s and widely promulgated at the authoritative and folk levels as well. There they now survive despite withdrawal of official endorsement. Let us note, for the historical record, that neither the priesthood ban itself nor its supporting doctrinal justifications were ever canon doctrines. No known revelation was ever promulgated to establish the ban, or even to tie it to the curse of the pharaohs in the book of Abraham, though that tie was at least "official."

The historical "career" of the priesthood ban and its accompanying doctrines suggests to us the importance of the principle of parsimony in our approach to doctrine. While accepting wholeheartedly the standard works of the church, we must be very reluctant to "canonize in our own hearts" any doctrines not explicitly included there. We may hold other doctrines as postulates, as long as we realize that they may in the long run prove erroneous, and that we have no right to consider their acceptance among the criteria of faithfulness. The premises of our church membership also oblige us to act in conformity to official policies and teachings of our church leaders; but here we are entitled to entertain reservations and express them to our leaders, since official statements can turn out to be wrong.[113] It is not blind faith that is required of us but only that we seek our own spiritual confirmation before questioning official instruction.

As for a teaching that is only authoritative, we owe it nothing more than respectful consideration, and we are perfectly free to reject it thereafter, even if it appears in a book entitled *Mormon Doctrine*. And toward folklore, we should be suspicious and require authentication, but we should never lose our sense of humor! A principle of parsimony thus applied by the Saints is ideally matched by restraint on the parts of leaders and teachers up and down the Church, and particularly on the parts of General Authorities, in the claims made for the authenticity of doctrines outside the four standard works. For despite sincerity and good intentions, much mischief can be done in a situation of doctrinal ambiguity when those in authority claim too much.

Reconsidering the Past

It has been noted that Mormons have yet to "come to terms" with polygamy; our ambivalence toward the "polygamy era" expresses itself in a studied (and sometimes puritanical) effort to "live it down," while still lionizing the polygamists in our past. How will we "come to terms" with our era of racial discrimination? We must begin, I think, by maintaining a comparative historical perspective. Before we jump too quickly to demand, "Isn't the Mormon heritage racist?" let us be sure to ask, "Compared to what?" A sense of historical balance and fairness calls for a comparison of Mormon ways with the ways of others in similar times, places, and circumstances.

Careful review of the history of Mormon racism will reveal that it has followed closely the comparable history for America as a whole, sad as that may be. Ambivalent expressions from our leaders about the status of blacks during our Missouri period were certainly understandable in a border state. After the move to Illinois, Joseph Smith and others who spoke on the subject seemed to share the dominant Northern sentiment of the time, a moderate and gradual abolitionism, rather than either a perpetuation of slavery or the more radical and precipitous solutions of the abolitionist movement itself. Even the outspoken racism of Brigham Young and some of his colleagues in Utah, and the relatively benign form of slavery permitted there in the 1850s and 1860s, were close to mainstream opinion in America at the time. Abraham Lincoln himself did not believe in social or political equality for blacks in those days.[114] After the Civil War, Jim Crow laws spread to Utah and remained entrenched there until the 1950s and 1960s, just as they did in the entire nation.[115] The Jim Crow tradition may have receded more slowly in some respects in Utah than in some other states but, in general, about as rapidly as in most places.[116] Mormon attitudes toward blacks, measured at the height of civil rights controversy in the society, differed little from national norms, given appropriate statistical "controls" for important demographic differences.[117] Thus, the peculiar Mormon priesthood ban did not demonstrably have any "carry-over" into secular, civil race relationships, despite the claims of the NAACP and other critics.[118]

Even the priesthood ban itself must be seen in comparative context. The pragmatic rather than theological fact of life is that the churches of America, like most other institutions, have all practiced racial discrimination. At least the major denominations had racially segregated congregations well into the age of civil rights, and blacks have never constituted more than a small proportion of the clergy of any denomination, even to this day.[119] As in medicine and law, a professional clergy can (and does) restrict black access to power and privilege by the more subtle means of restricting access to the specialized education by which alone the requisite credential (or ordination) can be obtained. In more egalitarian religions like Mormonism, which has no professional priesthood, the functional or sociological equivalent of such institutionalized racism was necessarily and ironically much less subtle: a categorical and formal denial of access to the priesthood altogether. For all of their moral posturing, then, in practice the "liberal" Christian denominations never had appreciably more blacks ordained than the Mormons did.

Let us, then, not look back to hang our heads. If we look back at all, let us do so only to remember the lessons suggested by our struggle with the race issue: the principle of parsimony both in what we believe and in what we teach, lest we again digest dubious doctrine in the service of temporary policy; the human element that must be recognized, appreciated, and endured in the conduct of even high Church office, lest we deify our prophets instead of sustain them; and the ultimate vindication of patient loyalty to our leadership, lest the office of prophet become the pawn of contemporary politics. Let us consider too, with deepest appreciation, the example of sacrifice and subtle efficacy provided all these years by our black brethren and sisters in the gospel. If we can do all these things, we will have nothing to live down but much to live up to.

NOTES

It is with deepest gratitude that I acknowledge how much my work has benefited by the generosity of many other scholars who have shared with me their knowledge, suggestions and criticisms. Besides those acknowledged in

177

various notes, other colleagues deserving of my special thanks are William G. Hartley, Newell Bringhurst, Gordon Irving, and, above all, Lester Bush.

1. Pearl of Great Price, Abr. 1:26-27. I have reordered the two verses.

2. The most important of these are Stephen G. Taggart, *Mormonism's Negro Policy: Social and Historical Origins* (Salt Lake City: University of Utah Press, 1970); Lester E. Bush, Jr., "Commentary on ... " Taggart's book in *Dialogue* 4 (Winter 1969): 86-103; then Bush's definitive "Mormonism's Negro Doctrine: An Historical Overview," *Dialogue* 8 (Spring 1973): 11-68; Ronald K. Esplin, "Brigham Young and Priesthood Denial to the Blacks," *BYU Studies* 19:3 (1979); and Newell G. Bringhurst, *Saints, Slaves, and Blacks: The Changing Place of Black People within Mormonism, 1820-1980* (Westport, Conn.: Greenwood Press, 1981); plus numerous shorter and/or less thoroughly researched articles cited, in turn, by these works.

3. Nelson had first been approached by church leaders for his assessment of the feasibility of opening missionary work in Cuba after World War II. His letter grew out of concerns about such an effort, given the Church's racial policy.

4. Excerpts from the exchange of correspondence between Nelson and the First Presidency are reproduced in John J. Stewart, *Mormonism and the Negro* (Orem, Utah: Bookmark Division, Community Press, 1960), pp. 33, 46, 47, 54. For more on Nelson's interaction with Church leaders during the 1940s, see his letter in *Dialogue* 2 (Autumn 1967): 8-9, and Bringhurst, *Saints, Slaves, and Blacks*, epilogue, and notes.

5. Stewart, *Mormonism and the Negro*, Part 2, pp. 16-18; Bush, "Mormonism's Negro Doctrine," pp. 43-44 and note 199.

6. Joseph Fielding Smith, *The Way to Perfection*, 11th ed. (Salt Lake City: the Genealogical Society, 1958), especially Chapters 7, 15, and 16. The first edition of this book appeared in 1931 and reflects the recorded teachings and opinions of the author's father and sixth church president, Joseph F. Smith, who in turn seems to have adopted many of the ideas of Brigham Young. All such teachings have been given prolonged credibility in more recent years by their repetition in Bruce R. McConkie's *Mormon Doctrine* 2nd ed. (Salt Lake City: Bookcraft, 1966), esp. pp. 526-28.

7. President McKay's private views on the matter over the years are discussed and documented in Bush, "Mormonism's Negro Doctrine," pp. 45-48, with accompanying notes.

8. Ibid., p. 46; and Roger O. Porter, "Educator Cites McKay Statement ... ," *Salt Lake Tribune*, 15 Jan. 1970.

9. One major consideration here, in my opinion, was President McKay's apparent preference for a colleagial style of administration, as opposed to a more autocratic or assertive one, so that he would not have been inclined to

insist very hard on his own policy preferences in the face of much resistance from his counselors or the Twelve.

10. See especially C.1. in the *South African Mission Proselyting Plan* Disc. #13, Dec. 1951, Elder Gilbert G. Tobler, comp., Mowbray, C.P. South Africa.

11. This transformation of policy in South Africa, and the importance in particular of President McKay's visit, is laid out in Farrell Ray Monson, "History of the South African Mission of the Church of Jesus Christ of Latter-day Saints, 1853-1970" (M.A. thesis, Brigham Young University, 1971), esp. pp. 42-46. See also A. Hamer Reiser, Oral History Interviews by William G. Hartley, 1974, vol. 2, pp. 165-69, James Moyle Oral History Program, Historical Department Archives, Church of Jesus Christ of Latter-day Saints, Salt Lake City, Utah.

12. See note 8 on McKay-McMurrin conversation. On deliberations among the General Authorities, also in 1954, see excerpt from Adam S. Bennion papers in Lester E. Bush Jr., "Compilation on the Negro in Mormonism," (1972, in LDS Church Archives or BYU library Special Collections) in which Apostle Bennion is thanked by Wallace R. Bennett for a recent talk reporting that "the Church leadership is even now undertaking a careful re-evaluation of our [Negro] doctrine." Bush p. 254 also reports an alleged re-evaluation about 1948, about the time of the Nelson correspondence. This may have led to the 1949 statement and a decision to give Negritos in the Philippines the priesthood. See note 14.

13. Lester E. Bush, Jr., "Introduction" to special section *Dialogue* 12 (Summer 1979), p. 12, note 1, and more details on church policy in and around Fiji in Norman Douglas, "Mormon Missionaries and the Fijian: Caution, Confusion, and Compromise," typescript, LDS Church Archives, where the inconsistencies in Fiji policies across time are set forth in some detail. See also Douglas, "The Sons of Levi and the Seed of Cain: Racial Myths in Mormon Scripture and their Relevance to the Pacific Islands," *Journal of Religious History* 8 (1974): 90-104. Additional information for this paragraph comes also from the Manuscript History of the Tonga Mission, 31 March 1959 Quarterly Report, via my personal interview with R. Lanier Britsch on 31 May 1981.

14. The information on the Negritos comes to me via a personal interview with John L. Sorenson, 31 May 1981, and a subsequent letter from him, 3 Aug. 1981. While a missionary in the Pacific in 1948, Sorenson was told by visiting Apostle Matthew Cowley that he was carrying a letter from the First Presidency authorizing the extension of the priesthood to all the peoples of the Philippines, explicitly including the Negritos. The reference to the delay for the West Irians of New Guinea is based on a letter in my files from the mission president in Singapore in 1973, letter of 3 Aug. 1981. He reported a

letter from the First Presidency in the mission files in which the priesthood was authorized for the West Irians as it had been earlier for other Micronesian and Melanesian peoples; signed by President Joseph Fielding Smith, Harold B. Lee, and N. Eldon Tanner, and dated either 1971 or early 1972.

15. Bush, "Mormonism's Negro Doctrine," p. 68, note 209.

16. As far as I can tell from personal interviews with missionaries who served in Brazil at various times in the 1950s and 1960s, the genealogical "burden of proof" was shifted from the Saints there to the Church during the term of Wm. Grant Bangerter as mission president (1958-63).

17. Personal conversation with Mark Grover, 6 June 1981. Grover, who served a mission in Brazil in the late 1960s, is currently working on a doctoral dissertation on church relationships with the Third World and has interviewed (or read interviews of) a number of the principals in the leadership of the church in Brazil since World War II. Also consulted in assessing the church racial experience in Brazil were transcripts of a dozen or so oral histories taken from various missionaries, mission presidents, and local church members who lived or served there and in other Latin American countries during the 1950s, 1960s, and 1970s. Since the race relations topic is still considered sensitive by many of these informants, nearly all of whom are still alive. I have deliberately avoided specifying in most cases which information derived from which interviews.

18. Ibid. For an example of one of the versions of the lineage lesson, see *Handbook: Brazil North Central Mission* (Sao Paulo, about 1970), pp. 39-42, which was still in use at least as late as 1975. Excerpts contributed to my files by Mark Grover.

19. Bush, "Mormonism's Negro Doctrine," p. 45 and p. 68, notes 207, 208. I also have personal knowledge of such cases among friends.

20. *The Nation* 174 (24 May 1952): pp. 488 ff.

21. McConkie's *Mormon Doctrine* was first published in 1958, though the second (1966) edition has had much greater circulation. See also e.g., Mark E. Petersen, "Race Problems—As They Affect the Church," an address given 27 Aug. 1954 at a Brigham Young University convention of religion teachers; Alvin R. Dyer, "For What Purpose?", an address given at a missionary conference held in Oslo, Norway, 18 March 1961; and Stewart, *Mormonism and the Negro*. An example of the same genre but published somewhat later was John L. Lund, *The Church and the Negro* (Jacksonville, Fla.: Paramount Publishers, 1967).

22. Bush, "Mormonism's Negro Doctrine," p. 42.

23. Thomas F. O'Dea, *The Mormons* (Chicago: University of Chicago Press, 1957), especially Ch. 9. O'Dea's 1972 essay on the Mormons discussed the race issue at some length, but by then it was obvious to everyone. See

O'Dea, "Sources of Strain in Mormon History Reconsidered" in Marvin S. Hill and James B. Allen, eds., *Mormonism and American Culture* (New York: Harper and Row, 1972).

24. See Charles S. McCoy, "The Churches and Protest Movements for Racial Justice," in Robert Lee and Martin Marty, eds., *Religion and Social Conflict* (New York: Oxford University Press, 1964) and Thomas F. Gossett, *Race: The History of an Idea in America* (New York: Schocken Books, 1965). Antiblack prejudice and some of its consequences among the clergy are described and measured in Rodney Stark et al., *Wayward Shepherds: Prejudice and the Protestant Clergy* (New York: Harper and Row, 1971), pp. 111-17.

25. E.g., G. W. Davidson, "Mormon Missionaries and the Race Question," *Christian Century*, 29 Sept. 1965; D. L. Foster, "Unique Gospel in Utah" *Christian Century* 14 July 1965; and several articles by Lester Kinsolving in the *San Francisco Chronicle*, 4 June 1966, p. 35; 24 June 1967, p. 26; 20 Dec. 1969, p. 15; and 21 March 1970, p. 17.

26. Utah Chapters, NAACP, "Proposed Resolution of Censure Regarding Discrimination Practiced by the Church of Jesus Christ of Latter-day Saints." See summary of this document in the *San Francisco Examiner*, 2 July 1965, p. 6.

27. E.g., Wallace Turner in various syndicated columns and in *The Mormon Establishment* (Boston: Houghton-Mifflin Co., 1966).

28. Among the most prominent were Sterling M. McMurrin, Stewart Udall, and Morris Udall. See the several examples of their critical comments in the epilogue to Bringhurst, *Saints, Slaves*, See also Stewart Udall's letter in *Dialogue* 2 (Summer 1967): 6-7, and the letter of Samuel W. Taylor in the *San Francisco Chronicle*, 11 July 1967, p. 32.

29. The lack of canonical basis for the priesthood policy and its supporting doctrines was a major argument advanced in my first article in *Dialogue* 2 (Winter 1967); see also Taggart, "Mormonism's Negro policy," and Bush, "Commentary on..."

30. This line of reasoning was articulated most fully in the Dec. 1969 statement of the First Presidency.

31. See Bringhurst, *Saints, Slaves*, epilogue, especially notes 50-57, where a number of other sources are cited on Romney's campaign and its implications for the Church at that time.

32. Sterling M. McMurrin, "A Note on the 1963 Civil Rights Statement," *Dialogue* 12 (Summer 1979): 60-63. It is unlikely, as McMurrin seems to imply (p. 61), that President Brown was unaware of the threat of demonstrations since the threat had been reported in the Salt Lake City papers (see e.g., the *Deseret News* for 5 Oct. 1963). For reiterations of the favorable

Church stand on civil rights after 1963, see April 1965 General Conference (*San Francisco Chronicle* 17 April 1965) and in 1966 April General Conference (*Dialogue* 1 [Summer 1966]: back page).

33. See note 26. Public demonstrations against the Church in 1965 are discussed also by Bringhurst in *Saints, Slaves*, epilogue, where he relies mainly on stories in the *Salt Lake Tribune* for 7-10 March 1965.

34. See accounts of these early Nigeria contacts in Bush, "Compilation," "The Nigerian Mission," pp. 360-68; Bush, "Mormonism's Negro Doctrine p. 45; *Time* magazine, 18 June 1965; Bringhurst, *Saints, Slaves* epilogue, including notes 69-72; and Bringhurst, "Mormonism in Black Africa; Changing Attitudes and Practices, 1830-1981," *Sunstone* 6 (May/June 1981): 17-18.

35. This incident was recounted to me by Eugene E. Campbell, who had read the minutes of the First Presidency meetings involved (letter in my files from Campbell, 7 April 1981).

36. E.g., Wallace Turner, "Mormons Weigh Stand on Negro—May End Ban on Complete Membership in Church," *New York Times* (western edition), 7 June 1963, an article widely disseminated in various newspapers around the same time.

37. "Mormon 'Fight' Over Civil Rights," *San Francisco Chronicle*, 17 April 1965, which refers to the rejection by President Brown of Elder Benson's publicly stated characterization of the civil rights movement as subversive or even Communist-inspired. The apparent pessimism of President McKay cited here is a reference to his widely quoted prediction during a 1964 visit to the Oakland (Calif.) Temple dedication, that a change in the priesthood policy would not come "in my lifetime or yours."

38. Hugh B. Brown, N. Eldon Tanner, Joseph Fielding Smith, Alvin R. Dyer and Thorpe B. Isaacson all served as counselors in the First Presidency during the final year or so of President McKay's life.

39. See notes 6, 21 above. Lee's views are treated briefly by Bush, "Mormonism's Negro Doctrine," p. 47, and notes 195, 217. The relevant developments during President Lee's later administration as church president remain an area of uncertainty in this history. Bush reports in personal correspondence a conversation with a General Authority in 1974 who informed him that Lee had announced in a general meeting of the authorities a decision to allow two black children to be sealed to white parents in response to a special request. It was the General Authority's feeling that Lee was perceived as moving surprisingly quickly on the whole black issue (given, one presumes, his objections to Brown's initiative in 1969). The inference was that the new insights of the scholarly articles appearing on the subject had played some modest role. Any further developments were aborted by Lee's unexpected death in December 1973.

40. The letter is reproduced in *Dialogue* 4 (Winter 1969), pp. 102-3. The incident which culminated in this letter came to me via Richard Poll, to whom it had been related by a close relative and confidant of a member of the First Presidency involved. I obtained direct verification from his source as recently as August 1981.

41. E.g., "LDS Leader Says Curb on Priesthood to Ease," in the *Salt Lake Tribune*, 25 Dec. 1969, p. 4-D; and a shorter version of the same article in the *San Francisco Chronicle*, 27 Dec. 1969, p. 22.

42. Mormons Hold to Doctrine—New Leaders Ban Changes," *San Francisco Sunday Examiner and Chronicle* , 25 Jan. 1970, p. 14-A.

43. Bush, "Mormonism's Negro Doctrine," pp. 46-47.

44. For a thorough, if biased, overview of the book of Abraham controversy, see Chapter 11 of Jerald and Sandra Tanner, *The Changing World of Mormonism* (Chicago: Moody Bible Institute, 1980). Examples of the scholarly analysis and commentary on the rediscovered papyrus fragments will be found in the following issues of *Dialogue* between 1967 and 1969: vol. 2, no. 4; vol. 3, 2; vol. 3, no. 3; 4, no. 1 and no. 4; articles by Hugh Nibley intermittently in the *Improvement Era* from January 1968 to May 1970; and Nibley's ponderous but not entirely relevant *The Message of the Joseph Smith Papyri: An Egyptian Endowment* (Salt Lake City: Deseret Book Co., 1975).

45. A generally fair review of the BYU controversy will be found in William F. Reed, "The Other Side of 'The Y'," *Sports Illustrated*, 26 Jan. 1970, pp. 38-39. Numerous newspaper articles on the controversy appeared around the West in late 1969 and early 1970, especially in the Utah papers, the San Francisco papers, and the Seattle papers; some of these were quite supportive of BYU (e.g. James J. Kilpatrick, "Stanford's Bigotry toward Mormons," *Chicago Daily News*, 11 Dec. 1969; and Dave Ruben, "Cards React 10 to 1 against Break with BYU," *San Francisco Chronicle*, 9 Dec. 1969, p. 5). See also *Saints, Slaves* epilogue, Bringhurst.

46. The ad can be found, for example, in the Spokane *Spokesman-Review*, 1 April 1970, p. 11.

47. See *Salt Lake Tribune*, 22 Feb. 1970; and almost daily, March 3 through 10, 1970. One indication of the total paralysis of any sense of humor during this episode was the apparently sober public reaction to a widely circulated claim by Jerry Rubin during a visit to Salt Lake City that both the Yippies and the Black Panthers were moving their headquarters to the city in order to join the war against the Mormons and that Eldredge Cleaver was already in hiding there!

48. William A. Wilson and Richard C. Poulsen, "The Curse of Cain and Other Stories: Blacks in Mormon Folklore," *Sunstone* 5 (Nov./Dec. 1980): 9-13.

49. Reported by Wallace Turner in "Mormons Ease Ban on Blacks," *San Francisco Chronicle*, 8 April 1972, p. 38 (*New York Times* News Service).

50. Lester Bush has reported to me that one of the Twelve expressed to him fear for the safety of church leaders even after this tense period. Better known, of course, is Ezra Taft Benson's claim during the late 1960s, often reiterated, that the civil rights movement was being used by the Communists; see his general conference address, 1967, *Improvement Era*, and note 37.

51. Press coverage disappeared abruptly about the end of March 1970.

52. A tendency to the parochial assumption that Utah or Great Basin Mormons are somehow representative of "the Mormons" can be seen in the handling of the "vigilantism" episode in Wilson and Poulsen "Curse of Cain," p. 10; and in O. Kendall White, Jr., & Daryl White, "Abandoning an Unpopular Policy: An Analysis of the Decision Granting the Mormon Priesthood to Blacks," *Sociological Analysis* 41 (Fall 1980): 231-45. The treatments in these two articles of Mormon collective reactions to black pressures in Utah indicate well enough the emotional intensity of some of those reactions, but the authors are in no position to judge the pervasiveness of the reactions, since they lack systematic data even from Utah, to say nothing of elsewhere. See my critique on White and White in *Sociological Analysis*, 42 (Fall 1981): 277-82.

53. In this respect, Lowry Nelson's misgivings expressed to the First Presidency in the 1940s proved prescient (see notes 3 and 4) and somewhat ironic.

54. Bush, "Mormonism's Negro Doctrine," p. 47, Turner, "Mormons Ease Ban," p. 38.

55. Bringhurst, *Saints, Slaves* epilogue.

56. Ibid.

57. Ibid., and *Lewiston Tribune* (Idaho), 19 July 1974, III-25.

58. An account of the excommunication of Douglas Wallace, and events leading up to it, are recounted in the Spokane (Washington) *Spokesman-Review*, 10 April 1976, p. 6. For the excommunication of Byron Marchant, see the *Lewiston* (Idaho) *Tribune*, 16 Oct. 1977, p. 8-D. Various papers around the country, especially in the West, carried corresponding stories about the same time. Marchant, interestingly, had been the Scoutmaster in the Boy Scout troop where the race issue had arisen three years earlier. A few other excommunications apparently occurred during this same general period or earlier over tactics used in opposing the Church's racial policy, but these other cases got little or no publicity outside of Utah. Subsequent to their excommunications, both Wallace and Marchant continued to make local news through their various attempts to draw public attention to their controversy with the Church. See accounts in Tanner and Tanner, *Changing World*, pp. 320-22, and newspaper stories cited there.

59. See Deseret News, *1975 Church Almanac*, p. F-3; 1980 *Church Almanac*, p. 263; and "Church Public Communications Program," *Annual Guidelines*, 1977-78 Salt Lake City, UT.; Corporation of the First Presidency of the Church of Jesus Christ of Latter-day Saints, 1977. (for Church officers).

60. William G. Hartley, Interview with Heber G. Wolsey, 14 May 1981; written summary in my files.

61. "Marketing the Mormon Image: An Interview with Wendell J. Ashton," *Dialogue* 10 (Spring, 1977): pp. 15-20. The interview was conducted in October 1976. also note 59.

62. A written excerpt from the NBC interview in my files, courtesy of Lester Bush. For his "explanation" of the Church's priesthood ban on blacks in this interview, Ashton simply fell back on the First Presidency letter of December 1969. In that connection, it is interesting to note the information in the Wolsey interview that the Public Communications Department, which reports directly to the First Presidency, is free to speak *for* the Presidency in any matter where the policy or position is already clearly established (as would have been the case with the reference by Ashton in 1973 to the 1969 First Presidency letter). In any other matter, Wolsey explains, First Presidency clearance must be sought for what the PCD publicly asserts. In either case, it would seem that the PCD speaks officially for the Church.

63. "Marketing the Mormon Image," pp. 18-19; and the transcript of the *Today Show* interview with President Kimball.

64. "Marketing the Mormon Image," p. 16. Compare Dennis L. Lythgoe, "The Changing Image of Mormonism," *Dialogue* 4 (Winter 1968): 45-58, esp. pp. 50-52, with Stephen Stathis and Dennis Lythgoe, "Mormonism in the 1970s: The Popular Perception," *Dialogue* 10 (Spring 1977): 95-113, esp. pp. 106-07.

65. Reed (note 45). Few blacks recruited to BYU lasted long until Keith Rice in 1977 (see BYU *Monday Magazine*, 23 Jan. 1978, p. 14). BYU recruiting appeals to black athletes and other students before 1970 seem to have been ambivalent. As reported in a BYU *Daily Universe* sports column for 31 Oct. 1969, young blacks were sometimes warned that they might not be happy in Provo with so few others of their own race. Also, I have from the files of Lester Bush a transcript of a document entitled, "Church Schools and Students of Color," obtained in 1968, ostensibly from the BYU president's office. It appears to be a set of instructions to university staff members involved with student recruiting and includes a sample letter to be sent to black applicants. Even the most optimistic and guileless black applicant would be hard put to find in this letter any other message than "don't come!"

66. Reed, "Other Side of the 'Y';" also "BYU-Washington Situation Unsettled," *BYU Today*, 1970 March, p. 1; and the *Spokane Daily Chronicle*, 26 Nov. 1969.

67. *BYU Today*, Aug. 1971.

68. *Deseret News*, 13 March 1976, p. 28A.

69. The relevant portion of Brooke's address can be found in *Dialogue* 11 (Summer 1978): p. 119-20. As late as 1969, if not later, BYU had an administrative policy permitting no more than two black speakers on campus per year, according to a report in the *Daily Universe* (5 May 1969). This policy resulted in denial of permission to invite both Ralph Abernathy and Julian Bond as speakers in the spring of 1969. The policy appears to have been changed, perhaps with the change of university presidents in the summer of 1971, but certainly by mid-decade. Senator Brooke's tone during the BYU address was typical of a more general tendency toward moderation apparent in the public comments on Mormons of many black people by the mid-1970s; see, e.g., "Blacks Discuss Lifestyle in Utah," *Deseret News*, 13 Mar. 1976, p. 28-A; and Sandra Haggerty (a black columnist), "Mormons and Black Folks," *Los Angeles Times* column in *Pacific Stars and Stripes*, 8 July 1974, p. 10.

70. *BYU Today*, March 1970, p. 4. In the same vein, there was a little-known expression of appreciation for Mormons (perhaps somewhat grudging) by the prominent black separatist, Wallace D. Muhammed (successor to Elijah Muhammed as leader of the Black Muslims) on 1 Oct. 1975, during a national PBS radio program called "Interface." Both Muhammeds cited the Mormons as an example, which they aspired as Muslims to emulate, of a people who had succeeded in building a nation within a nation. Somewhat earlier, a group of black civil rights activists who visited Utah came away expressing admiration for the political and economic separateness that they saw among the Mormons and for the ability of the latter to endure outside criticism without responding in kind, concluding "if we ever [hear] someone say anything against the Mormons again, we [will] defend them, even though they haven't really changed their views on us." See "Race and the City," Santa Barbara, Calif.: Center for the Study of Democratic Institutions, an interview in the early 1970s by Halleck Hoffman. The quotations are from Lou Smith.

71. Wynetta Martin Clark, *I am a Negro Mormon* (Ogden [Utah], 1970). See *BYU Today*, Feb. 1971, p. 5.

72. William G. Hartley, "Samuel D. Chambers," *Ensign* 4 (June 1974) was the first of these in an official Church magazine since 1966, when John Lamb (a black convert) published "My Responsibility," *Improvement Era* (69) Jan., 1966.

73. Debra E. Richards, "Open the Gates of the Temple," BYU *Daily Universe*, 12 April 1976, p. 3. Actually blacks had been permitted to do baptismal work in the temples since the turn of the century. However, a letter from the First Presidency to stake, ward, and mission priesthood leaders, dated 15 Aug. 1966, made it clear that higher ordinance work for deceased blacks was prohibited.

74. See note 71; also Carey C. Bowles, *A Mormon Negro Views the Church* (Maplewood, New Jersey, privately published pamphlet, 1968); Alan Gerald Cherry, *It's You and Me, Lord!* (Provo, Utah: Trilogy Arts Publication, 1970); and a somewhat more critical handling of the subject by Daily (David?) Oliver, *A Negro on Mormonism*, 1963. All of these tended to reject the theological rationales traditionally offered for the status of Negroes in the Church, but (except for Oliver) were nevertheless generally appreciative for their membership.

75. Sally Wright, "The Mormon Issue—Plain as Black and White," a two-part series in the *Concord Transcript* (California), 11 & 12 March 1970. Among other topics, these articles dealt with black Mormons in the area, particularly one Paul Gill, described as "black, proud, and a Mormon."

76. The information on the Genesis Group in the next several paragraphs comes from the following sources: (1) My interviews with Ruffin Bridgeforth, president of the Genesis Group, 20 Aug. 1975 and 2 June 1981; (2) a paper by Wayne Swensen, "The Genesis Group: The Beginning or the End?", submitted in August 1972 to Eugene E. Campbell for History 490 at BYU, a paper itself based largely on Swensen's interviews with the main leaders of the group during summer 1972; (3) an interview by Dennis L. Lythgoe with Lucille Bankhead, 10 Aug. 1972; (4) Peggy Olsen, "Ruffin Bridgeforth: Leader and Father to Mormon Blacks," *This People*, Winter 1980; and (5) *History of the Salt Lake Valley View Stake, 1965-1978* (Salt Lake City: Fine Arts Press, 1979), pp. 134, 282, 283.

77. As of mid-1981, the Genesis Group was thriving again, according to Bridgeforth, after having gone through a period of doldrums just prior to the June 1978, revelation. See "Black Mormon Group Dwindling," in *Monday Magazine* (Salt Lake City), 17 April 1978.

78. Lucille Bankhead, long-time Relief Society president for the Genesis Group, is obviously an exception to this generalization, having come from one of the oldest pioneer families. President Bridgeforth explained that in general it was easier for blacks converted as adults to remain active in the Church, since they had come in with the discriminatory policy already understood, rather than having to cope with it while growing up black and Mormon.

79. Oliver, *Negro on Mormonism*, p. 12, reports in 1956 an "Elder Peterson, of the Church Offices, held a number of cottage meetings in Negro homes for the purpose of finding out why so few Negroes belonged to the Mormon Church. One of such meetings was held in my home, at which he explained that if sufficient numbers of Negroes would join the Church, they would build them a chapel of their own, where they could worship to themselves." If this is Mark E. Petersen, the incident would seem to anticipate the Genesis Group. Oliver goes on to say, however, that "Elder Peterson" stipulated that the priesthood leadership of such a branch would all have to be white, though he

was hoping for a revelation soon that would make Negroes eligible for the priesthood.

80. The three apostles were Gordon B. Hinckley, Thomas S. Monson and Boyd K. Packer. At first the Genesis Group was placed under the jurisdiction of the Liberty Stake (like many other ethnic branches), but eventually it was transferred to the Valley View Stake.

81. The reference here is to the Southwest Los Angeles Branch, an independent branch in the Lawndale Stake of California (Watts area). Its 109 members are nearly all black, owing to the residential location of the branch, but there are also a few families of mixed race and about ten white members. This information was obtained in an interview with the branch president, Robert L. Lang, on 10 June 1981. At the time, the branch had been going for a year and a half and was considered by its president to be high in morale and activity of all kinds, including missionary work. Furthermore, President Lang said, "We're the only unit in the stake paid up on our budget!"

82. Lester Bush reports, furthermore, that as late as 1977, President Kimball still cited the book of Abraham as the basis for the traditional denial of the priesthood to blacks. That would, of course, still leave him the doctrinal flexibility to end the "pharaohs' curse" at any time.

83. Bruce R. McConkie, "All Are Alike Unto God," a speech delivered 18 Aug. 1978, at a BYU symposium of church educators; copy in my files.

84. See also various commentaries on the subject in the *Church News*, 6 Jan. 1979, p. 15, including President Kimball's own comments; and from the interview with his son Edward L. Kimball, *Dialogue* 11 (Winter 1978): 61.

85. Deseret News, *1975 Church Almanac*, A-7; *1980 Church Almanac*, p. 296, notes that the decision to build the Sao Paulo Temple was officially and publicly announced on 1 March 1975, during an area conference there. Obviously the decision had been made during the previous year.

86. These concerns had been expressed constantly since the 1940s. See Bringhurst, *Saints, Slaves, and Blacks*, especially notes 76 and 77, based upon the Adam S. Bennion papers, the full text of which is found in Bush, "Compilation," esp. p. 250. See also note 17 above. The closer one gets to 1978 in the recorded thoughts of these church leaders experienced in Brazil, the more pointed the dismay becomes about the futility of sorting out lineages.

87. Jan Shipps, "The Mormons: Looking Forward and Outward," *Christian Century* 95 (16-23 Aug 1978): 761-66; McConkie, "All are Alike," and Bush, "Introduction," p. 10 and note 3.

88. The information in these three paragraphs is based upon conversations with one of the principals. Although the Church's primary interest in obtaining the census records was unrelated to the race issue, there was some justification to the concerns expressed about other uses to which the data would be put.

89. First Presidency letter to priesthood leaders, 22 Feb. 1978.

90. See David Briscoe article in the Ogden (Utah) *Standard-Examiner*, 30 April 1978, p. 22A, quoting Heber G. Wolsey, Public Communications director for the Church.

91. The revelation was received by the president on 1 June 1978, ratified a week later by his immediate colleagues, and announced publicly on 9 June. The topic dominated the next issue of the *Church News* (17 June 1978), and the process is also discussed in some detail in McConkie's 1978 "All Are Alike." The *Church News* 6 Jan. 1979, p. 15, had a follow-up story. The handling of the initial coverage of the revelation and policy change in the June 17 *Church News* was curious, almost ambivalent: The cover of the issue featured a full-page picture of three LDS members of an Air Force band (the story of which was buried on page 10); and one of the prominent articles inside, without author byline, consisted of comments and quotations taken out of context from earlier statements by President Kimball advising against racial intermarriage (more on sociological than on theological grounds).

92. Leonard J. Arrington and Davis Bitton, *The Mormon Experience* (New York: Alfred Knopf Co., 1979), p. 324.

93. See my "Moderation in All Things: Political and Social Outlooks of Modern, Urban Mormons," *Dialogue* 7 (Spring 1972): 64.

94. Wilson and Poulsen, "Curse of Cain."

95. Hans Mol, *Religion and Race in New Zealand*, Christchurch, N.Z.: National Council of Churches, 1966, pp. 46, 47, and 59.

96. See Salt Lake City newspapers for 10-18 June 1978, especially, but other major city newspapers (e.g., in San Francisco) also provided fairly extensive news coverage and editorials during the same general period. See also both *Time* (p. 55) and *Newsweek* (p. 67) for 19 June 1978. Bringhurst, "Mormonism in Black Africa," refers to the publicity also covering new Church missionary initiatives in Africa in the months immediately following the new revelation (esp. p. 18 and notes 36-42).

97. Personal letter from William G. Hartley, 13 June 1978.

98. See article by Jan Hemming *Church News* 19 May 1979, p. 10, on the conversion of author Styne Slade after finishing her photo book, *The Mormon Way*. See also Mary Frances Sturlaugson, *A Soul So Rebellious* (Salt Lake City: Deseret Book Co., 1980), which was selling briskly around Utah in mid-1981.

99. Cleaver's serious contacts with the Church apparently have come partly by way of his participation with Cleon Skousen and others in the programs of the Freeman Institute. He was a featured speaker also at BYU in both February and July 1981, and has had some contacts with leaders of the Genesis Group, who assess his interest in the Church as genuine. See articles in

various large city newspapers during the first week of April 1981, e.g., *Deseret News* for 3 & 6 April 1981, where Cleaver is reported to have declared a definite intention to join the Church. See also Jo Scoffield, "'Symbol of Freedom' says Cleaver of U.S.," BYU *Daily Universe*, 13 Feb. 1981; and John Forster, "Cleaver Does About-face on Marxism," *Deseret News*, 12-13 Feb. 1981.

100. Rendell and Rachel Mabey, "A Mission to West Africa," *This People*, Sesquicentennial Issue (Spring?), 1980, pp. 24-37; and Bringhurst, "Mormonism in Black Africa."

101. See full-page advertisement by "Concerned Latter-day Saints" (Joseph Jenson, Chairman) in the *Salt Lake Tribune* for Sunday, July 23, 1978, p. A-6.

102. Among the most interesting of these "post-mortems" are several found in *Dialogue* 12 (Summer 1979); Janet Brigham, "to Every Worthy Member," *Sunstone* 3 (July-Aug. 1978): 11-15; interview with Lester Bush, "Mixed Messages on the Negro Doctrine," *Sunstone* 4 (May-June, 1979): 8-15; Wilson and Poulsen, "Curse of Cain;" White and White, "Abandoning an Unpopular Policy;" Jan Shipps, "Looking Forward;" and Bringhurst, *Saints, Slaves, and Blacks.*

103. See Note 96. Most of the comments in the press were fair and matter-of-fact. Partisan comments tended to partake mostly of the tone, "Well, it's about time those backward Mormons got their so-called 'revelation'!" or, from the excommunicants, "You see? We were right all along, and look how much misery we all went through in the meantime!"

104. Obvious from McConkie, *Mormon Doctrine* and "All Are Alike." President Kimball himself was very candid also about having "a great deal to fight... myself, largely, because I had grown up with... [the traditional beliefs]." See Gerry Avant, "Pres. Kimball says revelation was clear," *Church News*, 6 Jan. 1979.

105. See, e.g., White and White, "Abandoning an Unpopular Policy," and Tanner and Tanner, *Changing World*, Ch. 10.

106. Notice even the wording of the June, 1978, revelation: "He has heard our prayers, and *by revelation has confirmed* that the long promised day has come..." (italics added).

107. More or less literally translated, *aggiornamento* means "updating" or "modernizing," and was a term in vogue during the 1960s and 1970s to refer to modernizing tendencies in the Roman Catholic Church consequent to Vatican II.

108. Bush, "Mormonism's Negro Doctrine," Bringhurst, *Saints, Slaves, and Blacks.* Esplin, "Brigham Young," has made the most valiant effort to date to tie the origin of the black priesthood exclusion policy back to the Prophet Joseph Smith, but his evidence is only speculative and inferential, resting

mainly on the general assumption that everything Brigham Young taught he had learned from Joseph Smith.

109. See Acts 15:1-31, 16:3; Gal. 2:1-15, 5:2-6, 6:12-16. McConkie, "All Are Alike," also noted a parallel here between the ancient and the modern Church but more in terms of any Gentile access to the gospel at all, rather than in terms of the circumcision issue.

110. The full text of J. Reuben Clark's magnificent treatise on this subject is in *Dialogue* 12 (Summer 1979): 68-81.

111. McConkie, *Mormon Doctrine*, 2nd ed. (1979 paperback version), especially pp. 109, 214, 343, 526-529, and 616. On that last page, dark skin color is still explicitly tied to a "degenerate status" and to "racial degeneration," with what impact on our new black converts one can only wonder!

112. Gossett, *Race*, and H. Shelton Smith, *In His Image, But...: Racism in Southern Religion, 1780-1910* (Durham, N.C.: Duke University Press, 1972).

113. One has only to notice the number of times in a year that "corrections" are issued to earlier policy directives coming from the First Presidency to stake and ward leaders. In the case of the policy on blacks, furthermore, the official 1949 letter of the First Presidency explicitly endorsed Brigham Young's teaching that blacks would not get the priesthood until all the other descendants of Adam had done so—a position obviously proved wrong by the June 1978 revelation.

114. On development of Mormon attitudes toward blacks during the Missouri Period, see Bringhurst, *Saints, Slaves, and Blacks*, Ch. 2; also, of course, Bush, "Mormonism's Negro Doctrine," and Taggart, *Mormonism's Negro Policy*. On Lincoln's pre-war views, see Gossett, *Race*, p. 254.

115. C. Vann Woodward, *The Strange Career of Jim Crow* (New York: Oxford University Press, 1957).

116. The overturning of racially discriminatory laws and customs proceeded very unevenly around the entire nation and generally had to be fought out category by category (i.e. housing, jobs, education, etc. separately). The state of affairs was what produced the pressure, in fact, for the federal civil rights acts of 1964 and 1968. Even relatively "liberal" California in 1964 wiped away its entire slate of fair housing legislation with the passage of Proposition 14 by a 2-to-1 margin. It is a gross over-simplifcation of complex and subtle causal relationships to explain Utah's civil rights history, whatever it may be, by reference to Mormon theology, many critics to the contrary notwithstanding.

117. Reported in my "Mormonism and Secular Attitudes toward Negroes," *Pacific Sociological Review* 9 (Fall, 1966) and verified in general with more extensive data in my forthcoming *Mormons and Minorities*.

118. As far as I have been able to determine, none of the claims of

"carry-over" was ever substantiated by systematic research with the partial exception of David L. Brewer in a doctoral dissertation later summarized in "Religious Resistance to Changing Beliefs about Race," *Pacific Sociological Review* 13 (Summer 1970). Brewer, however, studied Utah *elites*, not church membership. All elites surveyed were, of course, largely Mormon in religion, but only among the *ecclesiastical* elite did denomination make a difference in racial attitudes; even here, Brewer failed to make appropriate comparisons by *age or generation*, obviously important with a Mormon ecclesiastical elite born disproportionately in the nineteenth century. In general, the available evidence simply does not support an indictment of more racism among Mormons than among others. The point has been made (e.g., Wilson and Poulsen, "Curse of Cain," p. 13) that we are entitled to but little comfort from a discovery that we are not worse than most others. This is true, but we are entitled to such comfort as we can take from impeaching the unduly racist picture that has been painted of us by critics inside and outside the Church. That our racism may have taken unique *forms* is apparent; but this is different from saying it is uniquely virulent or extensive.

119. I am, of course, excluding black clergymen serving only in segregated congregations. See McCoy, "Churches and Protest Movements."

Whence the Negro Doctrine?
A Review of
Ten Years of Answers

Lester E. Bush, Jr.

In this concluding essay, Lester Bush synthesizes his own research and that of others during the past decade. Finding the relevant documentary resources much more conclusive than ten years previously, he briefly evaluates the merits of recent hypotheses on the origins of Mormon teachings and practices and then offers his own detailed analysis. He concludes with a brief analysis of the final years of the priesthood ban.

It's now five years since the revelation of 1978 ended 131 years or more of Mormon priesthood discrimination against blacks. During this past half-decade, study of the "Negro doctrine" has lost both its urgency and, for many, its relevance. Yet few chapters in LDS history offer a more revealing window into the complexity of Mormon thought. At both the institutional and personal level, among rank-and-file as well as the elite, one finds in this singular subject a remarkable case study of the Mormon mind.

Historians, of course, have not abandoned the field. Articles, books, and even doctoral dissertations continue to appear, dealing with various aspects of the history of blacks and Mormons. Ronald K. Esplin, Newell G. Bringhurst, Ronald Coleman, and Armand Mauss in particular have brought important new data to light, while such disparate commentators as Klaus Hansen, Jan Shipps, Hugh Nibley, and Bruce R. McConkie have joined in the discussion.[1]

One persistently vexing question—and the one around which most recent controversy has centered—is that of when (and, thereby, why) the "Negro doctrine" actually originated. While the absence of a contemporary source specifically addressing this question explains part of the ongoing uncertainty, it also reflects at least two other problems: (1) a failure to consider systematically the wealth of relevant new data, and (2) a failure to distinguish analytically between the "practice" of priesthood restriction on the one hand, and the Negro "doctrine" which underlay this practice on the other.[2] Given all the new data which has appeared in the past decade, a history of the practice itself is now largely a straightforward descriptive exercise of what happened and when. One can come very close to providing final answers to these types of questions. The larger issue of doctrinal origins is more challenging and somewhat more subjective, though even here some observations can safely be made that partially reconcile the disparate recent commentary. Additional insights emerge from this early history which illuminate the recent demise of the priesthood ban as well as its origins.

A brief recapitulation of the arguments of the last few years will place the present analysis in perspective. When I looked into this issue over a decade ago, I was unable—despite over seventy years of previous unanimity in ascribing the priesthood restriction to Joseph Smith—to find any contemporary documentation that the Prophet implemented or even enunciated a general priesthood ban based on race. Brigham Young, by contrast, was unmistakably on record as espousing black priesthood denial no later than February 1849. The informal setting and casual wording of Young's remarks at the time, however, raised the question whether this really was the first statement of the policy. A suggestion that a restriction may have been in effect as early as 1847 was noted in a June 2 letter by mission president William Appleby.[3]

Newell Bringhurst later reached essentially the same conclusion in both a 1975 doctoral dissertation on Mormon attitudes toward blacks from 1830 to 1880, and a derivative 1978 essay. The following year, however, historian Ronald Esplin provided what he termed a circumstantial case for the traditional view that the restriction originated with Joseph Smith. In so doing, Esplin cited a newly uncovered talk by Parley Pratt, 25 April, 1847, belittling those wayward Saints who would follow a "Black man who has got the blood of Ham in him which lineage was cursed as regards the Priesthood."[4]

On the assumption that Pratt could only have learned of this implied restriction during the frenetic few preceding days at Winter Quarters (which Esplin judged unlikely), or prior to mid-1846—the times when Pratt and Young were together—Esplin felt comfortable pushing the apparent decision on blacks and the priesthood further back, "at least [to] 1843." This final leap was supported by two circumstantial assumptions: first, that despite the seeming originality of some of his teachings Brigham never went beyond the doctrines of Joseph; and second, that teachings which cannot be documented as originating with Joseph probably were part of those secret "temple-related teachings" of which we currently have no available records. However plausible this sounded, its scholarly merits were greatly limited by both the circularity of the first claim, and the inaccessibility of the second.

Bringhurst, meanwhile, in his comprehensive *Saints, Slaves, and*

Whence the Negro Doctrine?

Blacks: The Changing Place of Black People Within Mormonism (Greenwood Press, 1981), willingly accommodated the new 1847 material (Esplin later provided him with yet another late-1847 indication of a restriction on blacks), but found no compelling reason to join Esplin in locating the practice of priesthood denial in an even earlier period. He particularly emphasized the seemingly pivotal role of the black-Indian "prophet" William McCary to whom Pratt referred in his April remarks and whose early 1847 confrontation with the Mormon hierarchy appears circumstantially to have catalyzed Mormon thinking on blacks and the priesthood.[5]

Other knowledgeable students of Mormon history, such as Klaus Hansen and Richard Howard—and, one senses, Bringhurst himself— were nevertheless uncomfortable with the apparent exoneration of Joseph Smith that the 1847 date would seem to imply. Howard, for example, in a review of *Saints, Slaves, and Blacks*, found it "difficult . . . to imagine that Young's policies would have developed as they did . . . apart from the early antiabolitionist and racist positions of Mormonism's founder," while Hansen's 1980 chapter on "The Transformation of Racial Thought and Practice" strongly supported the notion that "[Smith's] Book of Abraham is indeed the linchpin in the Negro doctrine."[6]

With this as a backdrop let us turn to a chronology of what is now known of the key early events—a chronology which will show that there are few if any significant conflicts inherent in the data that Bringhurst (or I)—or Esplin—has presented, and the concerns of Hansen or Howard.

Development of Denial Practices

1830-June 1844
   • The Book of Mormon, published in 1830, clearly associated a "skin of blackness" with unrighteousness, though the subject was the ancestors of the Indians rather than Africans or others. In Joseph Smith's revision of the Bible, begun the following year, the book of Moses asserted the same association between "blackness" and unrighteousness among antediluvian peoples and identified the descendants of Cain as "black," (seemingly corroborating an early nineteenth-century notion that Africans were descended from Cain).[7]

   • Both the published and the private writings of early Church leaders concerned with the slavery-abolition debate left no question that they all—including Joseph Smith—accepted the conventional wisdom that blacks were descendants of Ham. Smith's revision of the Bible eventually added to the discussion of the curse on Ham's son Canaan that he had "a veil of darkness . . . cover him, that he shall be known among all men." The most complete statement of black genealogy was a W. W. Phelps letter in the March 1835 *Messenger and Advocate*, characterizing a "black skin" as a general indicator of apostasy and proposing that the "black seed" of Cain was passed through the Flood by Ham's having married "a black wife." While conceivably derivable from the extant book of Moses or contemporary folklore, this idea received its clearest apparent formal enunciation in the subsequent publication of the book of Abraham. Another relevant book of Abraham antecedent was suggested in Phelp's allusion, "Were or were not Pharaoh's 'priests,' (the real 'black coats' of Egypt...) the leaders of the great Gentile church in that day...."[8]

• Elijah Abel, a black member converted in 1832, was ordained an elder in 1836 and a seventy later the same year. He was well-known to Joseph Smith and the Mormon community in Kirtland, Nauvoo, and after 1842 in Cincinnati. His activities but not his priesthood status were discussed in leadership meetings in June 1839 (attended by Joseph Smith and other leading Mormons) and June 1843 (attended by Apostles Heber C. Kimball, John Page, and Orson Pratt).

• About the same time, book of Abraham passages noting that the lineage of the pharaoh was "cursed as to the priesthood" were translated (c 1837) and published (1842). This event logically related the priesthood curse to blacks, whom conventional wisdom, Phelps, and Mormons in general placed in the same basic lineage. On the other hand, as specifically set forth by Joseph Smith, this curse was a statement of historical circumstance, analogous to the related biblical curse of servitude placed on Canaan.

• Notwithstanding the publication of the book of Abraham in 1842, there is as yet no contemporary evidence that Joseph Smith enunciated a policy of priesthood restriction on blacks, or that any other leading Mormon during the Smith presidency referred to one. Similarly, biblical texts also accepted as scripture by Joseph and his contemporaries which—given the received genealogical traditions—might have provided sanction for the institution of Negro slavery were disregarded as the Prophet spoke openly and repeatedly against legalized slavery in the 1840s (this despite his use of these very scriptures the previous decade in an attack on abolitionism).

• Apostle Parley P. Pratt, speculating on the now discredited Kinderhook plates in May, 1843, was comfortable asserting that they were "filled with engravings in Egyptian language and contain the genealogy of one of the ancient Jaredites back to Ham the son of Noah..."—thereby placing a once righteous, priesthood-bearing people into the potentially suspect lineage.[9]

• At some point, apparently within a year or so prior to Joseph's death, at least one other black member, Walker Lewis, was ordained an elder in Lowell, Massachusetts, reportedly either by Apostle William Smith or Parley Pratt. While the date of Lewis's baptism and ordination is still uncertain, his support for local branch leaders was noted in passing by visiting Apostle Wilford Woodruff in November 1844.

June 1844-December 1847
●The area in which Elder Walker Lewis resided was visited repeatedly during 1844-45 by leading Mormons, including Wilford Woodruff, Brigham Young, and Ezra T. Benson, without more than passing reference to the presence of a black elder. Records of Elijah Abel's Cincinnati branch in June 1845 show him to have been active and a stalwart defender of the faith.

● Apostle Orson Hyde delivered a speech in Nauvoo in 1845 which he said was given "by permission" and based on the "mysteries of the kingdom." In it he referred to the "curse of slavery" resting on "Canaan, the son of Ham," and asserted that spirits who in the pre-mortal existence "lent an influence to the devil . . . come into the world and take bodies in the accursed lineage of Canaan; and hence the negro or African race." He warned his listeners, in the context of the Rigdon-vs.-the-Twelve debate, that "all those who are halting concerning who has the right to govern had better look at the fate of their brethren that have gone before them." While no explicit reference was made to a priesthood restriction, a question was perhaps implicit about the right of those cursed with servitude to assume positions of leadership, an argument made explicitly by Brigham Young a few years later. The best candidate for a "mystery" in this talk was the novel assertion that the alleged status of blacks in the preexistence justified their current predicament. (Some years later Brigham repudiated this as an adequate explanation for the priesthood ban, and also rejected other Hyde innovations including a "baby resurrection" and, possibly, the notion of a "guardian angel.")[10]

● The troublesome, self-proclaimed black-Indian "prophet," William McCary, arrived in Winter Quarters during the winter of 1846-47. While church leaders initially tolerated McCary's bizarre activities, by late March he was clearly in trouble. In a revealing confrontation with Brigham Young, and Apostles Richards, Orson Pratt, Benson, Woodruff, and others on 26 March, 1847, Young informed McCary, "its nothing to do with the blood for of one blood has God made all flesh, we have to repent (and) regain what we av lost—we av one of the best Elders an African in Lowell—[i.e., Walker Lewis]." McCary shortly after was expelled from the Mormon community but attracted some followers to his own curious schismatic brand of Mormonism.[11]

● Amid the concerns surrounding McCary's expulsion, Apostle Parley Pratt returned from a mission in England about 7 April. A week later, on 14 April, Brigham left Winter Quarters with the vanguard enroute for Salt Lake City. Just a few days later Pratt, who with another returned Apostle, John Taylor, had been left behind to oversee Winter Quarters, delivered his notable comments mocking any Saint unfaithful enough to follow "this Blackman [McCary] who has got the blood of Ham in him which lineage was cursed as regards the priesthood."[12]

• Coincidentally, in May 1847, mission president William Appleby encountered Walker Lewis in his Lowell branch, noted his priesthood status and the infant offspring of his interracially married son, and wrote Brigham Young on 2 June, 1847, asking if it were "the order of God, or tolerated, to ordain negroes to the priesthood and allow amalgamation. If it is, I desire to know it as I have yet to learn it." Under the date of May 19, but—according to Bringhurst—possibly not written until several years later, Appleby had noted in his journal that Lewis' ordination was "contrary... to the order of the Church... as descendants of Ham are not entitled to that privilege." (Appleby also had copied the relevant extract from the book of Abraham into his journal, shortly after it was published).[13]

• Brigham Young, who left Winter Quarters for the Great Basin well before Appleby's letter was written, apparently did not reply in writing. By the time Young returned to Winter Quarters, 31 October, Appleby also was there. Their presumed conversation is not recorded; but that Fall, Young was willing to rule, in Bringhurst's paraphrase, "that blacks in general were ineligible to participate in certain temple ordinances."[14]

December 1847-1877

• Vacancies in the Quorum of the Twelve created by the reorganization of the First Presidency late in December 1847 were not filled until 12 February, 1849, when four new apostles were set apart. One of these, Lorenzo Snow, asked Brigham the following day prior to a leadership meeting about the "chance of redemption... for the Africans." Young replied, in part, that "the Lord had cursed Cain's seed with blackness and prohibited them the Priesthood." This was, for years, the earliest known statement of priesthood denial to blacks; it remains the earliest explicit one.[15]

• At least twice in January 1852, Young as governor addressed the Utah Territorial Legislature on the question of legalizing Negro slavery. His position, repeatedly and emphatically reiterated over the next decade, despite an apparent personal aversion to the actual practice, was that the scriptural injunction of Genesis was clear: "In as much as we believe in the Bible, inasmuch as we believe in the ordenances of God, in the Preisthood and order and decrees of God, we must believe in Slavery." Moreover, "The seed of Canaan will inevitably carry the curse [of servitude] which was placed upon them, until the same authority which placed it there, shall see proper to have it removed."[16] On February 4 he signed into law Utah's "Act in relation to Service" formally legalizing African slavery in the territory. This act or its successors remained in effect until the Emancipation Proclamation a decade later.[17]

•The day after signing the act on slavery, Young again addressed the legislature, dwelling at some length on the impropriety of allowing the "children of old Cain" to hold ecclesiastical or civil office. During this speech Young made what is perhaps the first clear public statement of the priesthood ban: "If there never was a prophet or apostle of Jesus Christ spoke it before, I tell you, this people that are commonly called negroes are the children of old Cain. I know they are, I know that they cannot bear rule in the preisthood...." And, indeed, no leading Mormon throughout Young's presidency is known to have attributed this teaching to anyone else nor did Brigham Young himself do so. The closest Young came to citing a source was in this same 5 February address: "They are the true eternal principals the Lord Almighty has ordained, and who can help it, men cannot, the angels cannot, and all the powers of earth and hell cannot take it off, but thus saith the Eternal I am, what I am, I take it off at my pleasure, and not one partical of power can that posterity of Cain have, until the time comes the [sic] says he will have it taken away." The notion that a curse placed on Cain and his descendants was *the* explanation of this policy, evident in Young's comments both in 1849 and 1852, was found in virtually every one of his sermons or private comments on the subject. No other explanation, directly attributable to Brigham, has been discovered.[18]

1877-1901

• The circumstances surrounding the origin of the Negro doctrine were discussed in the leading councils of the Church on several occasions during the last third of the nineteenth century. In 1879 several meetings were held in response to an incorrect report that Zebedee Coltrin, a contemporary of Joseph Smith, had said that Joseph taught that blacks *could* hold the priesthood. Coltrin in fact had said just the opposite, claiming to have been told by Joseph in 1834 that "the Negro had no right nor cannot hold the Priesthood." Abraham Smoot, interviewed with Coltrin, volunteered his recollection that in 1838 and later, missionaries in the South had been advised that blacks (slaves?) were ineligible for the priesthood. While we can document an increasingly restrictive policy toward blacks in the South during these early years, Coltrin's broader claims were effectively refuted by Joseph F. Smith who had seen Elijah Abel's certification as a seventy, issued in 1841 and again in Salt Lake City. More damaging yet to Coltrin's story was Abel's correct recollection that Coltrin himself had ordained him a seventy in 1836 and that Joseph had told him he was "entitled to the priesthood." Abel's status as a priesthood holder in 1836 was further verified by consulting his patriarchal blessing, given by Joseph Smith, Sr., that year. Acting president John Taylor, an apostle with Joseph Smith for five years, was unable to offer anything more than the opinion that "probably" Abel had "been ordained before the will of the Lord had been fully understood, [and] it was allowed to remain."[19]

• In the 1890s, others attributed the Negro doctrine to Joseph Smith but without the specific detail of Coltrin. While the subject does not appear to have been of much concern, at no time did anyone who had served as a General Authority with Joseph ascribe the priesthood ban to him. Franklin D. Richards, who had known the Prophet as a young man and who became an Apostle at the same time as did Lorenzo Snow in 1849, seems in 1896 to have credited the Negro doctrine to Joseph Smith. Snow, however, who had asked about the chances for "the Africans" very early remained uncertain whether Brigham had learned his views from Joseph or originated them himself.[20]

• After 1900, it was generally accepted that Joseph originated the priesthood restriction on blacks.[21]

While not doing justice to the many subtleties in this history, this summary is probably sufficient to illustrate why the "when" and "where" of the priesthood ban is less a subject of confusion than it used to be. Notwithstanding the implied precedent of the book of Abraham, there was no hint of a practical concern about the priesthood status of Elijah Abel or Walker Lewis (or Ham's "descendants," the Jaredites!) through the mid-1840s. Indeed, substantial new evidence will be required to assert a policy of priesthood discrimination prior to the McCary encounter in early spring 1847. While some uncertainties remain, it presently appears that the policy of priesthood restriction crystallized in 1847, perhaps early in that spring but almost surely by fall. However, with no otherwise eligible black males at hand to prompt a public statement, what (probably little) discussion of the subject there was did not come until almost two years later in Utah by which time Brigham's views were clearly quite solid. Actual publicizing of the ban came three years later, when a variety of changed circumstances led to public statements on both slavery and priesthood.[22]

Origins of the Doctrine

The question of the origin of the "Negro doctrine" as distinct from the practice of priesthood discrimination—the "why"—is much more complicated. Most past "explanations" have begun with the unexamined assumption that the practice began with Joseph Smith and have polarized either into an "orthodox" view that God revealed the doctrine to Joseph or an "environmental" explanation that he originated it in response to the traumatic slave-related experiences in Missouri. In the absence of a concrete revelatory document on which to hang their claims, the orthodox —especially after the turn of the century—have cited the relevant book of Abraham passages and more recently the Coltrin account, plus the lengthening record of "inspired" reaffirmation by succeeding twentieth-century presidencies. In the absence of other support, exponents of the "Missouri thesis" were forced to rely on these same evidences,[23] adding only the important observation that the bridge between contemporary blacks and the scriptural curses on Cain, Ham, Canaan, or the pharaohs was the nineteenth-century conventional wisdom that tied these lineages together.

Research over the past decade or so uncovered serious problems with the Missouri thesis and its implied timetable. A mid-twentieth century perspective on Joseph's book of Abraham also found it insufficient to explain alone the advent of the Negro doctrine. Where faithful nineteenth-century minds had needed no explanation as to who comprised the modern descendants of Canaan, Ham, or Cain, this was no longer the case in 1970. The dismantling of the official orthodoxy on this subject has been detailed elsewhere.[24] Ultimately all that remained was an unanchored assumption that the doctrine originated with Joseph Smith and that its continuation was God's will. Since the revelation of 1978, one additional effort has been made in the "faithful" tradition to explain how and when Smith came to bar blacks from the priesthood—the Esplin hypothesis, which proposed without contemporary documentation that the Prophet reached this decision during a time when he was developing or elaborating on the more advanced temple rituals introduced at Nauvoo, during 1842-43.

Undermining the Missouri thesis also led to the formulation of more complex, less time-specific hypotheses by those who sought a possible nonrevelatory origin for the doctrine. The most extensive have been postulated by Hansen and Bringhurst. Hansen proposed as explanatory factors the sensitization of the Mormon leadership by their Missouri and Southern missionary experiences (a more broadly stated Missouri thesis); a developing "grandiose vision of the kingdom of God" into which "racial tolerance" fit less easily in terms of a scriptural injunction to maintain the purity of the chosen lineage; and concern about "the crisis of the family" and specific issues of "sex" and "miscegenation." While Hansen also asserted that Joseph "believed" in a direct link between the scriptures including the book of Abraham and "the modern Negro," he made no effort to document how either this assumption—or his other hypotheses —related in time or place to the many specifics known about the early history of blacks in the church. His essay, though built around an occasional historical datum, was principally a theoretical exercise seeking to accommodate some of what happened to an existing conceptual framework.[25]

Bringhurst, who shares many of Hansen's theoretical perceptions, was more specific as to time and circumstance in his analysis—and is thereby both more and less persuasive. He, too, found the metaphorical and sometimes literal racism of Mormon scripture a logical precursor to an increasing lineage consciousness among the early Mormons. While "whiteness" was perhaps symbolic, a quite literal "blackness" was associated with apostasy. This, Bringhurst felt, was both reflected in and generated by what he characterized as a major Mormon interest in "black Biblical counterfigures"—Cain, Ham, and Canaan. Concepts relating to these "counterfigures" in the books of Moses and Abraham were said to have "paved the way for implementation of black priesthood denial." While there was "little to suggest" that this policy was implemented "during the 1830s," these sources "would in time provide scriptural justification for these practices." Against this backdrop Bringhurst found also what he described as a "deterioration" after 1839 in the practical circumstances of blacks in both Mormon mind and community. And finally, he singled out as important the apparent social awkwardness of black elder Abel's priesthood presence among the Mormons and the scarcely veiled threat of black prophet McCary's priestly claims. While apprehensions relating to sex/miscegenation also figured prominently in Bringhurst's analysis, he suggested, because of the timing of the key Appleby letter, that these concerns served principally as an after-the-fact reinforcement to a decision taken shortly before.[26]

Notwithstanding the unanchored nature of Hansen's generalities and an ill-defined awkwardness of focus to Bringhurst's discussion, several of their postulated explanations seem to have real merit. Others are less persuasive. There appear also to be at least two conspicuous omissions: there is no in-depth consideration of either the relevant Mormon scriptures or of the personalities that interpreted them.[27] Another important problem with both works is a failure to analyze systematically —or occasionally even distinguish between—predisposing but insufficient early factors and those crucial later developments that led more or less directly to the priesthood ban.

It may be instructive to consider again the several relevant factors chronologically. Most will be seen to have taken place during the lifetime of Joseph Smith, thus explaining much of the later, retrospective identification of the Prophet as originator of the doctrine. In a sense this later judgment will be seen to be correct—despite Joseph's perhaps intentional failure to implement a policy of priesthood restriction.

As noted previously, publication of the Book of Mormon in 1830 reinforced the popular early nineteenth-century notion that racial characteristics could be traced directly to the moral calibre of various civilizations. Lamanites became "black" as they became depraved. Depravity, in turn, followed directly on the heels of apostasy. The entire process, however, was reversible; repentant peoples could again become "white and delightsome."[28] This popular contemporary assumption would not have been startling news to reasonably well-informed early readers of the Book of Mormon, nor were these points excessively emphasized in the Nephite history. They were rather passing illustrations indicative, with many other offered "proofs," of God's literal hand in the lives of both individuals and societies. More conspicuous by far was the theme of the gospel's universal message: it was for "all nations, kindreds, tongues, and people," extending not only to "black and white, bond and free, male and female," but also to "heathen . . . Jew and Gentile."[29]

Joseph Smith's revision of the Bible, undertaken later that year, continued in 1831 and was partially published in 1832. It introduced hundreds of changes or expansions into the text of the King James translation. Of these, three were related directly to "color" in contexts paralleling (but not even as central as) those relating to the subject in the Book of Mormon. Once again these passing additions would simply have confirmed opinions already held by many early nineteenth-century readers: "the seed of Cain" were "black," a "blackness came upon all the [explicitly unrighteous] children of Canaan," and Ham's cursed son Canaan was said to have had "a veil of darkness . . . cover him, that he may be known among all men." Noah's curse itself was left unchanged; Canaan was to be a "servant of servants" to his brethren.[30]

Any possible historical uncertainty about which contemporary group the early Mormons equated with cursed, black biblical lineages is emphatically clarified by the extensive antiabolitionist discourses carried in the April 1836 *Messenger and Advocate*. Among many other arguments Warren Parrish, Oliver Cowdery, and Joseph Smith each affirmed, in Smith's words, that "the curse is not yet taken off the sons of Canaan, neither will be until it is affected by as great power as caused it to come."[31] Perhaps reflecting some of the lingering Christian Primitivist phase of early Mormonism—or a diversity of opinion among the members— Joseph and the others added that the expressed opinions were the "sentiments I believe, as an individual."[32] It was, however, precisely this biblically-derived antiabolitionist phraseology in Joseph's essay which Brigham Young later used in calling for a legalization of Negro slavery in Utah. That the association of Negroes with Ham, Cain, or Canaan's curse of servitude had no necessary implications for free blacks was evidenced by the concurrent ordination of Elijah Abel to the priesthood and his participation in the early rituals initiated in the Kirtland Temple.

Nonetheless, Mormon sensitivities over the national slavery issue were substantially heightened by experiences in Missouri and elsewhere, as evidenced by a concurrent policy change limiting proselyting among slaves.[33]

Directly in the wake of these on-going developments came Joseph Smith's efforts to provide a translation of the Egyptian papyri recently acquired by himself on behalf of the Church. In retrospect, this proved a singularly pivotal effort in the history of what was to become the "Negro doctrine." However, while the resulting book of Abraham was ultimately to provide the proof-text for a policy of priesthood discrimination, one needs to examine the record closely before assuming it served this function either in the preparation phase (c1837) or at the time of publication (1842).

It is important to recall that despite the seeming novelty of the new scripture, much of it, as with the case of the book of Moses, was probably not substantively startling to those close to the Prophet when it was first written nor to the general membership five years later when parts were published. A major portion of the text was, after all, a relatively modest embellishment of the accepted Genesis account of creation.[34] Abraham admittedly figured much more prominently, but those familiar with the popular, contemporary editions of *Josephus' Complete Works* were already advised of Abraham's instrumental role, for example, in instructing the Egyptians in the "science of astronomy." Josephus' passing reference to "Egyptus" as an early Egyptian pharaoh, and Phelps's published proposal shortly before (noted above) on the Cain-Canaan genealogy would further have preempted the novelty (but none of the new prophetic authority) of Joseph's scripture.[35]

What was distinctively new in the book of Abraham was a creation account which accommodated a more fully developed Mormon theology and an extensive "midrash" concerned with the developing Mormon notion of priesthood authority. It was this latter textual expansion that included the references later central to the rationale for priesthood denial to blacks. The relevant verses, speaking of the pharaoh's ineligibility for the priesthood and various, often unspecified curses, unquestionably would have been understood as referring to the remote ancestors of African blacks. Canaanites, Hamites, and ancient Egyptians were all part of this same basic lineage. Yet these retrospectively prominent explanatory and genealogical points were not as doctrinally significant or central as other major points in the text.

The story of the Pharaoh's priesthood limitation was more particularly a vehicle for a message about authentic priesthood authority than a message about priesthood exclusion based on race per se. It clearly could have been both—and ultimately it was understood to be—but there is no necessary reason to assume this was originally the case or intent, or that if it were so in 1837, it still was so viewed in 1842. Possibly analagous, for example, was a related discussion in 1841 just a few months before the book of Abraham was published and the same year Elijah Abel was recertified as a seventy. In this discussion, the Prophet asserted that Canaan had been cursed with servitude "by the priesthood which [Noah] held, and the Lord had respect to his word, notwithstanding he was drunk."[36] Here the specifics of Joseph's illustration were clearly secondary to an underlying message about the power of the priesthood. In a real sense this very curse had to be discounted or explained away in some manner parallel to the case in point by all who supported abolishing slavery, for even among abolitionists the Ham-African genealogy was rarely in dispute. In 1836 Joseph appears not to have viewed the curse on Canaan in anything but literal, contemporary-relevant terms, but he apparently had changed his mind by the early 1840s when he began to speak out strongly against slavery.

Thus, while it is possible that Joseph contemplated denying blacks the priesthood at the time the earliest book of Abraham texts were in preparation—or at least considered this a rational implication of the text—it is highly relevant to note that he never publicly espoused this potential application of his scripture. Indeed, the very issue of the *Times and Seasons* in which these texts were first published also contained the first of Joseph's public proabolitionist, antislavery commentary.[37] In sum, at present we cannot confidently say what Joseph understood the implications of the book of Abraham to be for contemporary blacks, at any time between 1837 and his death in 1844. We can only say, as detailed previously, what we know about what he did in actual practice.

The elaboration of Mormon theology did not end with the advent of the book of Abraham. While later discussions of the "Negro doctrine" often end there, doctrinal developments in the final years of Joseph Smith's presidency were also relevant. In particular Esplin has focused attention on the new temple rituals, introduced and expanded in Nauvoo in the 1840s. While there may well be merit in linking black policies with temple development, it is still difficult to believe—given the apparent chronology of the actual practice—that a concrete policy of priesthood denial to blacks dated much before spring 1847. Nonetheless, the implications of earlier temple-related developments were probably relevant to priesthood denial to blacks *and* the underlying "Negro doctrine."

Joseph Smith's early view of the role of the temple, though perhaps initially elitist, was highly democratized by the time the first temple was dedicated in 1836.[38] This was reflected both in the inclusive "house rules" governing those in attendance and Elijah Abel's participation in the sacred ordinances introduced there.[39] Indeed, if any of the specifics of

Zebedee Coltrin's later recollections can be credited, a likely candidate is his statement that Abel was ordained to the priesthood because of his work on the temple. In the context of the universalism of the Book of Mormon, the highly inclusive lay structure of both the Mormon leadership and its salvation/exaltation theology, and the view that the millennium was virtually at hand, Abel's efforts probably were sufficient to overcome what must have been substantial social and cultural impediments to his being made (in the words of his patriarchal blessing) "equal to thy brethren."[40]

In the early 1840s, however, new temple rituals were introduced which, partly for social reasons, were much more exclusivist. These rituals were now intimately associated with another theological innovation: unorthodox and culturally suspect marriages between Mormon leaders and "celestial" or "spiritual" wives. There are a number of grounds on which one might reasonably argue that Joseph and his close advisers would have excluded blacks from these more sensitive and exclusive ordinances (if not from the priesthood per se), but there is no evidence that this was formally done. It is relevant to recall that by 1842 there were no longer any candidate blacks in the Nauvoo community. Abel had moved to Cincinnati in 1842, before the introduction of these later temple rituals.

A "democratization" of the more exclusive Nauvoo temple ordinances, or "endowments," probably envisioned by Joseph before his death, was carried out in practice in the years between the martyrdom and the exodus. Had there been eligible blacks petitioning for these "endowments" and marriage "sealings," a decision on black eligibility might have been forthcoming, but, as noted, there were none. Almost concurrent with the democratization of the endowment had been the implementation of yet another new, again exclusivist "second endowment" which unconditionally crowned selected initiates to be "gods." (In the first, they were "only" set apart conditionally to become gods.)[41] Given the sensitization of Mormon leaders by the escapades of McCary and the miscegenation of the Lewis family, it would not be hard to envision a policy restricting blacks thereafter from one or all of these Nauvoo-era temple ordinances—especially this "capstone" ritual—as suggested by Esplin's fall 1847 reference. By then there also had been other significant changes in perspective.

One key change seems to have been the degree of literalism with which some of the scriptures relating to blacks were understood and applied. Within a year of Joseph's death the *Times and Seasons* was again condemning blacks to divinely sanctioned servitude on the basis of a culturally conditioned, literalistic, scriptural interpretation of Genesis implicitly rejected by Joseph Smith.[42] The most striking illustration of this, of course, came with Brigham Young's assertion just a few years later that he had to believe in Negro slavery because he believed in the Bible.[43] As originator of the book of Abraham and of a variant revision of the Bible, Joseph clearly had the authority and confidence to interpret or reinterpret these scriptures in a way that modified the apparent "clear" meaning of the texts—and by implication he did so by not applying either to the actual practice of Negro slavery or priesthood eligibility. His successors seem not to have felt this same flexibility, and returned to a more literal (in a nineteenth-century context) reading of the texts.[44]

An obvious and clearly relevant illustration of this new or renewed literalism is found in the first known suggestion of a policy of priesthood restriction. The wording of Parley Pratt's 1847 characterization of McCary as having the "blood of Ham in him which lineage was cursed as regards the priesthood"—whether descriptive or proscriptive[45]—unmistakably derived in part from the book of Abraham. While the use of the book of Abraham as proof-text for the practice of priesthood denial was not to become popular for another half century, it is apparent from the appearance of the cadence "cursed as pertaining to the priesthood" in a handful of early sources that the priesthood restriction was very early understood in a book of Abraham context.[46] It is difficult to imagine that it would not have been, once the decision or interpretation had been made that the scriptural curses were still in effect.

Another relevant change between the pre-and post-Joseph Smith years, albeit a subtle one when viewed from 1983, is a clear deterioration in the way in which blacks were characterized by individual Mormon leaders. Prejudiced though all the early years may have been by modern standards, it is important to recall that where Brigham believed "nature" (as well as "nature's God") had prepared blacks only for servitude, Joseph apparently believed the status of blacks was environmentally mediated— and proposed placing them on a national equalization. Whatever Joseph's prejudices or true intent, he apparently never made a public statement parallel to Brigham's spring 1847 condemnation of his pioneer elders for abusing their priesthood by "stoop[ing] to dance like nigers."[47]

It is thus in a much richer context that one must consider such reasonably well-supported suggestions by Hansen and Bringhurst as the idea that growing lineage self-consciousness among the early Mormons also played an important role in the implementation of priesthood denial to blacks. While this no doubt was true, both it and their other suggestions were all threads in a demonstrably more complex fabric.

When Brigham finally made explicit the grounds for priesthood denial to blacks, he was very specific as to these grounds—and reiterated his explanation many times during the next two and half decades. As *descendants of Cain*, blacks were not entitled to the priesthood or to

participation in sacred temple ordinances.[48] Given the complex developments outlined above, his realization that this was the case must surely
have been the product of many factors. The sine qua non was no doubt
the full scriptural legacy left by Joseph Smith. For Brigham, one surmises,
no further revelation beyond the extant scriptures was necessary, as none
had been on the issue of black servitude. While there may have been a time
when this scriptural insight was not so self-evident, intervening events had
brought it into clearer focus. Once in focus there never was any further
question.

In a very real sense, Joseph Smith had provided a context which, in
his absence, inevitably led to a policy of priesthood denial to blacks.
Whether this would have occurred had Joseph not been killed is debatable.
He apparently had not felt it necessary to implement such a policy despite
the precedents provided while he lived, but later developments may have
changed his mind. It seems very unlikely that Brigham and his colleagues
perceived themselves as moving *away* from Joseph's lead, but they may
well have felt they were carrying it forward to its logical application.[49]

The Concluding Chapter

It may be instructive to consider briefly some events in the later years
of the priesthood restriction. Some of the final developments may be
understood somewhat more clearly in terms of the foregoing history.

Up to the mid-1880s, the Pearl of Great Price was not cited conspicuously in explanation of church policy on black restrictions. It would have
been very relevant but was also unnecessary for it merely affirmed an
association that was not in dispute. When the Pearl of Great Price did
come into vogue as a proof-text for church teachings, it ironically was
only anachronistically relevant. While it appeared to provide key evidence,
in fact it had been reduced logically to a mere link in a circular argument.
Since conventional wisdom no longer linked blacks to the ancient biblical
lineages, the Pearl of Great Price was called upon to do so. In essence,
modern blacks were asserted to be the descendants of Cain and Ham
because modern blacks were those against whom the ancient priesthood
ban was still in force; it was enforced against them because they were
descendants of Cain and Ham. A similarly circular argument soon
matched in popularity that of the Pearl of Great Price. This was the
notion that blacks were denied the priesthood because of some inadequacy
in the preexistence; the evidence for the inadequacy was that they were
denied the priesthood. By the time these twentieth century innovations
became popular, a long-established tradition of authoritative priesthood
denial readily bridged the breach in logic, much as conventional wisdom
about black genealogy had done so a century earlier.

In the final analysis, three principle factors sustained the priesthood ban in the twentieth century. In order of descending relevance, these were the authority of decades of vigorous and unwavering First Presidency endorsement of the policy; a preconceived and highly literalistic reading of several verses in the Pearl of Great Price; and an ambient culture which was indifferent to, if not supportive of, Mormon attitudes toward blacks. As formidable as these factors were, they were not the only influences at work.

Some of the very forces, initially set in motion by Joseph Smith, which originally led to the denial of the priesthood to blacks, eventually also helped assure that this ban would come to an end. In particular the central and essential role assigned to the temple in Mormon theology, and the pattern of progressive democratization of even the most exclusive of its rituals seem to have been major contributing factors at every significant step along the way. It was Elijah Abel's work on the Kirtland temple that apparently overcame whatever socio-cultural obstacles existed and led to his priesthood ordination. The institution of more culturally sensitive rituals with their connotations of unorthodox marriages, and their extension to rather large segments of the Mormon community was likely associated with the decision to deny to blacks both these rites and the priesthood which had come to assure access to them. A century later concern that black members in the vicinity of a South Pacific temple be allowed access to by-then much less sensitive temple rituals prompted one of the first serious reviews of church teachings on blacks in decades.[50] While no change in policy was made, just two decades later a similar review was prompted by the efforts of black members in the construction of yet another temple in Brazil; this time the decision was made that these worthy workers—like Elijah Abel 142 years before—be allowed to hold the priesthood so that they might enjoy the blessings of the temple.

A second major force set in motion by Joseph Smith was embodied in his notion of the universality of the gospel. This idea appears repeatedly in the Book of Mormon, in early Mormon sermons and hymns, the rules governing the Kirtland Temple, and the prospectus anticipating the opening of the Nauvoo temple. Mormonism, at least in theory, was a nationally and racially inclusive movement. Though apparently driven to a more self-conscious, exclusivist leadership style during its years of persecution, the heritage was still there. When the millennium didn't bring the nations of the earth flocking to Zion, Zion eventually sent forth its missionaries to the nations—with all their kindreds, tongues, and peoples. Eventually temples came to be built in areas where the cursed lineage was inextricably intertwined with the chosen. Black members in the international church figured prominently in leadership discussions in nearly every decade of the twentieth century. As noted, these were apparently temple-related discussions in the later '40s and again in 1978 when the priesthood ban finally came to an end.[51]

A final factor contributed by Joseph Smith to the ultimate termination of the priesthood ban was the exact wording he chose to use in setting forth the book of Abraham. While it can also be argued, as I did above, that this was part of the scriptural corpus which led to the implementation of the priesthood ban in the first place, in another sense it worked against its continuation. The problem was that, whatever the intent, the bridge that linked the cursed lineages of old to modern blacks was never made explicit in the book of Abraham. It would have been awkward, if not flagrantly anachronistic, to have done so, potentially undermining the antiquity ascribed to the whole endeavor. Given the conventional wisdom of the day, at the time it was also at the least unnecessary. When an explicit link *was* necessary a century later, it wasn't there—and the book of Abraham text itself thereby came to be used as evidence of its inapplicability to modern blacks.[52]

Why were these influences insufficient in the late 1940s, mid-1950s, or the mid-1960s when changes in policy received serious consideration—but adequate just a decade later?[53] The answer to this, I believe, lies with those three principal obstacles to change noted above: the authority (and by implication, integrity) of the First Presidency, an archaic reading of the Pearl of Great Price, and the cultural milieu.

Changes in the cultural milieu over the past three decades are both well known and well documented elsewhere. A rough indication of the transition which took place can be found within the Church by contrasting Apostle Petersen's 1954 attack on early civil rights advocates, "Race Relations as They Affect the Church," with statements by the First Presidency on the general subject in the next three decades. Embarrassing though the record may be, Mauss has shown that it was no more so than that of society at large.[54] The point is not to excuse this record but to note that no national hue and cry was to be expected from the 1949 First Presidency affirmation of church beliefs on blacks, and none was received. Two decades later, a much more "progressive" statement, including an endorsement of civil rights and shorn of the more offensive allusions to curses on Cain, *was* greeted with a great deal of national criticism if not overt hostility. The ascendancy to power in the Church of those preoccupied with its public image during the past decade or so amplified the effect of this realignment of the societal norms in which Mormonism operated. A variety of nondoctrinal accommodations ensued— reported elsewhere by Mauss—designed to enhance the image of Mormonism on the race issue. The process also prepared the membership itself for a radical change on the more fundamental issue of the priesthood ban. Thus the impact of the cultural milieu swung around to be just the opposite to that of a few decades before.

Whence the Negro Doctrine?

An inherent flaw in the use of the book of Abraham—the second major obstacle—as proof of the legitimacy of the "Negro doctrine" has been noted already. Several observers have suggested that even more serious was an attack in the late '60s on the whole notion of the historical authenticity of the book of Abraham. This argument derived from the discovery of fragments of the papyri which purportedly underlay key segments of the Abraham narrative. While this development may have affected a few "intellectuals" who were troubled over Church policy, it is doubtful that it swayed anyone of importance in the Church leadership. As difficult as it may have been to consider abandoning Church beliefs on blacks, this would surely have paled before the prerequisite task of discarding a formally canonized scripture. Concluding that the scripture previously had been misunderstood or misapplied was certainly more palatable—especially when this could be accomplished by implication, as in practice it actually was, though the simple omission of the timeworn book of Abraham argument from the formal defense of the priesthood ban.

How Church leaders came to conclude that the book of Abraham was not necessarily as relevant as previously thought is a question which cannot be completely answered at present. Little to nothing has been said publicly, and private insights may not be available for a number of years. One surmises that some leaders, such as Hugh B. Brown and possibly David O. McKay, had reached this conclusion in the '60s if not earlier. Others apparently were influenced by more recent scholarly examinations of the subject and their own resulting studies. In 1975, for example, one General Authority wrote privately that the historical work of the previous few years "probably has a far greater effect than [has been] acknowledged . . . or evidence[d]. Recent conversations suggest that this is so." Significantly, however, one who initially was apparently not impressed was President Kimball who continued to offer the book of Abraham as a proof-text for church policy as late as 1976.[55]

Even at the end, not every General Authority had abandoned the traditional beliefs. Apostle Bruce R. McConkie, for example, was widely commended for his humility when, shortly after the revelation, he called upon seminary and institute teachers to "forget everything I have said . . . that is contrary to the present revelation," adding that "it doesn't make a particle of difference what anybody ever said about the Negro matter before the first day of June 1978." The misimpression was created that he was disavowing much of his own extensive, though archaic dogma on the subject. As events have transpired, it is apparent that he had discarded only the claim that blacks would not be allowed to hold the priesthood in this lifetime—a modest enough concession under the circumstances. The next published version of his *Mormon Doctrine*, though incorporating word of the revelation, retained all the previous, traditional assertions about blacks. That this was no editorial oversight was made clear when McConkie published an expanded version of the seminary and institute talk in *Priesthood*, a collection of essays, in 1981. In setting the stage for his 1978 address, he had added, in part, "The ancient curse is no more. The seed of Cain and Ham and Egyptus and Pharaoh—all these now have power to rise up and bless Abraham as their father. All these, gentile in lineage, may now come and inherit by adoption all the blessings of Abraham, Isaac, and Jacob." Blacks thus were descendants of Cain after all![56]

At another extreme of this apparently multi-cornered spectrum resides defender-of-the-faith Hugh Nibley who unfortunately failed ever to publicly address Church teachings on blacks in the context of his book of Abraham studies. Now that the point is moot, he has published a new work, *Abraham in Egypt* (1981), which comes close to arguing that the Church never believed there was such a connection in the first place. "Why was Pharaoh . . . denied that priesthood which he 'would fain claim from Noah, through Ham' (1:27)," asks Nibley. "Certainly not because of Ham, 'a just man (who) walked with God'. . . ." Rather, he continues, it was because he traced his claim through the "*matriarchal* line" rather than the "patriarchal." "In all of which," concludes Nibley, "there is no mention of race, though enemies of the Church have declared with shock and outrage that these passages are proof of Mormon discrimination against blacks."[57]

The fading of the final remaining obstacle is probably the most difficult to access. The weight of many decades of authoritative reaffirmation of Church policy on blacks by the First Presidency created not only a self-perpetuating inertia but also posed a difficult obstacle to a radical change. A comparable change in Church policy on polygamy had been internally divisive and seemingly had undermined rather than enhanced the authority of the leadership. But the analogy to the Manifesto, though commonly drawn, is not really a very good one. The personal price paid by Mormons who entered into polygamous relationships and by those who were asked to abandon them were surely orders of magnitude greater than the intellectual and social awkwardness associated with a very belated, latter-day accusation of racism by only recently sensitized critics.

On the other hand, an accelerating tradition of leadership infallibility had been allowed to develop which largely dictated how any change might take place. No portion of the general tradition formally sanctioned by the First Presidency could be comfortably, affirmatively renounced. Thus, portions of the 1949 statement on blacks and the priesthood were simply omitted from the 1969 statement, thereby defining the new limits of church belief implicitly but without explicitly dealing with the discarded material. Similarly, the final First Presidency statement announcing the end of the priesthood ban in 1978 made no comment about the substance and legitimacy of any previous statement or belief. A revelatory experience was alluded to, the priesthood made available to all "worthy males," and the subject quietly but firmly declared dead.

Could this not have been done a decade earlier? Mauss presents data that suggests it almost was. He also suggests— correctly, I believe—that a major obstacle was concern on the part of the Church (i.e., the First Presidency) that this would have had the appearance of giving in to public pressure as the abandonment of polygamy clearly did. Thus no action was taken for almost a decade, by which time there was much less external agitation. Significantly, however—and perhaps providentially— during the interim the stature and authority of the First Presidency was asserted in unprecedented ways, through the canonization at their direction of new scripture. While the texts involved were neither new nor controversial, this action, I believe, was probably as significant as all the preparatory public relations efforts, for it effectively established the "authority" context within the Church for the abandonment of the priesthood ban.[58]

When the definitive analysis of the demise of the "Negro doctrine" is finally possible, I expect it to be a very complex weave, with the factors which came close to ending it in earlier years not necessarily those which ultimately led to the revelation of 1978. As in the beginning, there will no doubt be predisposing as well as precipitating factors, some of which will change while others continue to influence things. Some factors will be both predisposing in a general sense *and* precipitating in a specific application. The predisposing factors associated with the international church and the temple, for example, were jointly present from midcentury on. Those associated with the cultural milieu began a little later, and grew dramatically after 1970. These developments all pressed in one direction. Insights into the limits of the Pearl of Great Price, however, seem to have waxed and waned with the changing of key personalities throughout this period. Where this scripture may not have posed a major hurdle in the '60s, it appears to again have done so by the mid-'70s. Whether this view again changed in the final months or whether the force of the other factors—notably the compassion felt for blacks laboring for a temple in Brazil—simply carried the day has yet to be learned.

What is clear is that some combination of factors led President Kimball to conclude that it was time for a change *prior* to his revelation. One of the few notable things he has volunteered about the priesthood revelation of 1978 is that it was one of confirmation of a decision already reached.[59] Brigham apparently faced an analogous situation about 130 years earlier in a context of similar predisposing and precipitating factors. One can only wish he had sought a similar confirmation before acting on the conclusions he had reached about Cain and Ham—or, if he did so, that he had left a record of it along with the unfortunate policy legacy which resulted.

NOTES

1. Excluding newspaper and newsmagazine articles, about forty such essays related to some aspect of Mormons and blacks have appeared since the priesthood revelation in 1978. Several will be cited in this essay, and a comprehensive listing is included in "Chronological Bibliography on the Negro Doctrine," elsewhere in this volume.

2. Newell G. Bringhurst, the most prolific writer on this subject, comes closest to making this distinction in his comprehensive *Saints, Slaves, and Blacks: The Changing Place of Black People Within Mormonism* (Westport, Conn.: Greenwood, 1981). At no point, however, does he offer a focused analysis of this important issue.

3. Lester E. Bush, Jr., "Mormonism's Negro Doctrine: An Historical Overview," *Dialogue: A Journal of Mormon Thought* 8 (Spring 1973): 25, 56 note 85.

4. Newell G. Bringhurst, "'A Servant of Servants . . . Cursed as Pertaining to the Priesthood': Mormon Attitudes toward Slavery and the Black Man 1830-1880," Ph.D. dis., University of California, David, 1975, p. 121, and "An Ambiguous Decision: The Implementation of Mormon Priesthood Denial for the Black Man—A Re-examination," *Utah Historical Quarterly* 46 (Winter 1978): 47, 62-63; Ronald K. Esplin, "Brigham Young and Priesthood Denial to the Blacks: An Alternate View," *BYU Studies* 19:394-402. The Pratt quotation is from minutes, 15 Apr. 1847, Brigham Young Papers, Historical Department Archives, hereafter cited as LDS Church Archives Church of Jesus Christ of Latter-day Saints.

5. Bringhurst, *Saints, Slaves, and Blacks*, especially chapter five. Bringhurst paraphrases Esplin, without specific citation, as stating "Brigham Young . . . during the fall of 1847 . . . suggested that blacks in general were ineligible to participate in certain temple ordinances." (p. 86)

6. Richard Howard, review of *Saints, Slaves, and Blacks* in *The John Whitmer Historical Association Journal* 2 (1982): 63-64; Klaus Hansen, *Mormonism and the American Experience* (Chicago: The University of Chicago Press, 1980), p. 187, and Chapter 6 in general.

7. Hugh Nibley, *Since Cumorah: The Book of Mormon in the Modern World* (Salt Lake City: Deseret Book, 1967), pp. 246-51, argued that this "blackness" was to be understood only symbolically, but nineteenth-century

Mormon commentary indicates a quite literal understanding of the term. E.g., *Messenger and Advocate* 1 (Mar. 1835): 81-82, and *Times and Seasons* 6 (Apr. 1845): 857.

8. *Messenger and Advocate* 1 (Mar. 1835): 81-82. This letter, dated 6 Feb. 1835, also anticipates another theological innovation later found in the book of Abraham in its assumption about preexistence, but this idea was evident in then extant but unpublished portions of Joseph Smith's revision of the Bible.

9. Parley P. Pratt to John Van Cott, 7 May 1843, in Parley P. Pratt papers, LDS Church Archives. See also Bringhurst, *Saints, Slaves, and Blacks*, pp. 91, 92, and 104 note 47.

10. "Speech of Elder Orson Hyde, Delivered before the High Priests Quorum, in Nauvoo, April 27th 1845 . . ." (Liverpool, 1845). Similarly, this same month the *Times and Seasons* (6:857) carried "A Short Chapter on a Long Subject," which also moved away from Joseph's recent position by affirming that the servitude of blacks was a "curse of God" and one of the "decrees of eternal wisdom." Esplin, "Brigham Young," p. 398, disregards the fact that the only "curse" identified in Hyde's remarks was the "curse of slavery," and argues that they reflect knowledge of a priesthood ban at this early date. For Brigham's rejection of Hyde's neutrality thesis, see the Journal History of the Church of Jesus Christ of Latter-day Saints, 25 Dec. 1869 (LDS Church Archives). For further Hyde innovations, see Loretta L. Hefner, "From Apostle to Apostate: The Personal Struggle of Amasa Mason Lyman," *Dialogue* 16 (Spring 1983): 91.

11. This important March 1847 quotation, not previously published, was called to my attention by Ronald Esplin. It is found in minutes 26 Mar. 1847, Brigham Young Papers, LDS Church Archives. Its clear implication that there was no priesthood discrimination based on race at the time would seem to limit quite narrowly the time interval in which this practice was first enunciated. For a fuller treatment of McCary, see Bringhurst, *Saints, Slaves, and Blacks*, pp. 84-86, or Bringhurst, "Elijah Abel and the Changing Status of Blacks Within Mormonism," *Dialogue* 12 (Summer 1979): 26-28.

12. Esplin, "Brigham Young," p. 395.

13. William Appleby, Journal, 19 May 1847, LDS Church Archives. The book of Abraham abstract is under date of 5 May 1841. Bringhurst's concerns are noted in *Saints, Slaves, and Blacks*, p. 104 note 41.

14. See note 5. Appleby, about whom little has been written, merits further study. His particular concern with miscegenation is reflected in several journal entries. He later alluded rather harshly to blacks in an article he published on the book of Abraham. While Elijah Abel had been allowed in the Kirtland temple for the ordinance of washing and anointing in 1836, blacks who applied for temple ordinances after arrival in Utah were uniformly refused. On the evolution of Mormon thinking on these ordinances, see David John

Buerger. "'The Fulness of the Priesthood': The Second Annointing in Latter-day Saint Theology and Practice," *Dialogue* 16 (Spring 1983): 10-44.

15. Journal History, 13 Feb. 1849. The text of the earlier Pratt statement leaves the possibility that his remarks were historically descriptive, rather than currently proscriptive. While later events perhaps make this unlikely, it is important to recall that Joseph Smith could have made a comparable statement about Ham and servitude while yet opposing slavery. This in fact was the view of many abolitionists.

16. The first quotation, a remarkable though previously unpublished extract from a "Speach by Gov. Young in Counsel on a Bill relating to Affrican Slavery. Jan. 23d 1852"(LDS Church Archives) makes absolutely explicit the previously apparent source of Brigham's views on black slavery with obvious implications for his closely related views on priesthood. The second quotation is from Young's "Governor's Message, to the Legislative Assembly of Utah Territory, January 5, 1852"(LDS Church Archives). In this he follows Joseph Smith's 1836 antiabolitionist remarks: "The curse is not yet taken off the sons of Canaan, neither will be until it is affected by as great power as caused it to come." (*Messenger and Advocate* 2:290).

17. "An Act in relation to Service," approved 4 Feb. 1852. Brigham, of course, felt that neither the Civil War nor the Emancipation Proclamation would succeed in annulling God's decree. E.g., (6 Oct. 1863) *Journal of Discourses* 10:250.

18. Bush, "Mormonism's Negro Doctrine," pp. 25-26. It was in this context that Brigham replied to Lorenzo Snow in 1849; it was also the Cain ancestry which he asserted as the correct explanation in rebutting Hyde's "neutrality" thesis.

19. Ibid., pp. 31-32.

20. Ibid., pp. 61 note 134, 60 note 131.

21. Ibid., pp. 33-43.

22. In addition to the arrival of a growing number of blacks in Utah territory, Bringhurst, in *Saints, Slaves, and Blacks*, pp. 64-73, makes a case that the national political environment influenced the timing of Young's publication of Mormon views on slavery. Whatever the explanation, Young over a period of only a few months in 1852 presided over the initial publication of the Mormon position on polygamy, Adam-God, the legalization of slavery, and blacks and the priesthood. Young later commented that he once told Joseph Smith that "he had given us revelation enough to last us 20 years when that time is out I can give as good revelation as their is in the Doctrine & Covenants." As quoted in Gary James Bergera, "The Orson Pratt-Brigham Young Controversies: Conflict Within the Quorums, 1853 to 1868," *Dialogue* 13 (Summer 1980): 19.

23. Dennis Lythgoe, in reviewing *Saints, Slaves, and Blacks* for *The Journal of American History*, 69 (Sept. 1982): 421-22, has denied that a Missouri thesis ever existed, though one wonders how he can do so in the face of its clear articulation in, for example, Stephen G. Taggart's widely read *Mormonism's Negro Policy: Social and Historical Origins* (Salt Lake City: University of Utah Press, 1970).

24. Bush, "Mormonism's Negro Doctrine," pp. 39-49 and Armand L. Mauss, "The Fading of the Pharaohs' Curse: The Decline and Fall of the Priesthood Ban Against Blacks in the Mormon Church," *Dialogue* 14 (Fall 1981): 10-45. A major problem for the Missouri thesis has been that the verses of the book of Moses so intertwined with early Mormon thinking on blacks well precede any problems in Missouri.

25. Hansen, *Mormonism and the American Experience.*

26. Bringhurst, *Saints, Slaves, and Blacks*, pp. 45-46, 86-91.

27. If major fault is to be found with Bringhurst's very thorough treatment, it is with the way he couches his extraordinary wealth of descriptive material. My reading of the earliest relevant Mormon comments is that they were often spontaneous responses to the circumstances in which the Saints found themselves, delivered without much thought, and dealing with subjects at best incidental to any notion of Mormon "doctrine." *Saints, Slaves, and Blacks* perhaps inadvertantly conveys the impression that most pre-Utah Mormon commentary relating to blacks was deliberate, if not premeditated, and that it somehow reflected an underlying, conscious effort to formulate a policy on race. This is particularly evident in the use of such terms as "church spokesmen," or "Mormon racism," or "Mormonism's initial attitude," or even "Mormon racist theories" at a time when there was often no such thing as a "Mormon" spokesman or theory relating to blacks—or almost any other subject. This in turn obscures an already complex problem by failing to distinguish systematically between the views expressed in letters to the editor from "average" members, on the one hand, and the views of acknowledged Church leaders on the other. Nor is any effort made to sort out the diverse (but often consistent over time) views of individual prominent Mormons. Perhaps most important, no distinction is made between views self-labelled as "personal" and those put forth with some semblance of institutional authority. Overall this is much less a problem in the materials relating to the early Utah experience and the development of slavery among the Mormons, a circumstance Bringhurst has shown to be at once more complex and self-aware than previously realized. In this instance Bringhurst's data support much more convincingly a case that the words and actions of church leaders *were* deliberate and well thought out.

28. Despite recent changes in the 1981 edition, see 2 Ne. 5:21-23; Jac. 3:5, 8-10; Alma 3:6-9; 3 Ne. 2:14-15; and Morm. 5:15.

29. Examples are, 1 Ne. 17:35, 19:17, 22:28; 2 Ne. 26:26-28; 3 Ne. 28:29, among many.

30. Moses 7:22, 7:8; and Gen. 9:30 Joseph Smith Translation (JST).

31. *Messenger and Advocate* 2:290.

32. Ibid., p. 289.

33. Proselyting restrictions among slaves were announced in 1835 and further tightened the following year.

34. On this general issue see Anthony A. Hutchison, "A Redaction Critical Approach to LDS Creation Narratives," paper delivered at the Mormon History Association annual meeting, Omaha, Nebraska, 6 May 1983.

35. *Josephus: Complete Works*, trans. William Whiston (Grand Rapids, Mich.: Kregel Publications, 1960), pp. xi (Introduction), 33 (Antiquities of the Jews), 612 (Flavius Josephus against Apion).

36. Joseph Smith, *History of the Church of Jesus Christ of Latter-day Saints*, ed. B. H. Roberts, 7 vols. (Salt Lake City: Deseret Book Company, 1966) 4:445-46, entry for 1 Nov. 1841.

37. *Times & Seasons* 3 (1 Mar. 1842): 705, 722-25.

38. See Buerger, "Fulness of the Priesthood," pp. 14-16.

39. *History of the Church* 2:368-69; and Council Meeting Minutes, 4 June 1879, Adam S. Bennion Papers, Lee Library, Brigham Young University, Provo, Utah.

40. Joseph Smith's Patriarchal Blessing Record, p. 88, as cited in Council Meeting Minutes, 4 June 1879, Adam S. Bennion Papers.

41. Buerger, "'Fulness of the Priesthood,'" pp. 22-26.

42. Both the "Short Chapter" of *Times & Seasons* 6 (1 Apr. 1845): 857, and the contemporaneous Orson Hyde talk to the same effect are cited in note 10 above.

43. See note 16 and accompanying text.

44. Similar flexibility has been noted on the part of Joseph Smith in other instances (e.g., polygamy) in which he eventually led the church markedly away from the theology introduced through the Book of Mormon or his other early revelations.

45. Not until 1879 does one find this distinction clearly made even on the issue of slavery. At that time Franklin D. Richards observed, in part, "[Noah] said they should be servants of servants among their brethren, making their servitude the fulfilment of prophecy, whether according to the will of God or not." *Journal of Discourses* 20:312.

46. E.g., *The Seer* 1 (1853): 56, *The Mormon*, 12 Sept. 1857.

47. Bush, "Mormonism's Negro Doctrine," pp. 20-21, 54 note 65, 28-29. While Bringhurst has convincingly made the point that at no time were the early Mormon leaders very progressive on race by modern standards, he has not, as suggested in *Saints, Slaves, and Blacks*, produced data to show a net change in attitude immediately after 1839. The clearest "deterioration" in the status of blacks is evident in the 1845-47 period.

48. As noted previously, this is the only explanation ever offered by Brigham Young for the priesthood restriction; he reiterated it virtually every time he addressed the subject.

49. The concurrent action on slavery, however, suggests that in this instance, at least, a literalist allegiance to Joseph's scripture predominated over a strict adherence to his point of view. As noted, during his lifetime Joseph seems to have reversed this precedence.

50. This, in the late 1940s following a visit to the area served by the Hawaiian temple by Apostle Matthew Cowley and reportedly in anticipation of eventually building a temple in New Zealand.

51. Specific concerns during these years related to South Africa, Fiji, Tonga, Hawaii, West Irian, the Philippines, Brazil, and Cuba. See, for example, Mauss, "The Fading of the Pharaohs' Curse," pp. 12-14; Bringhurst, "Mormonism in Black Africa: Changing Attitudes and Practices, 1830-1981," *Sunstone* 6 (May-June 1981): 15-21; Norman Douglas, "The Sons of Lehi and the Seed of Cain: Racial Myths in the Mormon Scriptures and Their Relevance to the Pacific Islands," *Journal of Religious History* 8 (June 1974): 90-104; and Mark L. Grover, "The Lineage of Cain in the Land of Racial Democracy: The Mormon Priesthood and the Brazilian of African Descent," paper given during the Mormon History Association annual meeting, Omaha, Nebraska, 7 May 1983.

52. A related problem which loomed increasingly larger in the mid-twentieth century was that of identifying exactly which groups were to be denied the priesthood, i.e., who comprised the descendants of Cain. Given traditional assumptions, this had been relatively easy in nineteenth-century America but proved difficult if not impossible in the international, twentieth-century church. The history of this problem is discussed at some length in my "Response to Mark Grover's Essay on 'The Lineage of Cain in the Land of Racial Democracy,'" Mormon History Association annual meeting, Omaha, Nebraska, 7 May 1983.

53. Extensive discussions in these earlier years led to a narrowing of the formal orthodoxy on the subject of the priesthood ban through First Presidency statements (1949, 1969) and to some change in which races qualified for the ban; but in the final analysis, the core practice was always publicly reaffirmed.

54. Armand L. Mauss, "Mormonism and Secular Attitudes Toward Negroes," *Pacific Sociological Review* 9 (Fall 1966): 91-99.

55. Mauss, "The Fading of the Pharaoh's Curse," offers the most complete discussion of these events to date. Much remains to be learned about leadership thinking on this subject, during the '70s especially.

56. See Bruce R. McConkie, "The New Revelation on Priesthood," in *Priesthood* (Salt Lake City: Deseret Book, 1981), pp. 126-37, esp. p. 128. The partial revisions in his *Mormon Doctrine*, 2nd ed. (Bookcraft: Salt Lake City, 1966) are to be found in the 27th printing.

57. Hugh Nibley, *Abraham in Egypt* (Salt Lake City: Deseret Book, 1981), esp. p. 134.

58. Doctrine & Covenants 137 and 138 were presented for sustaining votes as scripture in general conference, April 1976.

59. Most of what has been published is summarized in my "Introduction" to a special issue on the priesthood revelation of 1978, *Dialogue* 12 (Summer 1979): 9-12.

Appendix

Authoritative Statements on the Status of Blacks

August 17, 1949

The attitude of the Church with reference to Negroes remains as it has always stood. It is not a matter of the declaration of a policy but of direct commandment from the Lord, on which is founded the doctrine of the Church from the days of its organization, to the effect that Negroes may become members of the Church but that they are not entitled to the priesthood at the present time. The prophets of the Lord have made several statements as to the operation of the principle. President Brigham Young said: "Why are so many of the inhabitants of the earth cursed with a skin of blackness? It comes in consequence of their fathers rejecting the power of the holy priesthood, and the law of God. They will go down to death. And when all the rest of the children have received their blessings in the holy priesthood, then that curse will be removed from the seed of Cain, and they will then come up and possess the priesthood, and receive all the blessings which we now are entitled to."

President Wilford Woodruff made the following statement: "The day will come when all that race will be redeemed and possess all the blessings which we now have."

The position of the Church regarding the Negro may be understood when another doctrine of the Church is kept in mind, namely, that the conduct of spirits in the premortal existence has some determining effect upon the conditions and circumstances under which these spirits take on mortality and that while the details of this principle have not been made known, the mortality is a privilege that is given to those who maintain their first estate; and that the worth of the privilege is so great that spirits are willing to come to earth and take on bodies no matter what the handicap may be as to the kind of bodies they are to secure; and that among the handicaps, failure of the right to enjoy in mortality the blessings of the priesthood is a handicap which spirits are willing to assume in order that they might come to earth. Under this principle there is no injustice whatsoever involved in this deprivation as to the holding of the priesthood by the Negroes.

The First Presidency

Neither White nor Black

December 15, 1969

To General Authorities, Regional Representatives of the Twelve,
Stake Presidents, Mission Presidents, and Bishops.

Dear Brethren:

In view of confusion that has arisen, it was decided at a meeting of
the First Presidency and the Quorum of the Twelve to restate the position
of the Church with regard to the Negro both in society and in the Church.

First, may we say that we know something of the sufferings of those
who are discriminated against in a denial of their civil rights and Constitutional privileges. Our early history as a church is a tragic story of persecution and oppression. Our people repeatedly were denied the protection of
the law. They were driven and plundered, robbed and murdered by mobs,
who in many instances were aided and abetted by those sworn to uphold
the law. We as a people have experienced the bitter fruits of civil discrimination and mob violence.

We believe that the Constitution of the United States was divinely
inspired, that it was produced by "wise men" whom God raised up for this
"very purpose," and that the principles embodied in the Constitution are
so fundamental and important that, if possible, they should be extended
"for the rights and protection" of all mankind.

In revelations received by the first prophet of the Church in this
dispensation, Joseph Smith (1805-1844), the Lord made it clear that it is
"not right that any man should be in bondage one to another." These
words were spoken prior to the Civil War. From these and other revelations have sprung the Church's deep and historic concern with man's free
agency and our commitment to the sacred principles of the Constitution.

It follows, therefore, that we believe the Negro, as well as those of
other races, should have his full Constitutional privileges as a member of
society, and we hope that members of the Church everywhere will do their
part as citizens to see that these rights are held inviolate. Each citizen must
have equal opportunities and protection under the law with reference to
civil rights.

However, matters of faith, conscience, and theology are not within
the purview of the civil law. The first amendment to the Constitution
specifically provides that "Congress shall make no law respecting an
establishment of religion, or prohibiting the free exercise thereof."

The position of the Church of Jesus Christ of Latter-day Saints
affecting those of the Negro race who choose to join the Church falls
wholly within the category of religion. It has no bearing upon matters of
civil rights. In no case or degree does it deny to the Negro his full privileges
as a citizen of the nation.

This position has no relevancy whatever to those who do not wish to

222

join the Church. Those individuals, we suppose, do not believe in the divine origin and nature of the church, nor that we have the priesthood of God. Therefore, if they feel we have no priesthood, they should have no concern with any aspect of our theology on priesthood so long as that theology does not deny any man his Constitutional privileges.

A word of explanation concerning the position of the Church.

The Church of Jesus Christ of Latter-day Saints owes its origin, its existence, and its hope for the future to the principle of continuous revelation. "We believe all that God has revealed, all that He does now reveal, and we believe that He will yet reveal many great and important things pertaining to the Kingdom of God."

From the beginning of this dispensation, Joseph Smith and all succeeding presidents of the Church have taught that Negroes, while spirit children of a common Father, and the progeny of our earthly parents Adam and Eve, were not yet to receive the priesthood, for reasons which we believe are known to God, but which He has not made fully known to man.

Our living prophet, President David O. McKay, has said, "The seeming discrimination by the Church toward the Negro is not something which originated with man; but goes back into the beginning with God . . . .

"Revelation assures us that this plan antedates man's mortal existence, extending back to man's pre-existent state."

President McKay has also said, "Sometime in God's eternal plan, the Negro will be given the right to hold the priesthood."

Until God reveals His will in this matter, to him whom we sustain as a prophet, we are bound by that same will. Priesthood, when it is conferred on any man comes as a blessing from God, not of men.

We feel nothing but love, compassion, and the deepest appreciation for the rich talents, endowments, and the earnest strivings of our Negro brothers and sisters. We are eager to share with men of all races the blessings of the Gospel. We have no racially-segregated congregations.

Were we the leaders of an enterprise created by ourselves and operated only according to our own earthly wisdom, it would be a simple thing to act according to popular will. But we believe that this work is directed by God and that the conferring of the priesthood must await His revelation. To do otherwise would be to deny the very premise on which the Church is established.

We recognize that those who do not accept the principle of modern revelation may oppose our point of view. We repeat that such would not wish for membership in the Church, and therefore the question of priesthood should hold no interest for them. Without prejudice they should grant us the privilege afforded under the Constitution to exercise our chosen form of religion just as we must grant all others a similar privilege. They must recognize that the question of bestowing or withholding priesthood in the Church is a matter of religion and not a matter of Constitutional right.

We extend the hand of friendship to men everywhere and the hand of fellowship to all who wish to join the Church and partake of the many rewarding opportunities to be found therein.

We join with those throughout the world who pray that all of the blessings of the gospel of Jesus Christ may in due time of the Lord become available to men of faith everywhere. Until that time comes we must trust in God, in His wisdom and in His tender mercy.

Meanwhile we must strive harder to emulate His Son, the Lord Jesus Christ, whose new commandment it was that we should love one another. In developing that love and concern for one another, while awaiting revelations yet to come, let us hope that with respect to these religious differences, we may gain reinforcement for understanding and appreciation for such differences. They challenge our common similarities, as children of one Father, to enlarge the out-reachings of our divine souls.

Faithfully your brethren,

The First Presidency
By Hugh B. Brown
N. Eldon Tanner

June 8, 1978

To All General and Local Priesthood Officers of The Church of Jesus Christ of Latter-day Saints Throughout the World

Dear Brethren:

As we have witnessed the expansion of the work of the Lord over the earth, we have been grateful that people of many nations have responded to the message of the restored gospel, and have joined the Church in ever-increasing numbers. This, in turn, has inspired us with a desire to extend to every worthy member of the Church all of the privileges and blessings which the gospel affords.

Aware of the promises made by the prophets and presidents of the Church who have preceded us that at some time, in God's eternal plan, all of our brethren who are worthy may receive the priesthood, and witnessing the faithfulness of those from whom the priesthood has been withheld, we have pleaded long and earnestly in behalf of these, our faithful brethren, spending many hours in the Upper Room of the Temple supplicating the Lord for divine guidance.

He has heard our prayers, and by revelation has confirmed that the long-promised day has come when every faithful, worthy man in the Church may receive the holy priesthood, with power to exercise its divine authority, and enjoy with his loved ones every blessing that flows therefrom, including the blessings of the temple. Accordingly, all worthy male members of the Church may be ordained to the priesthood without regard for race or color. Priesthood leaders are instructed to follow the policy of carefully interviewing all candidates for ordination to either the Aaronic or the Melchizedek Priesthood to insure that they meet the established standards for worthiness.

We declare with soberness that the Lord has now made known His will for the blessing of all His children throughout the earth who will hearken to the voice of His authorized servants, and prepare themselves to receive every blessing of the gospel.

Sincerely yours,

The First Presidency
Spencer W. Kimball
N. Eldon Tanner
Marion G. Romney

Chronological Bibliography
on the Negro Doctrine

The past two decades have seen such a remarkable number of studies on Mormon attitudes toward blacks that it is easy to forget that the subject did not originate in the mid-sixties. The following bibliography offers a reasonably comprehensive, though not exhaustive, chronology of the most significant secondary source literature on this subject. It does not attempt to include the equally voluminous newspaper and news magazine coverage which also began in earnest during the mid-sixties. Those interested in this news media side of the history should consult Dennis L. Lythgoe, "The Changing Image of Mormonism," *Dialogue* 3 (Winter 1968): 45-58; Stephen W. Stathis and Dennis L. Lythgoe, "Mormonism in the Nineteen-Seventies: The Popular Perception," *Dialogue* 10 (Spring 1977): 95-113; "Among the Mormons" press bibliographies by Linda Thatcher in *Dialogue* 11 (Winter 1978): 104-11 and 12 (Winter 1979): 114-26; and Stephen W. Stathis, "Mormonism and the Periodical Press: A Change is Underway," *Dialogue* 14 (Summer 1981): 48-73.

1900-1949

"Are Negroes Children of Adam?" *Millennial Star* 65 (3 Dec. 1903): 776-78.

"The Negro and the Priesthood." *Liahona, The Elders' Journal* 5 (1908): 1164-67.

Smith, Joseph Fielding, Jr., "The Negro and the Priesthood," *Improvement Era* 27 (April 1924): 564-65.

Beller, Jack, "Negro Slaves in Utah," *Utah Historical Quarterly* 2 (Oct. 1929): 123-26.

Smith, Joseph Fielding, Jr., *The Way to Perfection*. Salt Lake City: Deseret Book, 1931, esp. ch. 7 ("Appointment of Lineage"), 15 ("The Seed of Cain"), and 16 ("The Seed of Cain After the Flood").

Brodie, Fawn M. *No Man Knows My History: The Life of Joseph Smith*. New York: Alfred A. Knopf, 1945.

Christensen, James Boyd. "A Social Survey of the Negro Population of Salt Lake City, Utah" (M.A. thesis, University of Utah, 1948).

First Presidency of the Church of Jesus Christ of Latter-day Saints, "First Presidency Statement [on blacks], August 17, 1949," Historical Department Library and Archives Church of Jesus Christ of Latter-day

Saints, hereafter LDS Church Archives. See text in Appendix.

1950-59

Nelson, Lowry. "Mormons and the Negro." *The Nation* 174 (24 May 1952): 488.

Bennett, Wallace R. "The Negro in Utah." *Utah Law Review* 3 (Spring 1953): 340-48.

Petersen, Mark E. "Race Problems—As They Affect the Church." Address at Brigham Young University, 27 Aug. 1954. LDS Church Archives.

Bennett, Wallace R. "The Legal Status of the Negro in Utah," in Symposium on the Negro in Utah, Utah Academy of Sciences, Arts, and Letters, Weber College, 20 Nov. 1954.

Cole, Harmon O. "The Status of the Negro in Utah." Ibid.

Smith, Elmer R. "The Social Status of the Negro in Utah." Ibid.

Kirkpatrick, L. H. "The Negro and the L.D.S. Church." *Pen Magazine*, Winter 1954, pp. 12-13, 29.

Smith, Elmer R., *The Status of the Negro in Utah*. Salt Lake City NAACP Salt Lake Branch, 1956.

Richardson, Arthur M. *That Ye May Not Be Deceived* Salt Lake City, 1957?.

Christenson, J. B. "Negro Slavery in the Utah Territory." *Phylon Quarterly* 13 (Oct. 1957): 298-305.

McConkie, Bruce R., *Mormon Doctrine*. Salt Lake City: Bookcraft, 1958, esp. entries on "Negroes," "Cain," Ham," "Pre-existence," "Priesthood," and "Races of Men."

Caldwell, Gaylon L. "Moral and Religious Aspects of the Status of the Negro in Utah." *Western Humanities Review* 13 (1959): 102-6.

1960-64

Stewart, John J. *Mormonism and the Negro*. Orem, Utah: Community Press, 1960.

Berrett, William E., "The Church and the Negroid People." Ibid., pp. 1-24.

Dyer, Alvin R., "For What Purpose?" Address to a missionary conference, Oslo, Norway, 18 March 1961. Widely distributed in typescript. LDS Church Archives.

Moyle, Henry D., "What of the Negro?" Address to the French East Mission, Geneva, Switzerland, 30 Oct. 1961. LDS Church Archives.

Shipps, Jan B. "Second-Class Saints." *Colorado Quarterly* 11 (1962-63): 183-90.

Oliver, David H., *A Negro on Mormonism*. Salt Lake City: D. H. Oliver, 1963). Experiences of a non-Mormon black in Salt Lake City.

Tanner, Jerald and Sandra Tanner. *The Negro in Mormon Theology*. Salt Lake City: Modern Microfilm Co., 1963.

Nye, Jeff, "Memo from a Mormon," *Look* 27 (22 Oct. 1963): 74-78.

Duncan, Adam M. "Civil Rights in Utah: A Concept of Race and an Attitude." Utah Academy of Sciences, Art, and Letters, Utah State University, 9 Nov. 1963.

Frame, Robert M. *The Negro Question*. N.p., May 1964.

Dutson, Roldo Van Leuven. "A Study of the Attitude of the Latter-day Saint Church, in the Territory of Utah, Toward Slavery as it Pertained to the Indian as well as the Negro from 1847 to 1865." Ph.D. diss., Brigham Young University, 1964.

Heywood, Yates, *The Negro Question Resolved*. Salt Lake City: Paragon Press, 1964.

1965-69

Foster, Donald L. "Unique Gospel in Utah." *Christian Century* 82 (14 July 1965): 890-92.

Davidson, Glen W. "Mormon Missionaries and the Race Question." *Christian Century* 82 (29 Sept. 1965): 1183-1186.

Carter, Kate B., *The Negro Pioneer*. Salt Lake City: Daughters of the Utah Pioneers, 1965.

Tanner, Jerald and Tanner, Sandra. *Joseph Smith's Curse Upon the Negro*. Salt Lake City: Modern Microfilm Co., 1965.

Lamb, John. "My Responsibility." *Improvement Era* 69 (Jan. 1966): 36-37. Experience of a black Mormon.

Brewer, David L., "Utah Elites and Utah Racial Norms." Ph.D. diss., University of Utah, 1966.

Brodie, Fawn M. *No Man Knows My History*. 2nd ed. New York: Alfred A. Knopf, 1966, esp. supplement.

Eddins, Boyd L. "The Mormons and the Civil War," M.A. thesis, Utah State University, 1966.

Lythgoe, Dennis L. "Negro Slavery in Utah." M.A. thesis, University of Utah, 1966.

Woodbury, Naomi Felicia. "A Legacy of Intolerance: Nineteenth Century Pro-slavery Propaganda and the Mormon Church Today." M.A. thesis, UCLA, 1966.

Mauss, Armand L., "Mormonism and Secular Attitudes toward Negroes." *Pacific Sociological Review* 9 (Fall 1966): 91-99.

Turner, Wallace. *The Mormon Establishment.* Boston: Houghton Mifflin Co., 1966, esp. ch. 8 ("The Anti-Negro Doctrine") and 9 ("Will the Negro Doctrine Change?").

McConkie, Bruce R. *Mormon Doctrine.* 2nd ed. Salt Lake City: Bookcraft, 1966. See 1958 ed.

"Negroes and Mormons, Romney and God." *Reveille* 2 (April 1967): 6-10.

Lund, John L. *The Church and the Negro: A Discussion of Mormons, Negroes and the Priesthood.* Salt Lake City: Paramount Publishers, 1967.

Tanner, Jerald and Sandra Tanner. *The Negro in Mormon Theology.* Salt Lake City: Modern Microfilm Co., 1967.

Jennings, Warren A. "Factors in the Destruction of the Mormon Press in Missouri, 1833." *Utah Historical Quarterly* 35 (Winter 1967): 56-76.

Lythgoe, Dennis L. "Negro Slavery and Mormon Doctrine." *Western Humanities Review* 21 (1967): 327-38.

Mauss, Armand L., "Mormonism and the Negro: Faith, Folklore and Civil Rights." *Dialogue* 4 (1967): 19-39.

Whalen, William J. *The Latter-day Saints in the Modern Day World.* rev. ed. Notre Dame: University of Notre Dame Press, 1967, esp. Ch. 16 ("Mormonism and the Negro"), pp. 245-57.

McMurrin, Sterling M. "The Negroes Among the Mormons." Address to the Annual Banquet, Salt Lake Chapter NAACP, 21 June 1968.

Maag, Margaret J. "Discrimination Against the Negro in Utah and Institutional Efforts to Eliminate It." M.A. thesis, University of Utah, 1968.

Ramjoue, George. "The Negro in Utah: A Geographical Study in Population." M.A. thesis, University of Utah, 1968.

Bowles, Carey C. *A Mormon Negro Views the Church.* Maplewood, N.J.: Carey Bowles, 1968. Experiences of a black Mormon.

Benson, Ezra Taft. *Civil Rights: Tool of Communist Deception.* Salt Lake City: Deseret Book, 1968.

Douglas, Ella Lewis, and Armand L. Mauss. "Religious and Secular Factors in the Race Attitudes of Logan, Utah, Residents." *Proceedings* of the Utah Academy of Sciences, Arts, and Letters 45:2 (1968).

First Presidency of the Church of Jesus Christ of Latter-day Saints, "First Presidency Statement [on blacks], December 15, 1969," LDS Church Archives. Quoted in Appendix.

Bush, Lester E., Jr. "A Commentary on Stephen G. Taggart's *Mormonism's Negro Policy: Social and Historical Origins.*" *Dialogue* 4 (Winter 1969): 86-103.

1970-74

Reed, William F. "The Other Side of the 'Y'." *Sports Illustrated*, 26 Jan. 1970, pp. 38-39.

Mauss, Armand L. "Mormonism and Minorities." Ph.D. diss., University of California, Berkeley, 1970.

Clark, Wynetta Martin. *I am a Negro Mormon*. Ogden, Utah: n. pub., 1970). Experiences of a black Mormon.

Taggart, Stephen G. *Mormonism's Negro Policy: Social and Historical Origins*. Salt Lake City: University of Utah Press, 1970.

Tanner, Jerald and Sandra Tanner. *Mormons and Negroes*. Salt Lake City: Modern Microfilm Co., 1970.

Brewer, David L. "Religious Resistance to Changing Beliefs about Race." *Pacific Sociological Review* 13 (Summer 1970): 163-70.

Brodie, Fawn M., "Can We Manipulate the Past?" First Annual American West Lecture, University of Utah, 3 Oct. 1970.

Cherry, Alan Gerald. *It's You and Me, Lord!* Provo, Utah: Trilogy Arts Publication, 1970. Experiences of a black Mormon.

Trank, Douglas M. "The Negro and the Mormons: A Church in Conflict." *Western Speech* 35 (Fall 1970): 220-30.

Walton, Brian. "A University's Dilemma: B.Y.U. and Blacks." *Dialogue* 6 (Spring 1971): 31-36.

Monson, Farrell Ray. "History of the South African Mission of the Church of Jesus Christ of Latter-day Saints, 1853-1970." M.A. thesis, Brigham Young University, 1971.

Lythgoe, Dennis L. "Negro Slavery in Utah." *Utah Historical Quarterly* 39 (Winter 1971): 40-54.

Cherry, Alan, "A Negro's Life Changed." In Hartman Rector and Connie Rector, eds, *No More Strangers*. Salt Lake City: Bookcraft, 1971, pp. 90-99. Experiences of a black Mormon.

Brodie, Fawn M. *No Man Knows My History: The Life of Joseph Smith*. 2nd ed. New York: Alfred A. Knopf, 1971, esp. supplement.

Mauss, Armand L. "Moderation in All Things: Political and Social Outlooks of Modern Urban Mormons." *Dialogue* 7 (Spring 1972): 57-69. Esp. pp. 61-67, "The Race Question."

Martin, Wynetta Willis. *Black Mormon Tells Her Story*. Salt Lake City: Hawkes Publications, 1972, revised 1972. Experiences of a black Mormon.

Hawkes, John D. "Why Can't the Negro Hold the Priesthood?" Ibid., pp. 81-94.

Bush, Lester E., Jr., "Compilation on the Negro in Mormonism." 1972 Documentary sourcebook. Lee Library Special Collections, Brigham Young University; and LDS Church Archives.

White, O. Kendall, Jr. "Mormonism's Anti-Black Policy and Prospects for Change." *Journal of Religious Thought* 29 (Autumn-Winter, 1972): 39-60.

O'Dea, Thomas F. "Sources of Strain in Mormon History Reconsidered." in Marvin S. Hill and James B. Allen, eds. *Mormonism and American Culture.* New York: Harper & Row, 1972.

Bush, Lester E., Jr. "Mormonism's Negro Doctrine: An Historical Overview." *Dialogue* 8 (Spring 1973): 11-68.

England, Eugene. "The Mormon Cross." *Dialogue* 8 (Spring 1973): 78-86.

Nibley, Hugh. "The Best Possible Test." *Dialogue* 8 (Spring 1973): 73-77.

Thomasson, Gordon C. "Lester Bush's Historical Overview: Other Perspectives." *Dialogue* 8 (Spring 1973): 69-72.

Trank, Douglas Monty. "A Rhetorical Analysis of the Rhetoric Emerging from the Mormon-Black Controversy." Ph.D. diss., University of Utah, 1973.

Douglas, Norman. "The Sons of Lehi and the Seed of Cain: Racial Myths in the Mormon Scriptures and their Relevance to the Pacific Islands." *Journal of Religious History* 8 (June 1974): 90-104.

Hartley, William G. "Samuel D. Chambers." *New Era* 4 (June 1974): 46-50.

Nelson, Lowry. "Mormons and Blacks." *Christian Century* 91 (Oct. 1974): 949-50.

1975-79

Bringhurst, Newell G. "'A Servant of Servants . . . Cursed as Pertaining to the Priesthood': Mormon Attitudes toward Slavery and the Black Man 1830-1880." Ph.D. diss., University of California, Davis, 1975.

Wolfinger, Henry J. "A Test of Faith: Jane Elizabeth James and the Origins of the Utah Black Community." Clark S. Knowlton, ed., *Social Accommodation in Utah.* American West Occasional Papers. Salt Lake City, 1975: 126-72.

Coleman, Ronald G. "Blacks in Utah History: An Unknown Legacy." In Helen Z. Papanikolas, ed. *The Peoples of Utah.* Salt Lake City: Utah State Historical Society, 1976.

Wells, Elmer E. "Unjustifiable Denial of Priesthood to Black Mormons." *Negro History Bulletin* 40 (July 1977): 725-27.

Bringhurst, Newell G. "Forgotten Mormon Perspectives: Slavery, Race, and the Black Man as Issues Among Non-Utah Latter-day Saints, 1844-1873." *Michigan History* 61 (Winter 1977): 353-70.

Hill, Donna. *Joseph Smith: The First Mormon.* Garden City: Doubleday & Co., 1977, esp. ch. 12 ("Blacks in the Early Church"), pp. 379-94.

Clark, Michael J. "Improbable Ambassadors: Black Soldiers at Fort Douglas, 1896-99." *Utah Historical Quarterly* 46 (Summer 1978): 282-301.

Coleman, Ronald G. "Utah's Black Pioneers: 1847-1869." *UMOJA: A Scholarly Journal of Black Studies*, new series, 11 (Summer 1978): 95-110.

Bringhurst, Newell G. "An Ambiguous Decision: The Implementation of Mormon Priesthood Denial for the Black Man—A Re-examination." *Utah Historical Quarterly* 46 (Winter 1978): 45-64.

First Presidency of the Church of Jesus Christ of Latter-day Saints, "First Presidency Statement [on blacks], February 22, 1978." LDS Church Archives.

First Presidency of the Church of Jesus Christ of Latter-day Saints, "First Presidency Statement [on priesthood], June 8, 1978." LDS Church Archives, also quoted in full in the Appendix.

Briscoe, David, and George Buck. "Black Friday." *Utah Holiday* 7 (July 1978): 38-40.

Brigham, Janet. "'to every worthy member,'" *Sunstone* 3 (July/Aug. 1978): 11-15.

Walters, Wesley P. *Interview with Mormon Apostle LeGrand Richards Concerning 1978 Negro "Revelation."* 16 Aug. 1978. Phoenix, Ariz.: Ex-Mormons for Jesus, 1978.

McConkie, Bruce R., "All Are Alike Unto God," address to Seminary & Institute of Religion personnel, Brigham Young University, 18 Aug. 1978.

Shipps, Jan B. "The Mormons: Looking Forward and Outward." 95 (16-23 Aug. 1978): 761-766. Priesthood revelation of 1978.

Esplin, Ronald K. "Brigham Young and Priesthood Denial to the Blacks: An Alternate View." *BYU Studies* 19 (Spring 1979): 394-402.

Young, Thane. "Mixed Messages on the Negro Doctrine: An Interview with Lester Bush." *Sunstone* 4 (May-June 1979): 8-15.

Bringhurst, Newell G. "Elijah Abel and the Mark of Cain." *American Heritage* 39 (June/July 1979): 111.

Bush, Lester E., Jr. "Introduction [to issue on the priesthood revelation of 1978]," *Dialogue* 12 (Summer 1979): 9-12.

Bringhurst, Newell G. "Elijah Abel and the Changing Status of Blacks Within Mormonism." *Dialogue* 12 (Summer 1979): 22-36.

Eastmond, J. Nicholls, Jr. "The New Revelation: A Personal View." *Dialogue* 12 (Summer 1979): 50-53.

[Hartley, William G.], "Saint Without Priesthood: The Collected Testimonies of Ex-slave Samuel D. Chambers." *Dialogue* 12 (Summer 1979): 13-21.

McMurrin, Sterling M. "A Note on the 1963 Civil Rights Statement." *Dialogue* 12 (Summer 1979): 60-63.

Russell, William D. "A Priestly Role for a Prophetic Church: The RLDS Church and Black Americans." *Dialogue* 12 (Summer 1979): 37-49.

Smart, M. Neff. "The Challenge of Africa." *Dialogue* 12 (Summer 1979): 54-57.

Smith, George D., Jr. "The Negro Doctrine—An Afterview." *Dialogue* 12 (Summer 1979): 64-67.

Kunz, Phillip R. "Blacks and Mormonism: A Social Distance Change." *Psychological Reports* 45 (August 1979): 81-82.

Newell, Linda King, and Valeen Tippetts Avery. "Jane Manning James: Black Saint, 1847 Pioneer." *Ensign* 9 (Aug. 1979): 26-29.

Palmer, Spencer J. "Mormons in West Africa; New Terrain for the Sesquicentennial Church." Annual Religion Faculty Lecture, Brigham Young University, 27 Sept. 1979, typescript, Brigham Young University Publications.

Coleman, Ronald G. "The Buffalo Soldiers: Guardians of the Uintah Frontier, 1886-1901." *Utah Historical Quarterly* 47 (Fall 1979): 421-39.

Haroldsen, E. O., and Harvey, K. "Diffusion of Shocking Good News." *Journalism Quarterly* 56 (Winter 1979): 771-75. Priesthood revelation of 1978.

Freeman, Joseph. *In the Lord's Due Time*. Salt Lake City: Bookcraft, 1979. Experiences of a black Mormon.

Wangeman, William Carl. *The Blackman: A Son of God*. Bountiful, Utah: Horizon Publishers, c1979.

1980-1983

Brigham, Janet. "Nigeria and Ghana: A Miracle Precedes the Messengers." *Ensign* 10 (Feb. 1980): 73-76.

Lye, William, "From Burundi to Zaire: Taking the Gospel to Africa." *Ensign* 10 (March 1980): 10-15.

Mabey, Randell, and Rachel Mabey. "A Mission to West Africa." *This People*, Spring 1980, pp. 24-37.

Coleman, Ronald G. "A History of Blacks in Utah, 1825-1910." Ph.D. diss., University of Utah, 1980.

White, O. Kendall, Jr., and Daryl White. "Abandoning an Unpopular Policy: An Analysis of the Decision Granting the Mormon Priesthood to Blacks." *Sociological Analysis* 41 (Fall 1980): 231-45.

Wilson, William A., and Richard C. Poulsen. "The Curse of Cain and Other Stories: Blacks in Mormon Folklore." *Sunstone* 5 (Nov.-Dec. 1980): 9-13.

White, O. Kendall, Jr. "Boundary Maintenance, Blacks, and the Mormon Priesthood." *Journal of Religious Thought* 37 (Fall-Winter, 1980): 30-44.

Obinna, Anthony Uzodimma. "Voice from Nigeria." *Ensign* 10 (Dec. 1980): 28-30. Experiences of a black Mormon.

Olsen, Peggy. "Ruffin Bridgeforth: Leader and Father to Mormon Blacks." *This People*, Winter 1980.

Hansen, Klaus. *Mormonism and the American Experience*. Chicago: University of Chicago Press, 1980, esp. Ch. 6 ("The Transformation of Racial Thought and Practice").

Sturlaugson, Mary. *A Soul So Rebellious*. Salt Lake City: Deseret Book, 1980. Experiences of a black Mormon.

Tanner, Jerald and Sandra Tanner. *The Changing World of Mormonism*. Chicago: Moody Bible Institute, 1980. esp. Ch. 10, "Changing the Anti-Black Doctrine."

Bringhurst, Newell G. "Mormonism in Black Africa: Changing Attitudes and Practices, 1830-1981." *Sunstone* 6 (May-June 1981): 15-21.

Mauss, Armand L. "Comments: White on Black Among the Mormons: A Critique of White & White." *Sociological Analysis* 42 (Fall 1981): 277-83.

White, O. Kendall, Jr. and Daryl White. "Reply to Mauss' Critique of Our Analysis of Admitting Blacks into the Mormon Priesthood." *Sociological Analysis* 42 (Fall 1981): 283-88.

Mauss, Armand L. "The Fading of the Pharaoh's Curse: The Decline and Fall of the Priesthood Ban Against Blacks in the Mormon Church." *Dialogue* 14 (Fall 1981): 10-45.

Bringhurst, Newell G. "The Mormons and Black Slavery—A Closer Look." *Pacific Historical Review* 50 (Nov. 1981): 329-38. "Charles B. Thompson and the Issues of Slavery and Race." *Journal of Mormon History* 8 (1981): 37-47. "'The Descendants of Ham' in Zion:

Discrimination Against Blacks along the Shifting Mormon Frontier, 1830-1920." *Nevada Historical Quarterly* 24 (Winter 1981): 298-318.

McConkie, Bruce R. "The New Revelation on Priesthood." In *Priesthood.* Salt Lake City: Deseret Book, 1981, pp. 126-37.

Bringhurst, Newell G. *Saints, Slaves and Blacks: The Changing Place of Black People Within Mormonism.* Westport, Conn.: Greenwood Press, 1981.

Long, E.B. *The Saints and the Union: Utah Territory during the Civil War.* Urbana: University of Illinois Press, 1981.

Gerlach, Larry R. *Blazing Crosses in Zion: The Ku Klux Klan in Utah* Logan, Utah: Utah State University Press, 1982.

Sturlaugson, Mary. *He Restoreth My Soul.* Salt Lake City: Deseret Book, 1982. Experiences of a black Mormon.

Grover, Mark L. "The Lineage of Cain in the Land of Racial Democracy: The Mormon Priesthood and the Brazilian of African Descent," paper presented at the Mormon History Association annual meeting, Omaha, Nebraska, 5-8 May 1983.

Quinn, D. Michael. *J. Reuben Clark: The Church Years.* Provo, Utah: Brigham Young University Press, 1983, esp. ch. 10 ("All Nations, and Kindreds, and People, and Tongues"), pp. 221-236.

Alphabetical Bibliography:
Published and Unpublished

Publications

"Are Negroes Children of Adam?" *Millennial Star* 65 (3 Dec. 1903): 776-778.

Beller, Jack. "Negro Slaves in Utah." *Utah Historical Quarterly* 2 (Oct. 1929): 123-26.

Bennett, Wallace R. "The Negro in Utah." *Utah Law Review* 3 (Spring 1953): 340-48.

Benson, Ezra Taft. *Civil Rights, Tool of Communist Deception*. Salt Lake City: Deseret Book, 1968.

Berrett, William E. "The Church and the Negroid People." In John J. Stewart. *Mormonism and the Negro*. (1960), pp. 1-24.

Bowles, Carey C. *A Mormon Negro Views the Church*. Maplewood, N. J.: Carey Bowles, 1968. Experiences of a black Mormon.

Brewer, David L. "Religious Resistance to Changing Beliefs about Race." *Pacific Sociological Review* 13 (Summer 1970): 163-70.

Brigham, Janet. "'to every worthy member.'" *Sunstone* 3 (July/Aug. 1978): 11-15. "Nigeria and Ghana: A Miracle Precedes the Messenger." *Ensign* 10 (Feb. 1980): 73-76.

Bringhurst, Newell G. "Forgotten Mormon Perspectives: Slavery, Race, and the Black Man as Issues Among Non-Utah Latter-day Saints, 1844-1873." *Michigan History* 61 (Winter 1977): 353-70. "An Ambiguous Decision: The Implementation of Mormon Priesthood Denial for the Black Man—A Re-examination." *Utah Historical Quarterly* 46 (Winter 1978): 45-64. "Elijah Abel and the Changing Status of Blacks Within Mormonism," *Dialogue* 12 (Summer 1979): 22-36. "Elijah Abel and the Mark of Cain." *American Heritage* 39 (June/July 1979): 111. "Mormonism in Black Africa: Changing Attitudes and Practices, 1830-1981." *Sunstone* 6 (May-June 1981): 15-21. "The Mormons and Black Slavery—A Closer Look." *Pacific Historical Review* 50 (Nov. 1981): 329-338. *Saints, Slaves, and Blacks: The Changing Place of Black People Within Mormonism*. Westport, Conn.: Greenwood Press, 1981. "Charles B. Thompson and the Issues of Slavery and Race." *Journal of Mormon History* 8 (1981): 37-47. "'The Descendants of Ham' in Zion: Discrimination Against Blacks Along the Shifting Mormon Frontier, 1830-1920." *Nevada*

Bibliography: Published and Unpublished

Historical Quarterly 24 (Winter 1981): 298-318.

Briscoe, David, and George Buck. "Black Friday." *Utah Holiday* 7 (July 1978): 38-40.

Brodie, Fawn M., *No Man Knows My History* 2nd ed. New York: Alfred A. Knopf, 1966, esp. supplement. "Can We Manipulate the Past?" First Annual American West Lecture, University of Utah, 3 Oct. 1970.

Bush, Lester E., Jr. "A Commentary on Stephen G. Taggart's *Mormonism's Negro Policy: Social and Historical Origins*," *Dialogue* 4 (Winter 1969): 86-103. "Mormonism's Negro Doctrine: An Historical Overview." *Dialogue* 8 (Spring 1973): 11-68. "Introduction [to issue on the priesthood revelation of 1978]." *Dialogue* 12 (Summer 1979): 9-12.

Caldwell, Gaylon L. "Moral and Religious Aspects of the Status of the Negro in Utah." *Western Humanities Review* 13 (1959): 102-106.

Carter, Kate B. *The Negro Pioneer.* Salt Lake City: Daughters of the Utah Pioneers, 1965.

Cherry, Alan Gerald. *It's You and Me, Lord!* Provo, Utah: Trilogy Arts Publication, 1970. "A Negro's Life Changed," in Hartman Rector, and Connie Rector, eds., *No More Strangers.* Salt Lake City: Bookcraft, 1971, pp. 90-99. Experiences of a black Mormon.

Christenson, J. B. "Negro Slavery in the Utah Territory." *Phylon Quarterly* 13 (Oct. 1957): 298-305.

Clark, Michael J. "Improbable Ambassadors: Black Soldiers at Fort Douglas, 1896-99." *Utah Historical Quarterly* 46 (Summer 1978): 282-301.

Clark, Wynetta Martin. *I am a Negro Mormon.* Ogden, Utah: n. pub., 1970. Experiences of a black Mormon.

Coleman, Ronald G. "Blacks in Utah History: An Unknown Legacy." in Helen Z. Papanikolas, ed., *The Peoples of Utah.* Salt Lake City, Utah State Historical Society, 1976. "Utah's Black Pioneers: 1847-1869." *UMOJA: A Scholarly Journal of Black Studies,* new series 11 (Summer 1978): 95-110. "The Buffalo Soldiers: Guardians of the Uintah Frontier, 1886-1901." *Utah Historical Quarterly* 47 (Fall 1979): 421-39.

Davidson, Glen W. "Mormon Missionaries and the Race Question." *Christian Century* 82 (29 Sept. 1965): 1183-86.

Douglas, Ella Lewis, and Armand L. Mauss. "Religious and Secular Factors in the Race Attitudes of Logan, Utah, Residents." *Proceedings* of the Utah Academy of Sciences, Arts, and Letters 45:2 (1968).

Douglas, Norman. "The Sons of Lehi and the Seed of Cain: Racial Myths in the Mormon Scriptures and Their Relevance to the Pacific Islands." *Journal of Religious History* 8 (June 1974): 90-104.

Eastmond, J. Nicholls, Jr. "The New Revelation: A Personal View." *Dialogue* 12 (Summer 1979): 50-53.

England, Eugene. "The Mormon Cross." *Dialogue* 8 (Spring 1973): 78-86.

Esplin, Ronald K. "Brigham Young and Priesthood Denial to the Blacks: An Alternative View." *BYU Studies* 19 (Spring 1979): 394-402.

Foster, Donald L. "Unique Gospel in Utah." *Christian Century* 82 (14 July 1965): 890-92.

Frame, Robert M. *The Negro Question.* N.p., May 1964.

Freeman, Joseph. *In the Lord's Due Time.* Salt Lake City: Bookcraft, 1979. Experiences of a black Mormon.

Gerlach, Larry R. *Blazing Crosses in Zion: The Ku Klux Klan in Utah.* Logan: Utah State University Press, 1982).

Hansen, Klaus. *Mormonism and the American Experience.* Chicago: University of Chicago Press, 1980), esp. Ch. 6 ("The Transformation of Racial Thought and Practice").

Haroldsen, E. O., and Harvey, K. "Diffusion of Shocking Good News." *Journalism Quarterly* 56 (Winter 1979): 771-75. Priesthood revelation of 1978.

Hartley, William G., "Samuel D. Chambers." *New Era* 4 (June 1974): 46-50. "Saint Without Priesthood: The Collected Testimonies of Ex-slave Samuel D. Chambers," *Dialogue* 12 (Summer 1979): 13-21.

Hawkes, John D. "Why Can't the Negro Hold the Priesthood?" In Wynetta Willis Martin, *Black Mormon Tells Her Story.* (Salt Lake City: Hawkes Publications, 1972), pp. 81-94.

Heywood, Yates, *The Negro Question Resolved.* Salt Lake City: Paragon Press, 1964.

Hill, Donna. *Joseph Smith: The First Mormon.* Garden City: Doubleday & Co., 1977, esp. Ch. 12 ("Blacks in the Early Church"), pp. 379-94.

Jennings, Warren A. "Factors in the Destruction of the Mormon Press in Missouri, 1833." *Utah Historical Quarterly* 35 (Winter 1967): 56-76.

Kirkpatrick, L. H. "The Negro and the L.D.S. Church." *Pen Magazine,* Winter 1954, pp. 12-13, 29.

Kunz, Phillip R. "Blacks and Mormonism: A Social Distance Change." *Psychological Reports* 45 (Aug. 1979): 81-82.

Lamb, John. "My Responsibility." *Improvement Era* 69 (Jan. 1966): 36-37. Experience of a black Mormon.

Bibliography: Published and Unpublished

Long, E. B. *The Saints and the Union: Utah Territory during the Civil War*. Urbana: University of Illinois Press, 1981.

Lund, John L. *The Church and the Negro: A Discussion of Mormons, Negroes and the Priesthood*. Salt Lake City: Paramount Publishers, 1967.

Lye, William. "From Burundi to Zaire: Taking the Gospel to Africa." *Ensign*, 10 (March 1980): 10-15.

Lythgoe, Dennis L. "Negro Slavery and Mormon Doctrine. *Western Humanities Review* 21 (1957): 327-38. "Negro Slavery in Utah." *Utah Historical Quarterly* 39 (Winter 1971): 40-54.

Mabey, Randell, and Rachel Mabey. "A Mission to West Africa." *This People*, Spring 1980, pp. 24-37.

Martin, Wynetta Willis. *Black Mormon Tells Her Story*. Salt Lake City: Hawkes Publications, 1972, rev. 1972. Experiences of a black Mormon.

Mauss, Armand L. "Mormonism and Secular Attitudes Toward Negroes." *Pacific Sociological Review* 9 (Fall 1966): 91-99. "Mormonism and the Negro: Faith, Folklore and Civil Rights." *Dialogue* 4 (Winter 1967): 19-39. "Moderation in All Things: Political and Social Outlooks of Modern Urban Mormons." *Dialogue* 7 (Spring 1972): 57-69, esp. pp. 61-67 on "The Race Question." "Comments: White on Black Among the Mormons: A Critique of White & White." *Sociological Analysis* 42 (Fall 1981): 277-83. "The Fading of the Pharaoh's Curse: The Decline and Fall of the Priesthood Ban Against Blacks in the Mormon Church." *Dialogue* 14 (Fall 1981): 10-45.

McConkie, Bruce R. *Mormon Doctrine*. 2nd ed. Salt Lake City: Bookcraft, 1966, esp. sections on "Negroes," "Cain," "Ham," "Pre-existence," "Priesthood," and "Races of Men." "The New Revelation on Priesthood." In *Priesthood*. Salt Lake City: Deseret Book, 1981, pp. 126-37.

McMurrin, Sterling M. "A Note on the 1963 Civil Rights Statement." *Dialogue* 12 (Summer 1979): 60-63.

"Negroes and Mormons, Romney and God." *Reveille* 2 (April 1967): 6-10.

Nelson, Lowry. "Mormons and the Negro." *Nation* 174 (24 May 1952): 488. "Mormons and Blacks." *Christian Century* 91 (Oct. 1974): 949-50.

Newell, Linda King, and Valeen Tippetts Avery, "Jane Manning James Black Saint, 1847 Pioneer." *Ensign* 9 (Aug. 1979): 26-29.

Nibley, Hugh. "The Best Possible Test." *Dialogue* 8 (Spring 1973): 73-77.

Nye, Jeff. "Memo from a Mormon." *Look* 27 (22 Oct. 1963): 74-78.

Obinna, Anthony Uzodimma. "Voice from Nigeria." *Ensign* 10 (Dec. 1980): 18-30. Experiences of a black Mormon.

O'Dea, Thomas F. "Sources of Strain in Mormon History Reconsidered." In Marvin S. Hill, and James B. Allen, eds., *Mormonism and American Culture*. New York: Harper & Row, 1972.

Oliver, David H. *A Negro on Mormonism*. Salt Lake City: D. H. Oliver, 1963. Experiences of a non-Mormon in Salt Lake City.

Olsen, Peggy, "Ruffin Bridgeforth: Leader and Father to Mormon Blacks." *This People*, Winter 1980.

Quinn, D. Michael. *J. Reuben Clark: The Church Years*. Provo, Utah: Brigham Young University Press, 1983, esp. ch. 10. ("All Nations, and Kindreds, and People, and Tongues"), pp. 221-236.

Richardson, Arthur M. *That Ye May Not Be Deceived*. Salt Lake City: n. pub., 1957?.

Reed, William F. "The Other Side of the 'Y'." *Sports Illustrated*. 26 Jan. 1970, pp. 38-39.

Russell, William D. "A Priestly Role for a Prophetic Church: The RLDS Church and Black Americans," *Dialogue* 12 (Summer 1979): 37-49.

Shipps, Jan B. "Second-Class Saints." *Colorado Quarterly* 11 (1962-63): 183-90. "The Mormons: Looking Forward and Outward." 95 (16-23 Aug. 1978): 761-66. Priesthood revelation of 1978.

Smart, M. Neff. "The Challenge of Africa." *Dialogue* 12 (Summer 1979): 54-57.

Smith, Elmer R. *The Status of the Negro in Utah*. Salt Lake City: NAACP Salt Lake Branch, 1956.

Smith, George D., Jr. "The Negro Doctrine—An Afterview." *Dialogue* 12 (Summer 1979): 64-67.

Smith, Joseph Fielding, Jr. "The Negro and the Priesthood." *Improvement Era* 27 (April 1924): 564-65. *The Way to Perfection*. Salt Lake City: Deseret Book, 1931, esp. ch. 7 ("Appointment of Lineage"), 15 ("The Seed of Cain"), and 16 ("The Seed of Cain After the Flood").

Stewart, John J. *Mormonism and the Negro*. Orem, Utah: Community Press, 1960.

Sturlaugson, Mary. *A Soul So Rebellious*. Salt Lake City: Deseret Book, 1980. *He Restoreth My Soul*. Salt Lake City: Deseret Book, 1982. Experiences of a black Mormon.

Taggart, Stephen G. *Mormonism's Negro Policy: Social and Historical Origins*. Salt Lake City: University of Utah Press, 1970.

Tanner, Jerald, and Sandra Tanner. *The Negro in Mormon Theology*.

Bibliography: Published and Unpublished

Salt Lake City: Modern Microfilm Co., 1963. Joseph Smith's Curse upon the Negro. Salt Lake City: Modern Microfilm Co., 1965. *The Negro in Mormon Theology.* Salt Lake City: Modern Microfilm Co., 1967. *Mormons and Negroes.* Salt Lake City: Modern Microfilm Co., 1970. *The Changing World of Mormonism.* Chicago: Moody Bible Institute, 1980. Esp. Ch. 10, "Changing the Anti-Black Doctrine."

"The Negro and the Priesthood." *Liahona, The Elders' Journal* 5 (1908): 1164-67.

Thomasson, Gordon C. "Lester Bush's Historical Overview: Other Perspectives." *Dialogue* 8 (Spring 1973): 69-72.

Trank, Douglas M. "The Negro and the Mormons: A Church in Conflict." *Western Speech* 35 (Fall 1971): 220-30.

Turner, Wallace. *The Mormon Establishment.* Boston: Houghton Mifflin Co., 1966, esp. Ch. 8 "The Anti-Negro Doctrine," and 9 "Will the Negro Doctrine Change?".

Walters, Wesley P. *Interview with Mormon Apostle LeGrand Richards Concerning 1978 Negro "Revelation."* 16 Aug. 1978. Phoenix: Ex-Mormons for Jesus, 1978.

Walton, Brian. "A University's Dilemma: BYU and Blacks." *Dialogue* 6 (Spring 1971): 31-36.

Wangeman, William Carl. *The Blackman: A Son of God.* Bountiful, Utah: Horizon Publishers, c1979.

Wells, Elmer E. "Unjustifiable Denial of Priesthood to Black Mormons." *Negro History Bulletin* 40 (July 1977): 725-27.

Whalen, William J. *The Latter-day Saints in the Modern Day World* rev. ed. Notre Dame: University of Notre Dame Press, 1967. Esp. Ch. 16 ("Mormonism and the Negro"), pp. 245-57.

Wilson, William A., and Richard C. Poulsen. "The Curse of Cain and Other Stories: Blacks in Mormon Folklore." *Sunstone* 5 (Nov.-Dec. 1980): 9-13.

White, O. Kendall, Jr. "Mormonism's Anti-Black Policy and Prospects for Change." *Journal of Religious Thought* 29 (Autumn-Winter, 1972): 39-60. "Boundary Maintenance, Blacks, and the Mormon Priesthood." *Journal of Religious Thought* 37 (Fall-Winter 1980-81): 30-44.

White, O. Kendall, Jr., and Daryl White. "Abandoning an Unpopular Policy: An Analysis of the Decision Granting the Mormon Priesthood to Blacks." *Sociological Analysis* 41 (Fall 1980): 231-45. "Reply to Mauss' Critique of Our Analysis of Admitting Blacks into the Mormon Priesthood. *Sociological Analysis* 42 (Fall 1981): 283-88.

Bibliography: Published and Unpublished

Wolfinger, Henry J. "A Test of Faith: Jane Elizabeth James and the Origins of the Utah Black Community." In Clark S. Knowlton, ed., *Social Accommodation in Utah*. American West Occasional Papers. Salt Lake City, Utah, 1975: 126-172.

Young, Thane "Mixed Messages on the Negro Doctrine: An Interview with Lester Bush." *Sunstone* 4 (May-June 1979): 8-15.

Unpublished Works

Bennett, Wallace R. "The Legal Status of the Negro in Utah." In Symposium on the Negro in Utah, Utah Academy of Sciences, Arts, and Letters, Weber College, 20 Nov. 1954.

Bush, Lester E., Jr. "Compilation on the Negro in Mormonism." 1972. [Documentary sourcebook] Lee Library Special Collections, Brigham Young University, and LDS Historical Department Library Archives.

Brewer, David L. "Utah Elites and Utah Racial Norms." Ph.D. diss., University of Utah, 1966.

Bringhurst, Newell G. "'A Servant of Servants . . . Cursed as Pertaining to the Priesthood': Mormon Attitudes toward Slavery and the Black Man 1830-1880." Ph.D. diss., University of California, Davis, 1975.

Christensen, James Boyd. "A Social Survey of the Negro Population of Salt Lake City, Utah." M.A. thesis, University of Utah, 1948.

Cole, Harmon O. "The Status of the Negro in Utah." In Symposium on the Negro in Utah, Utah Academy of Sciences, Art, and Letters, Weber College, 20 Nov. 1954.

Coleman, Ronald G. "A History of Blacks in Utah, 1825-1910." Ph.D. diss., University of Utah, 1980.

Duncan, Adam M. "Civil Rights in Utah: A Concept of Race and an Attitude." Utah Academy of Sciences, Arts and Letters, Utah State University, 9 Nov. 1963.

Dutson, Roldo Van Leuven. "A Study of the Attitude of the Latter-day Saint Church, in the Territory of Utah, Toward Slavery as it Pertained to the Indian as Well as the Negro from 1847 to 1865." Ph.D. diss., Brigham Young University, 1964.

Dyer, Alvin R. "For What Purpose?" Address to missionary conference, Oslo, Norway, 18 March 1961, widely distributed in typescript. LDS Church Archives.

Eddins, Boyd L. "The Mormons and the Civil War." M.A. thesis, Utah State University, 1966.

First Presidency of the Church of Jesus Christ of Latter-day Saints. "First Presidency Statement [on blacks], August 17, 1949." LDS Church Archives. See Appendix.

First Presidency of the Church of Jesus Christ of Latter-day Saints. "First Presidency Statement [on blacks], December 15, 1969." LDS Church Archives. See Appendix.

First Presidency of the Church of Jesus Christ of Latter-day Saints, "First Presidency Statement [on blacks], February 22, 1978." LDS Church Archives.

First Presidency of the Church of Jesus Christ of Latter-day Saints. "First Presidency Statement [on priesthood], June 8, 1978." LDS Church Archives. See Appendix.

Grover, Mark L. "The Lineage of Cain in the Land of Racial Democracy: The Mormon Priesthood and the Brazilian of African Descent." Paper presented at the Mormon History Association annual meeting, Omaha, Nebraska, 5-8 May 1983.

Lythgoe, Dennis L. "Negro Slavery in Utah," M.A. thesis, University of Utah, 1966.

Maag, Margaret J. "Discrimination Against the Negro in Utah and Institutional Efforts to Eliminate It." M.S. thesis, University of Utah, 1968.

Mauss, Armand L. "Mormonism and Minorities." Ph.D. diss., University of California, Berkeley, 1970.

McConkie, Bruce R. "All Are Alike Unto God." Address to Seminary & Institute of Religion personnel. Brigham Young University, 18 Aug. 1978.

McMurrin, Sterling M. "The Negroes Among the Mormons." Address to the Annual Banquet, Salt Lake Chapter NAACP, 21 June 1968.

Monson, Farrell Ray. "History of the South African Mission of the Church of Jesus Christ of Latter-day Saints, 1853-1970." M.A. thesis, Brigham Young University, 1971.

Moyle, Henry D. "What of the Negro?" Address to French East Mission, Geneva, Switzerland, 30 Oct. 1961. LDS Church Archives.

Palmer, Spencer J. "Mormons in West Africa: New Terrain for the Sesquicentennial Church." Annual Religion Faculty Lecture, Brigham Young University, 27 Sept. 1979. Typescript, Brigham Young University Publications.

Petersen, Mark E. "Race Problems—As They Affect the Church." Address at Brigham Young University, 27 Aug. 1954. LDS Church Archives.

Ramjoue, George. "The Negro in Utah: A Geographical Study in Population." M.A. thesis, University of Utah, 1968.

Smith, Elmer R. "The Social Status of the Negro in Utah." In Symposium on the Negro in Utah, Utah Academy of Sciences, Arts, and Letters, Weber College, 20 Nov. 1954.

Trank, Douglas Monty. "A Rhetorical Analysis of the Rhetoric Emerging from the Mormon-Black Controversy." Ph.D. diss., University of Utah, 1973.

Woodbury, Naomi Felicia. "A Legacy of Intolerance: Nineteenth Century Pro-slavery Propaganda and the Mormon Church Today." M.A. thesis, UCLA, 1966.

Index

Index

Index

Tullidge, Edward, 1
Turner, Nat, 54

U

Udall, Stewart, 4-5, 15-16
University of Arizona, 158
University of Utah, 166
University of Washington, 158
U. S. Census, 166

V

Vernon, Glenn, 5

W

War in Heaven, 10, 12-13, 15, 72, 87.
    See also preexistence
Washington, D. C., Mormon blacks
    in, 90
Watts, California, 3, 165
Way to Perfection, The, 87, 150
Welch, Robert, 19
West Africa, missionary work in, 170
Western Athletic Conference, 158
Wilkinson, Ernest L., 158
Williams, A. Cecil, 17-18
Winter Quarters, 135-6
Wolsey, Heber G., 161
Women's Issues, 160, 162. *See also*
    Equal Rights Amendment
World War II, 150
Woodruff, Wilford, 70, 76, 78-9, 83,
    91, 134, 197, 221

Y

Young, Brigham, 38, 40-41, 65-71,
    74, 78, 83, 87-8, 91, 97, 134-37, 140,
    173, 175-6, 194, 198-200, 203,
    207-8, 213, 221
Young, Brigham, Jr., 38